ULTIMATE SPIDER-MAN

WAR OF THE SYMBIOTES

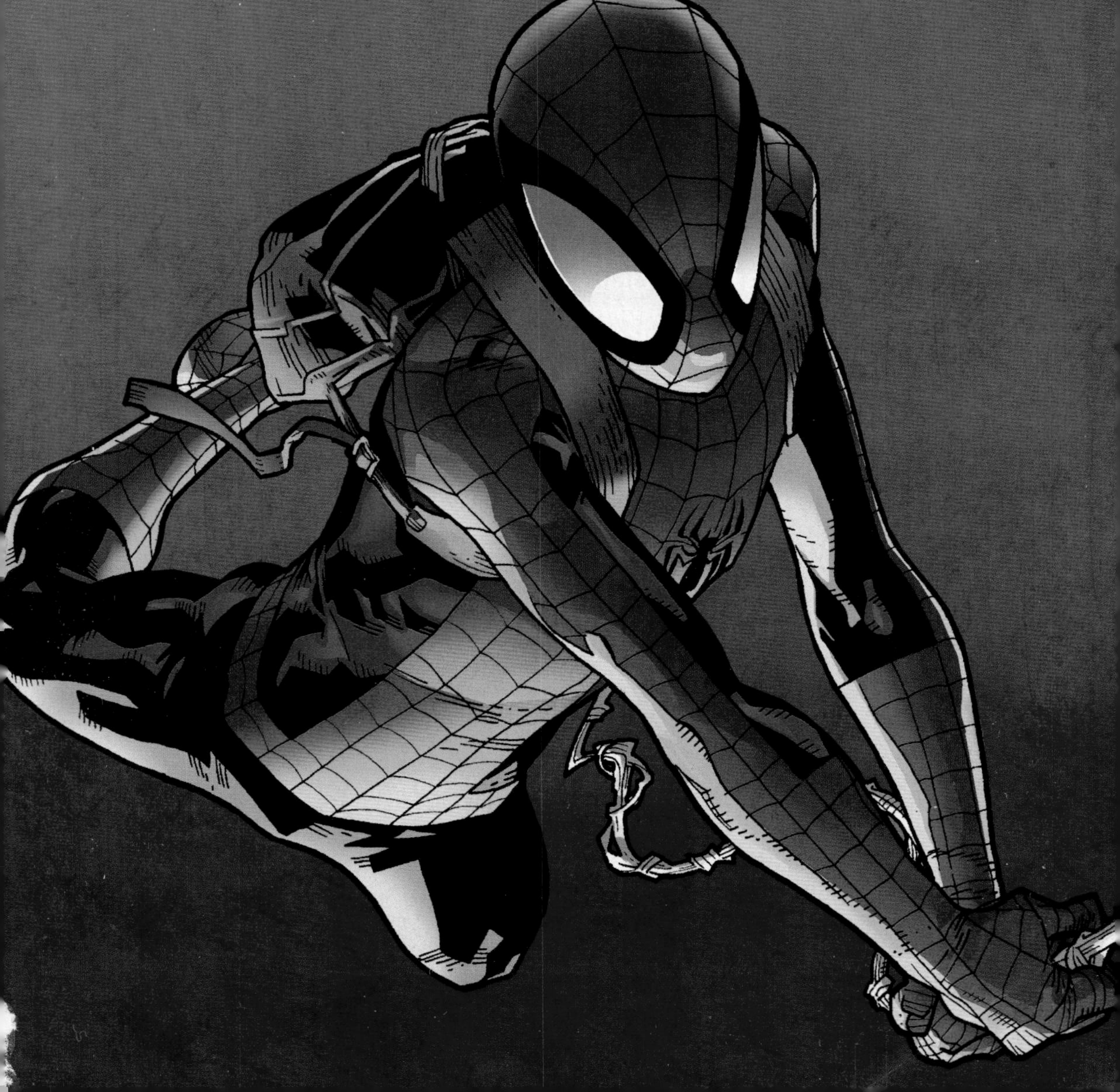

ULTIMATE
SPIDER-MAN
WAR OF THE SYMBIOTES

writer
BRIAN MICHAEL BENDIS
pencils
STUART IMMONEN
inks
WADE VON GRAWBADGER
colors
JUSTIN PONSOR
letters
VIRTUAL CALLIGRAPHY'S CORY PETIT
cover art
STUART IMMONEN & RICHARD ISANOVE
assistant editors
LAUREN SANKOVITCH & LAUREN HENRY
editors
BILL ROSEMANN, RALPH MACCHIO & MARK PANICCIA

collection editor
JENNIFER GRÜNWALD
editorial assistant
ALEX STARBUCK
assistant editors
CORY LEVINE & JOHN DENNING
editor, special projects
MARK D. BEAZLEY
senior editor, special projects
JEFF YOUNGQUIST
senior vice president of sales
DAVID GABRIEL
vice president of creative
TOM MARVELLI

editor in chief
JOE QUESADA
publisher
DAN BUCKLEY

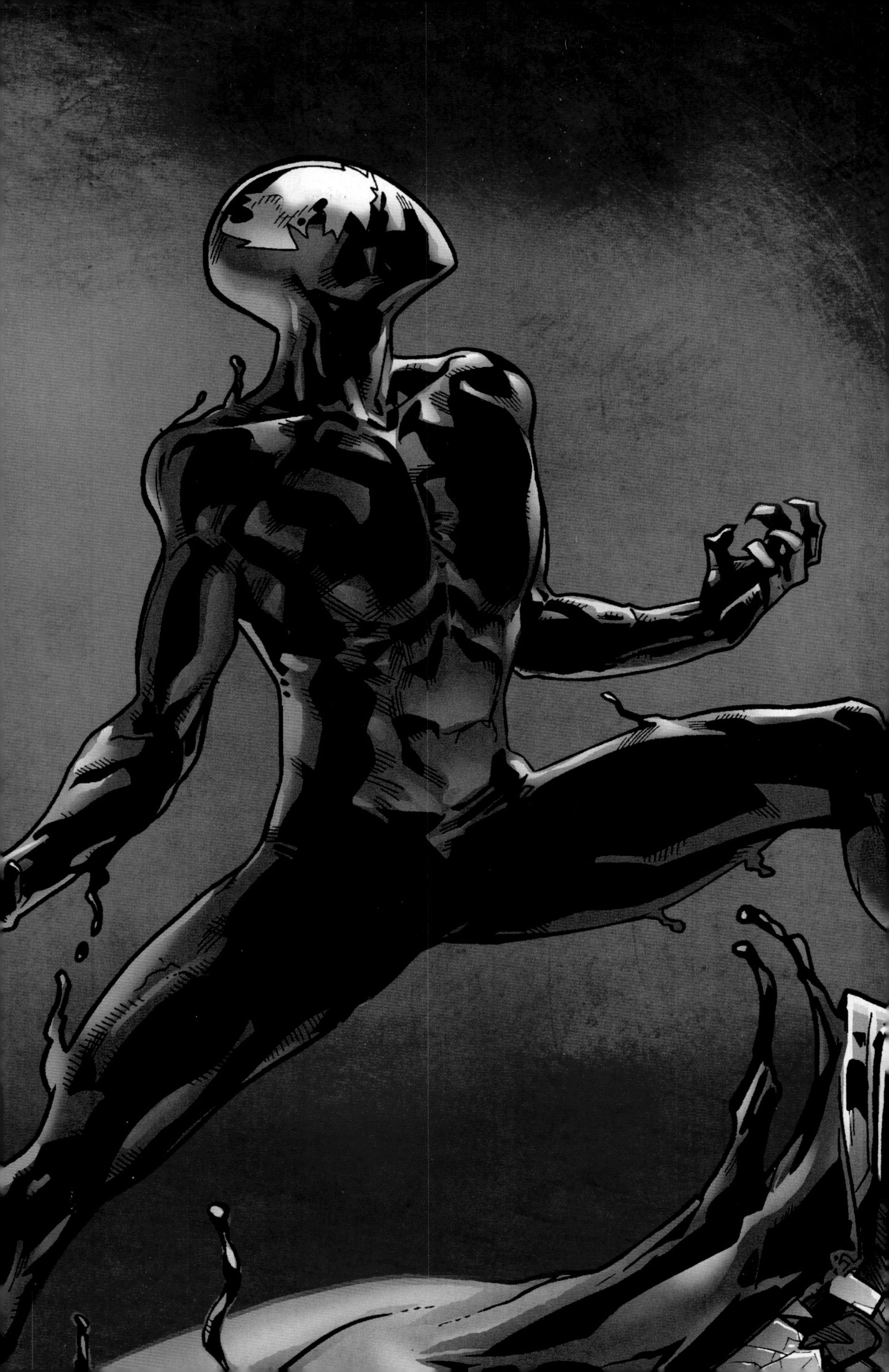

PREVIOUSLY

The bite of a genetically altered spider granted high-school student Peter Parker incredible arach nid-like powers! When a burglar killed his beloved Uncle Ben, a grief-stricken Peter vowed to use his amazing abilities to protect his fellow man. He learned the invaluable lesson that with great power there must also come great responsibility!

Now the fledgling super hero tries to balance a full high-school curriculum, a night job as a web designer for the Daily Bugle tabloid, a relationship with the beautiful Mary Jane Watson, and swing time as the misunderstood, web-slinging Spider-Man!

Peter Parker and Mary Jane have gotten back together, leaving his troubled relationship with Kitty Pryde (of the world-famous X-Men) in shambles. To complicate matters even further, Kitty who was kicked out of the X-Men, now goes to school with them!

But that's not the end of his problems!

Some time ago, Peter was attacked by his good friend Eddie Brock, who, under the control of the dangerous organism known as Venom, has a vendetta against Spider-Man. Managing to escape Venom's assault, Peter discovered that the Venom organism was accidentally created years before by none other than Peter and Eddie's fathers. This deadly legacy has now caught up to Peter, and though he thinks Venom is gone from his life, things are about to change...

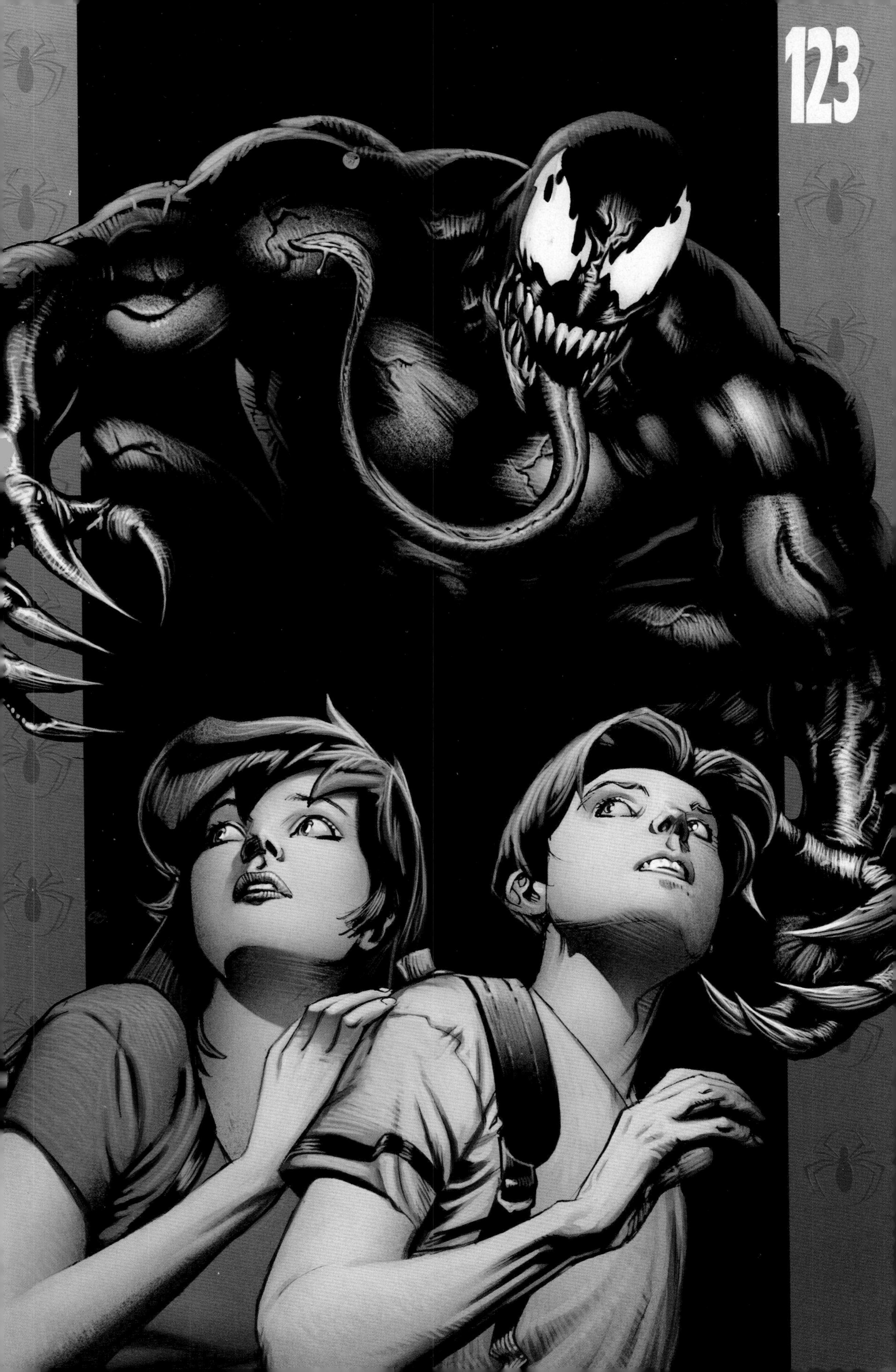
123

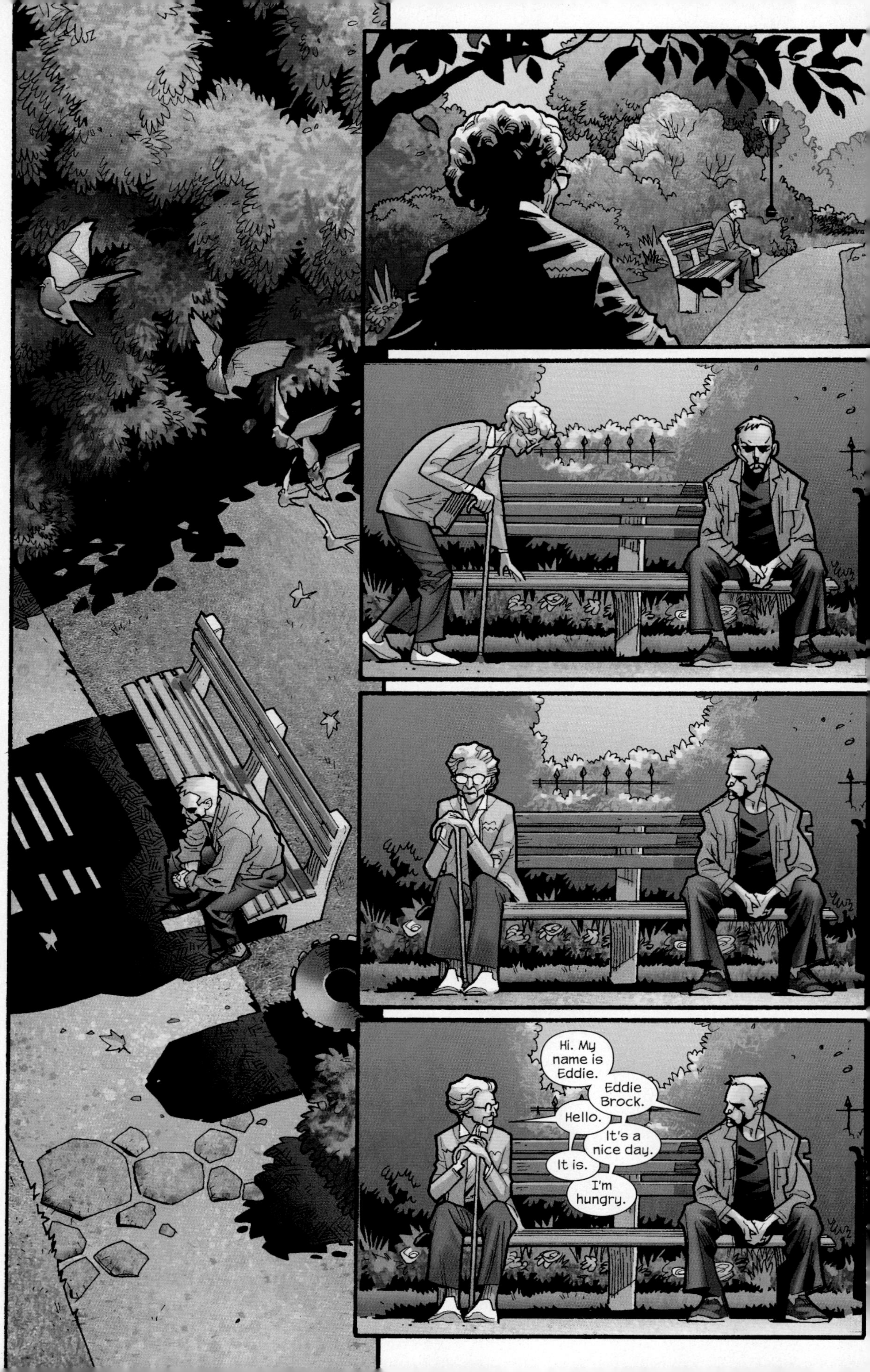
Hi. My name is Eddie.
Eddie Brock.
Hello.
It's a nice day.
It is.
I'm hungry.

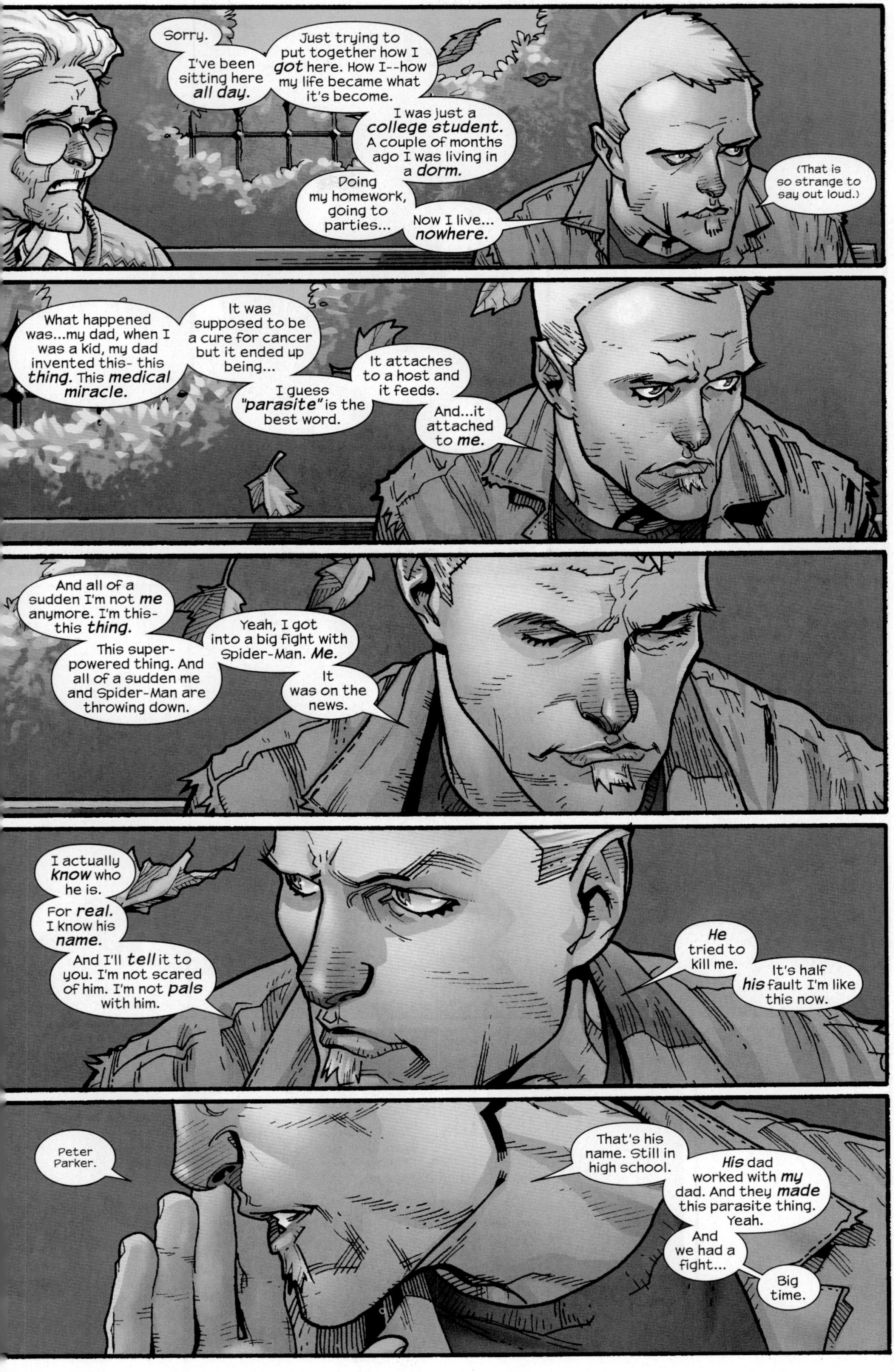
Sorry.
I've been sitting here all day.
Just trying to put together how I got here. How I--how my life became what it's become.
I was just a college student. A couple of months ago I was living in a dorm.
Doing my homework, going to parties...
Now I live... nowhere.
(That is so strange to say out loud.)
What happened was...my dad, when I was a kid, my dad invented this- this thing. This medical miracle.
It was supposed to be a cure for cancer but it ended up being...
I guess "parasite" is the best word.
It attaches to a host and it feeds.
And...it attached to me.
And all of a sudden I'm not me anymore. I'm this- this thing.
This super-powered thing. And all of a sudden me and Spider-Man are throwing down.
Yeah, I got into a big fight with Spider-Man. Me.
It was on the news.
I actually know who he is.
For real. I know his name.
And I'll tell it to you. I'm not scared of him. I'm not pals with him.
He tried to kill me.
It's half his fault I'm like this now.
Peter Parker.
That's his name. Still in high school.
His dad worked with my dad. And they made this parasite thing. Yeah.
And we had a fight...
Big time.

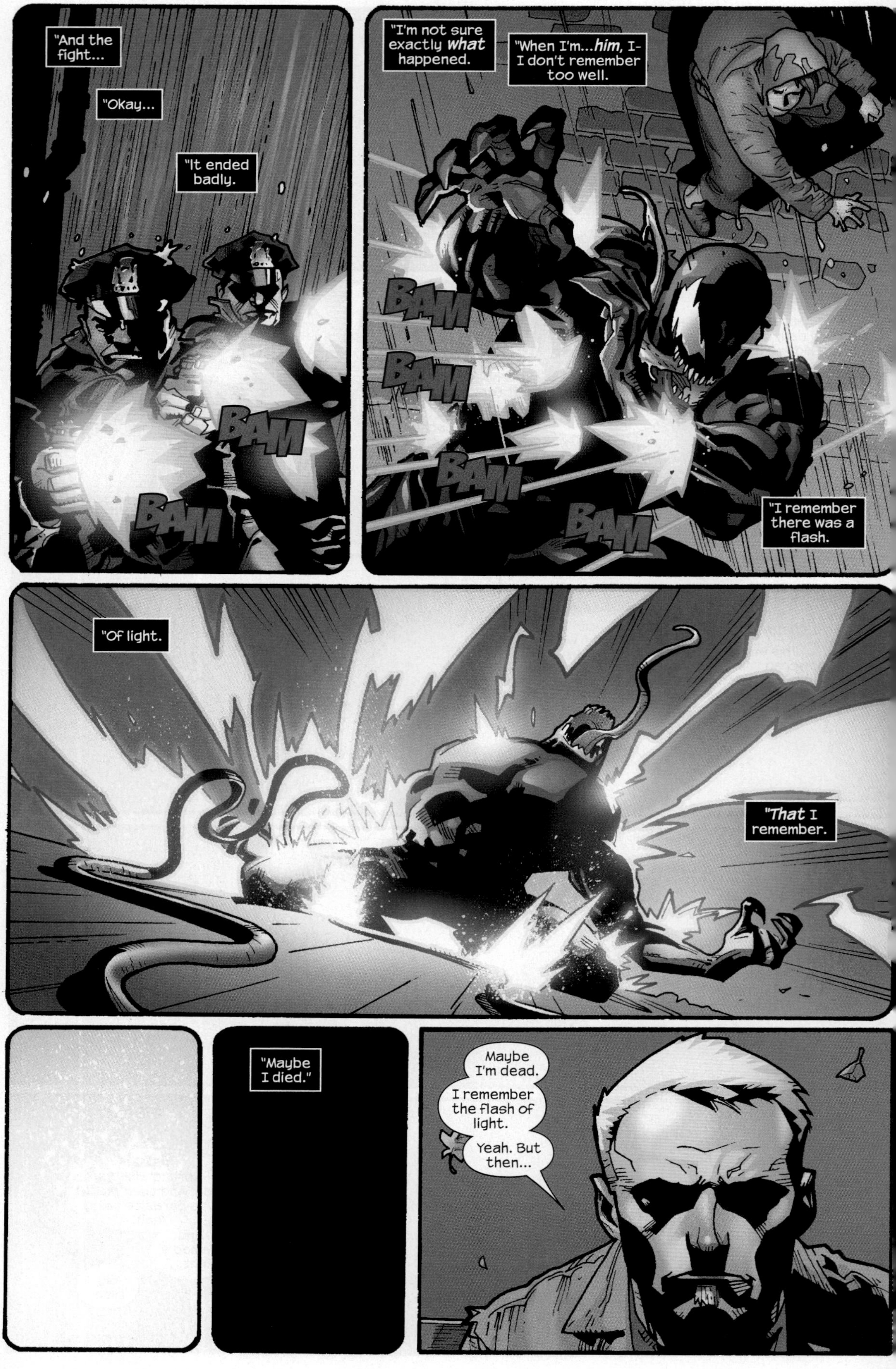
"And the fight...
"Okay...
"It ended badly.
BAM
BAM
"I'm not sure exactly *what* happened.
"When I'm...*him*, I-I don't remember too well.
BAM
BAM
BAM
BAM
"I remember there was a flash.
"Of light.
"*That* I remember.
"Maybe I died."
Maybe I'm dead.
I remember the flash of light.
Yeah. But then...

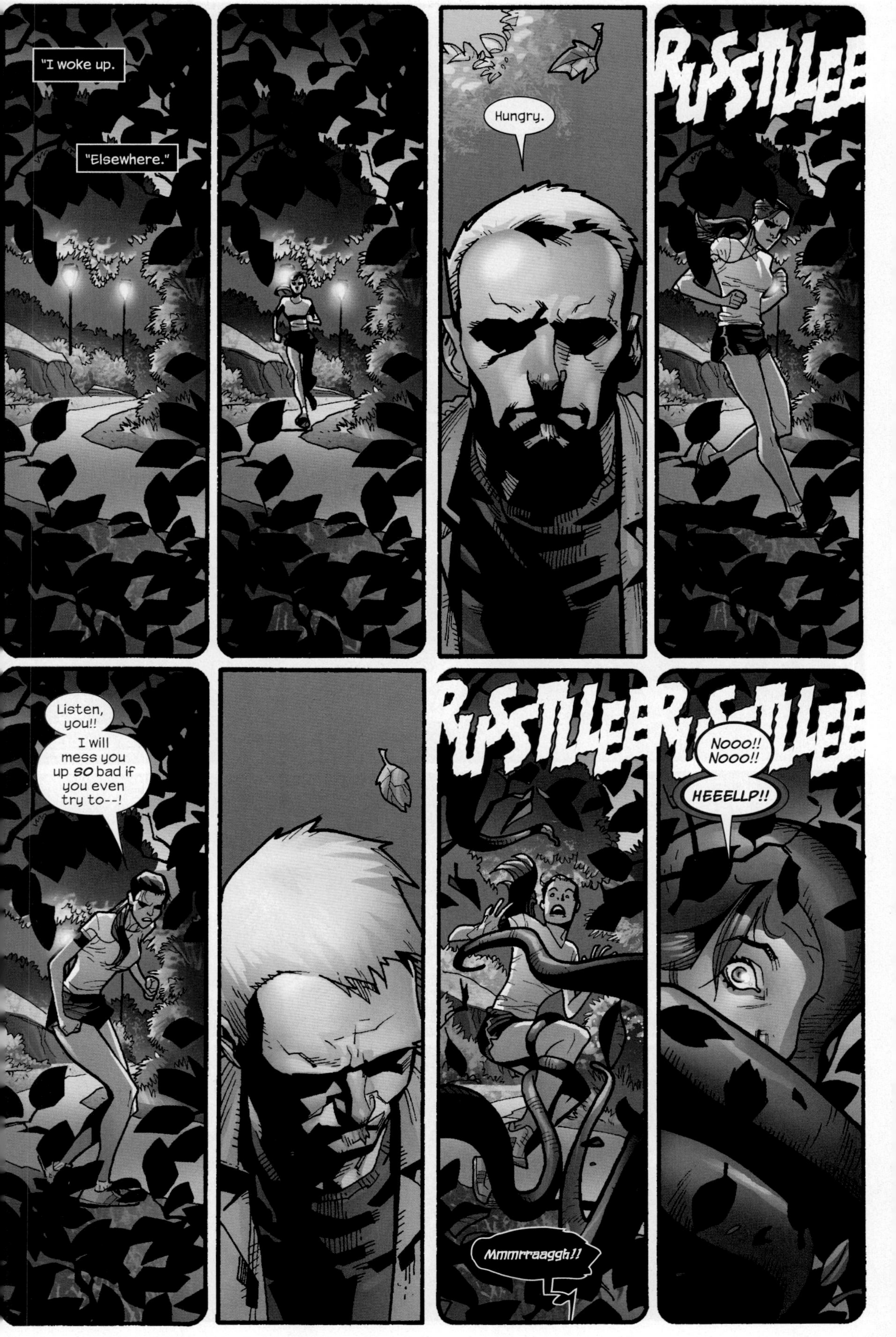
"I woke up.
"Elsewhere."
Hungry.
RUSTLLEE
Listen, you!! I will mess you up SO bad if you even try to--!
RUSTLLEER
RUSTLLEE
Nooo!! Nooo!!
HEEELLP!!
Mmmrraaggh!!

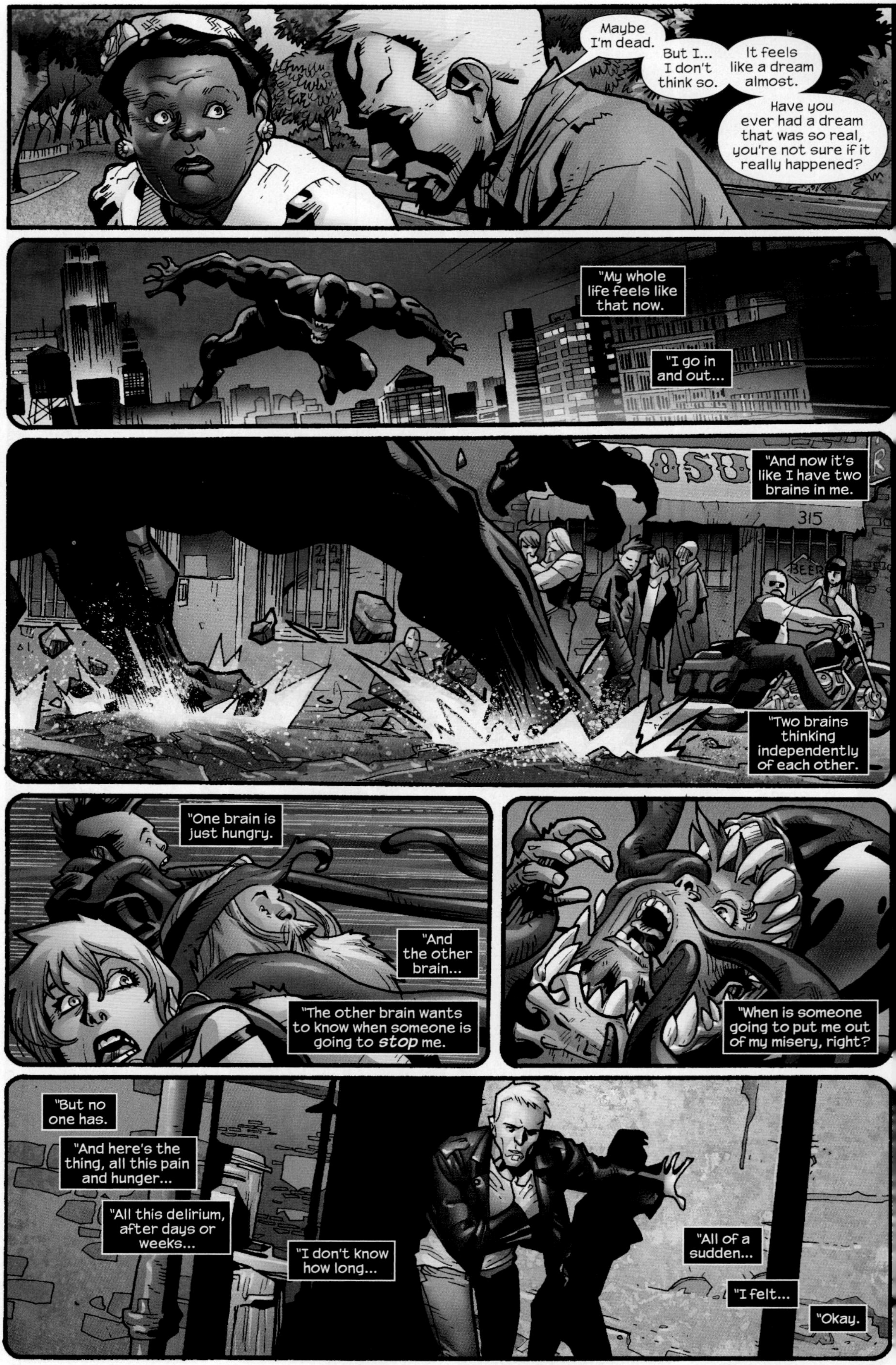
Maybe I'm dead.
But I... I don't think so.
It feels like a dream almost.
Have you ever had a dream that was so real, you're not sure if it really happened?
"My whole life feels like that now.
"I go in and out...
"And now it's like I have two brains in me.
315
BEER
"Two brains thinking independently of each other.
"One brain is just hungry.
"And the other brain...
"The other brain wants to know when someone is going to *stop* me.
"When is someone going to put me out of my misery, right?
"But no one has.
"And here's the thing, all this pain and hunger...
"All this delirium, after days or weeks...
"I don't know how long...
"All of a sudden...
"I felt...
"Okay.

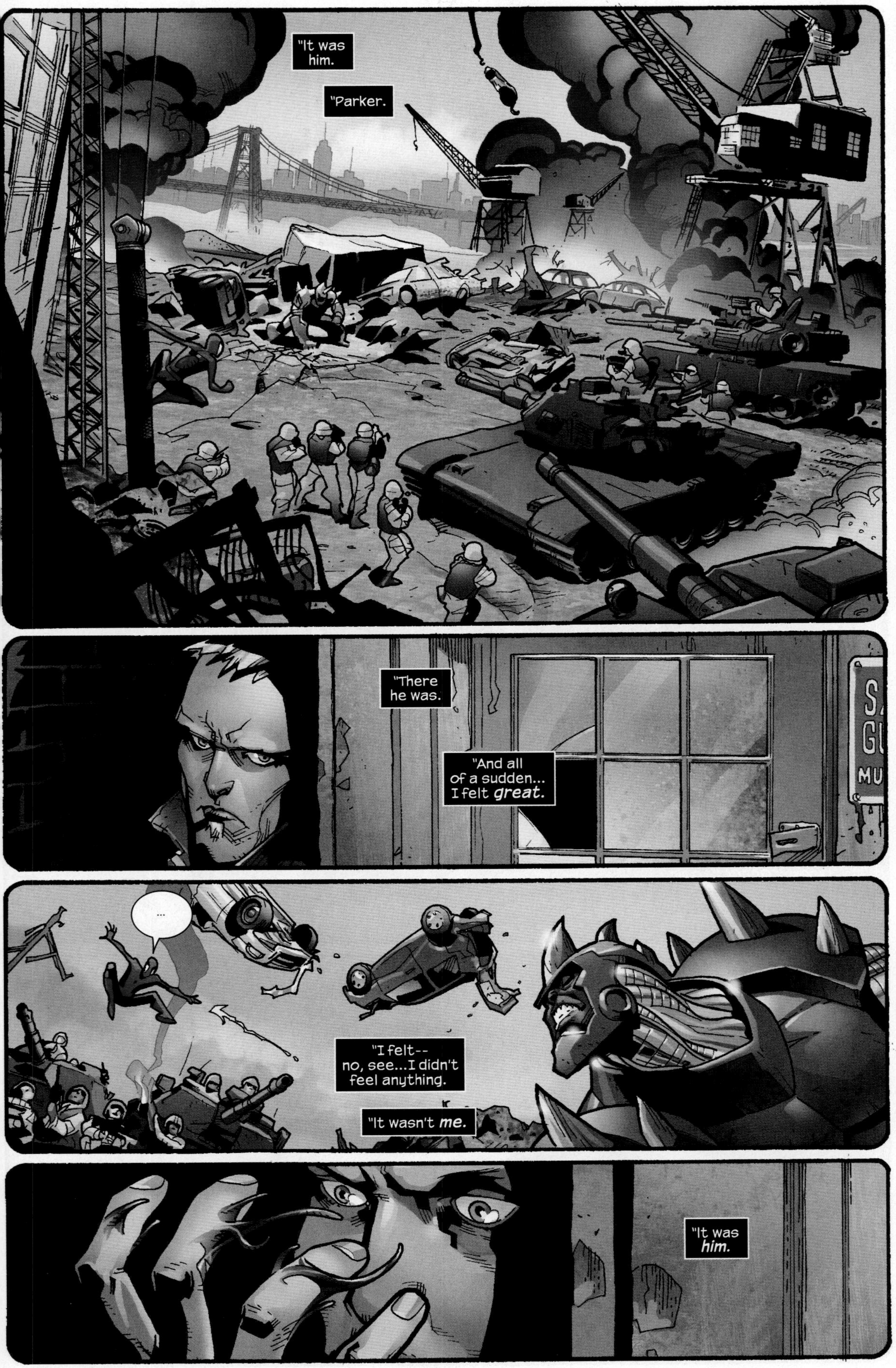
"It was him.
"Parker.
"There he was.
"And all of a sudden... I felt *great.*
...
"I felt-- no, see... I didn't feel anything.
"It wasn't *me.*
"It was *him.*

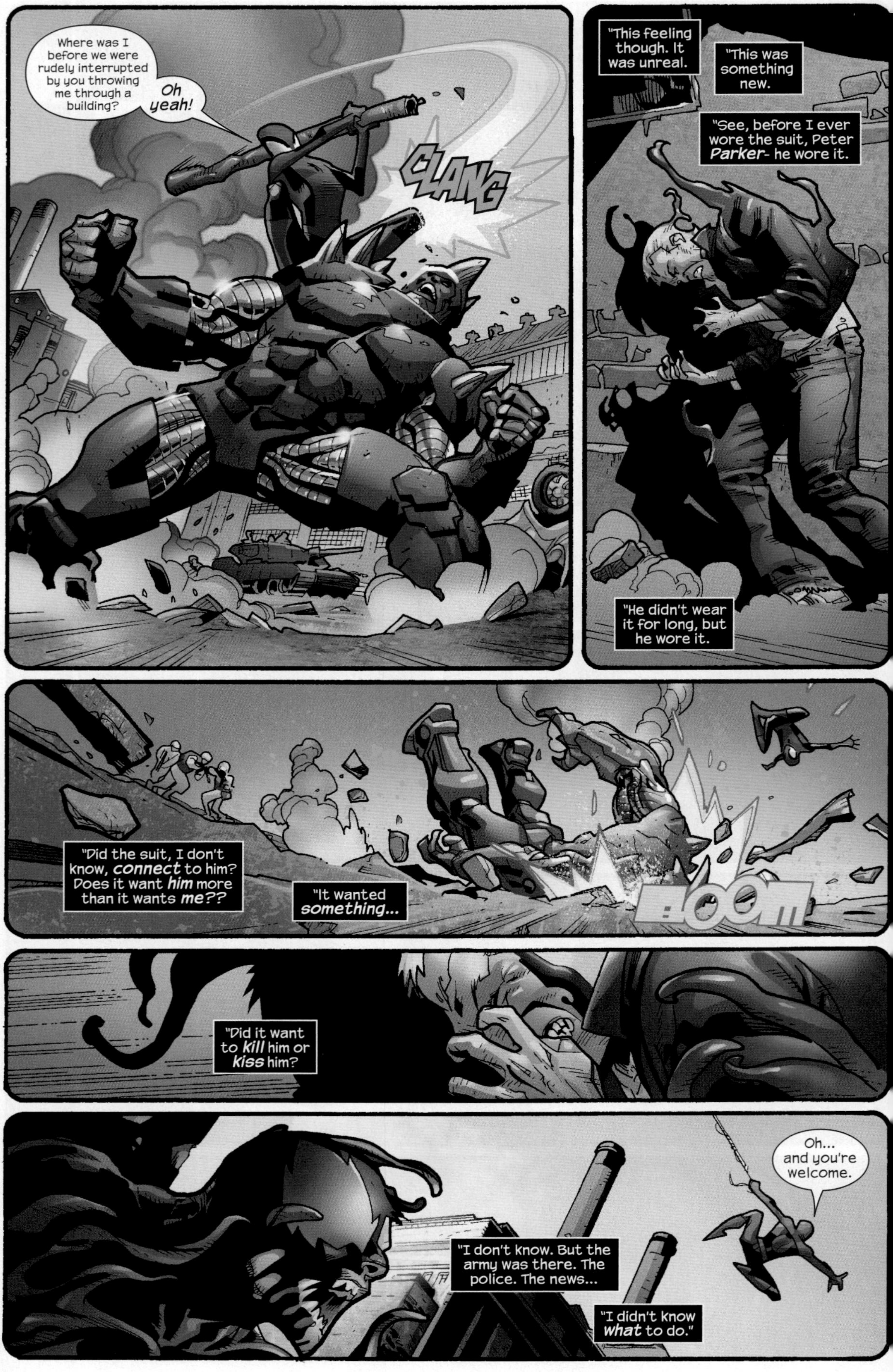
Where was I before we were rudely interrupted by you throwing me through a building?
Oh yeah!
CLANG
"This feeling though. It was unreal.
"This was something new.
"See, before I ever wore the suit, Peter Parker- he wore it.
"He didn't wear it for long, but he wore it.
"Did the suit, I don't know, connect to him? Does it want him more than it wants me??
"It wanted something...
BOOM
"Did it want to kill him or kiss him?
"I don't know. But the army was there. The police. The news...
"I didn't know what to do."
Oh... and you're welcome.

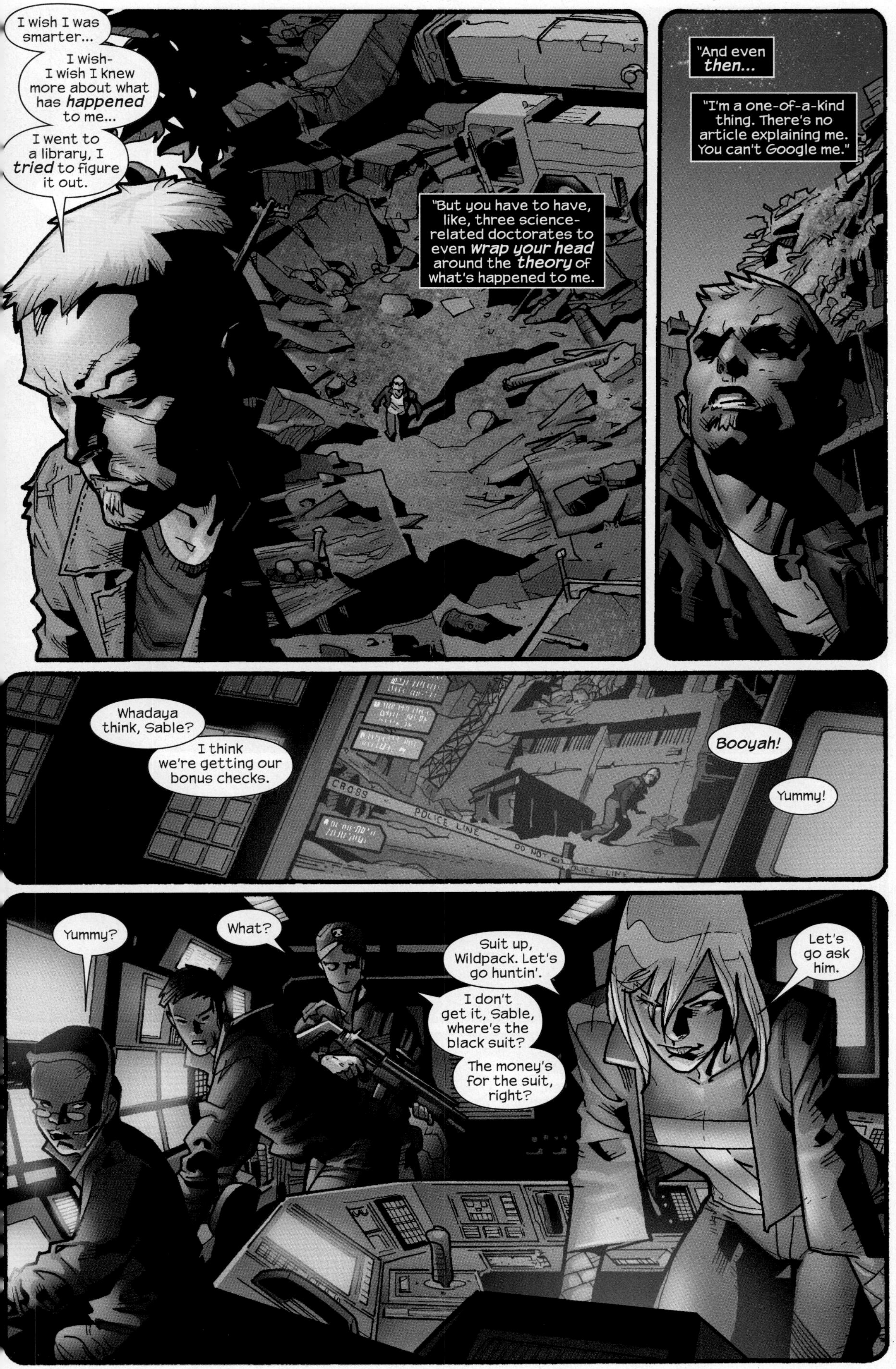

I wish I was smarter...
I wish- I wish I knew more about what has *happened* to me...
I went to a library, I *tried* to figure it out.
"But you have to have, like, three science-related doctorates to even *wrap your head* around the *theory* of what's happened to me.
"And even *then...*
"I'm a one-of-a-kind thing. There's no article explaining me. You can't Google me."
Whadaya think, Sable?
I think we're getting our bonus checks.
Booyah!
Yummy!
CROSS
POLICE LINE
DO NOT
Yummy?
What?
Suit up, Wildpack. Let's go huntin'.
I don't get it, Sable, where's the black suit?
The money's for the suit, right?
Let's go ask him.

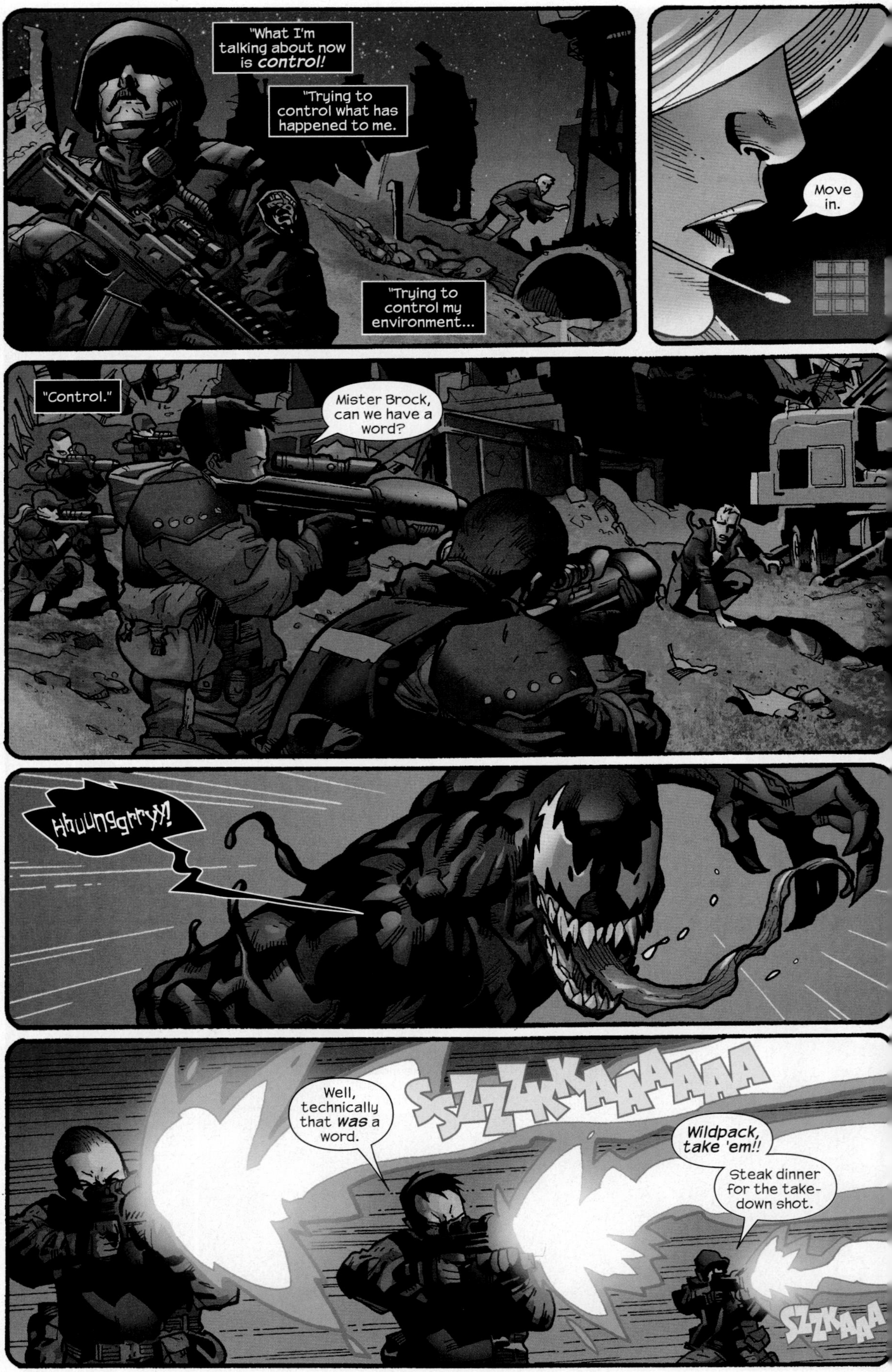
"What I'm talking about now is *control!*
"Trying to control what has happened to me.
"Trying to control my environment...
Move in.
"Control."
Mister Brock, can we have a word?
Hhuuungrryy!
SSZZZKKAAAAAA
Well, technically that *was* a word.
Wildpack, take 'em!!
Steak dinner for the take-down shot.
SZZKAAA

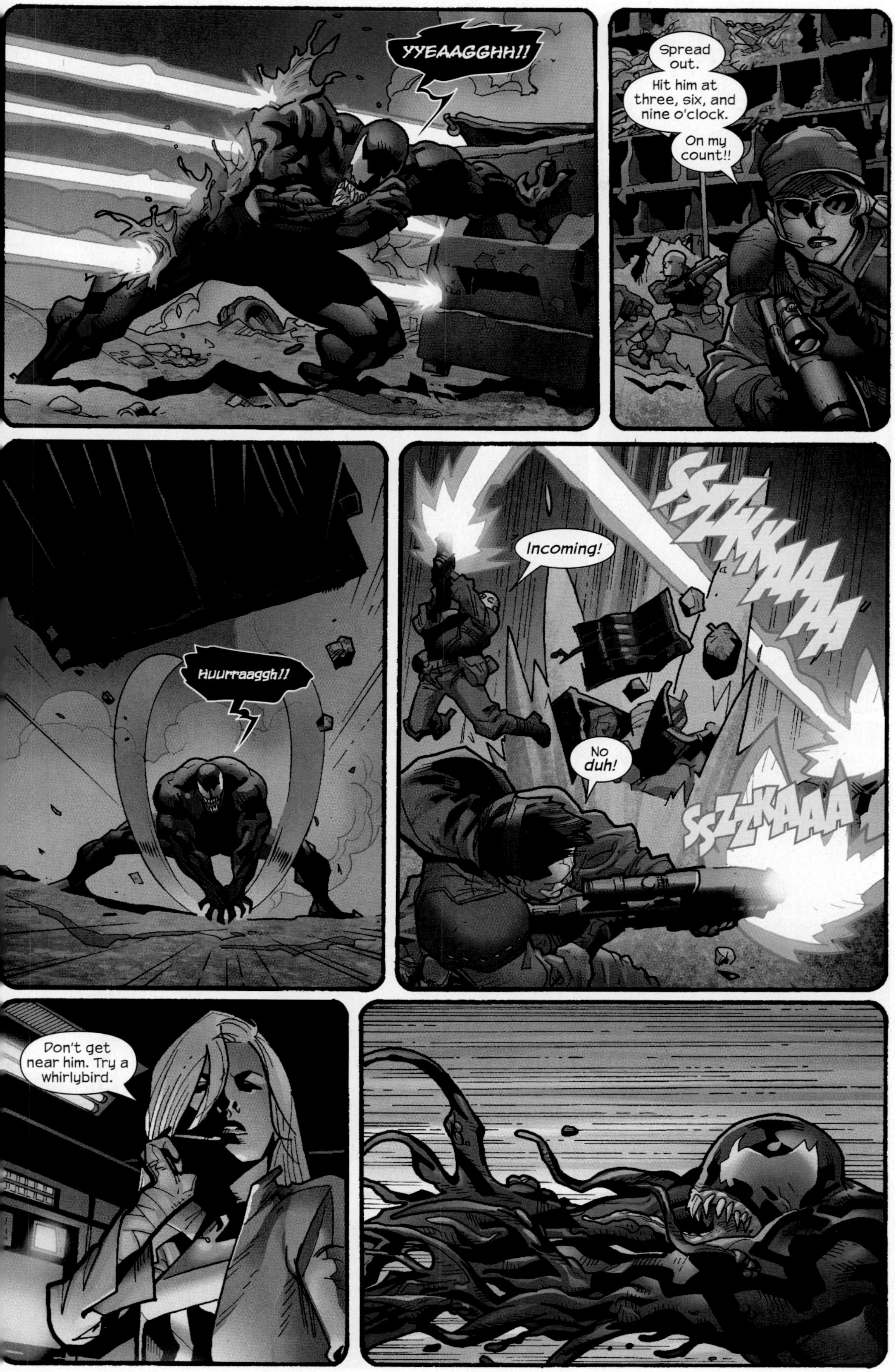
YYEAAGGHH!!
Spread out.
Hit him at three, six, and nine o'clock.
On my count!!
Huurraaggh!!
Incoming!
SSZZKKAAAA
No duh!
SSZZKAAA
Don't get near him. Try a whirlybird.

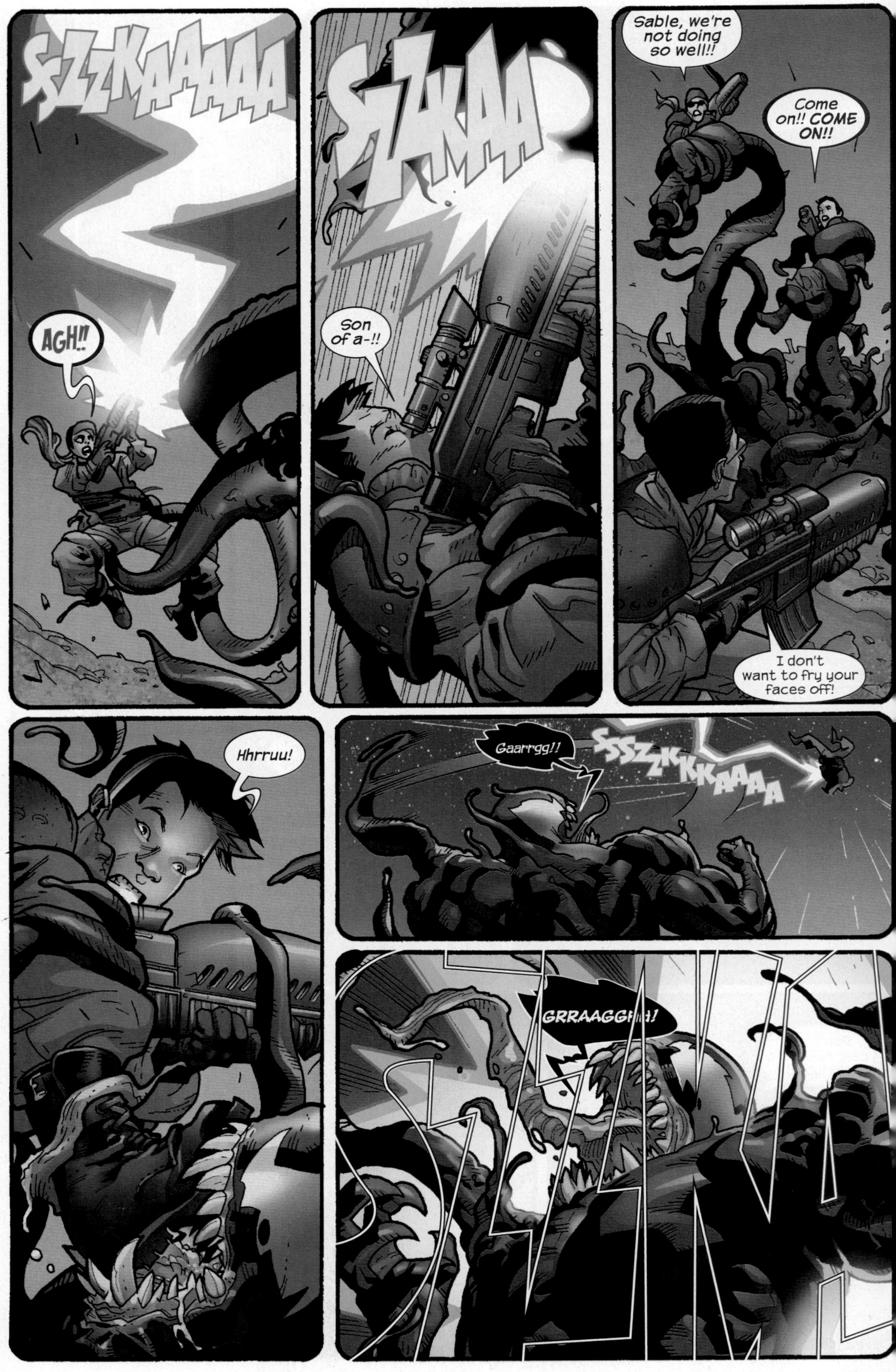

SZZKAAAAAA
AGH!!
SZKAA
Son of a-!!
Sable, we're not doing so well!!
Come on!! COME ON!!
I don't want to fry your faces off!
Hhrruu!
Gaarrgg!!
SSSZKKKAAAAA

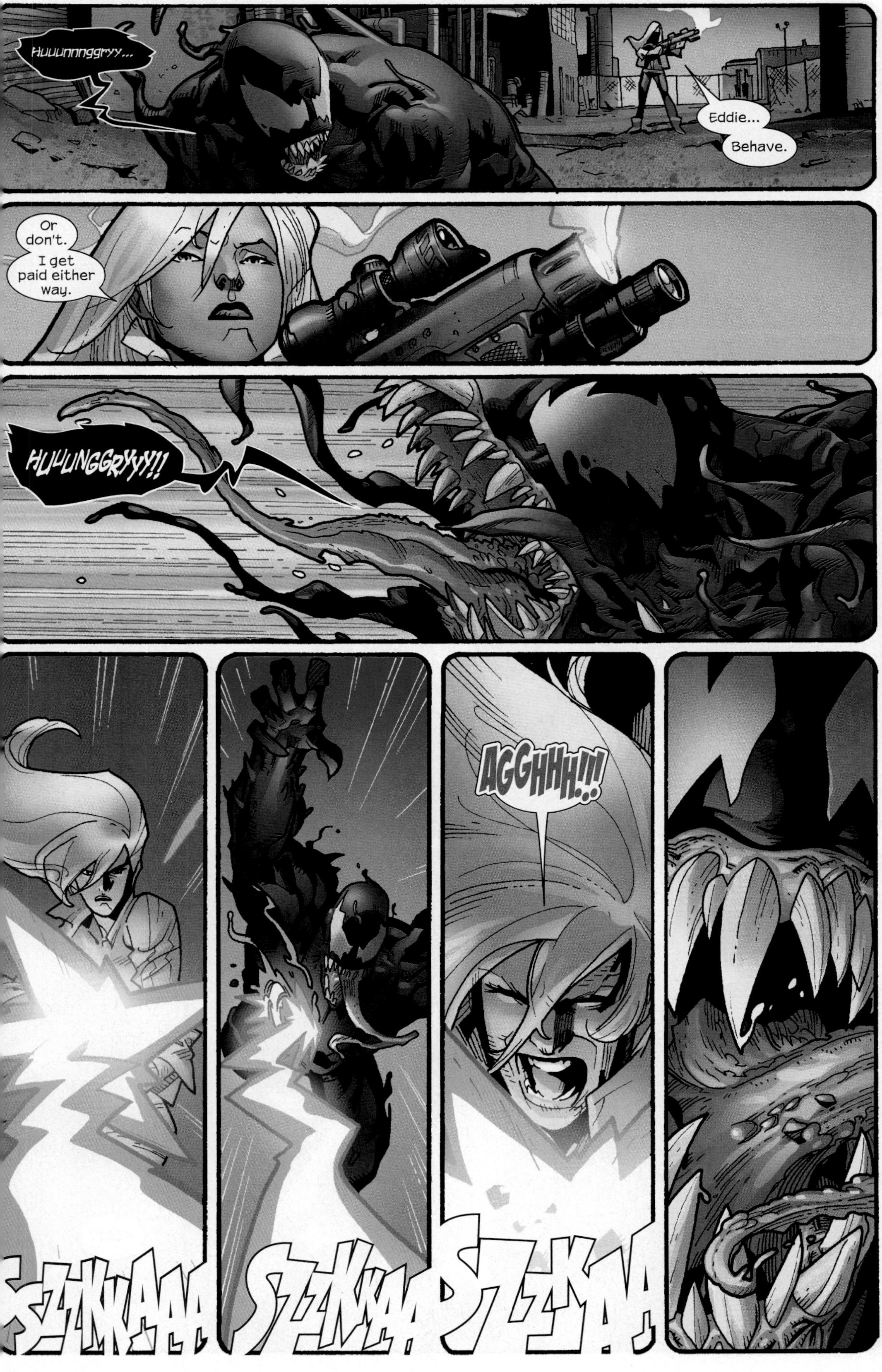
Huuunnnggryy...
Eddie...
Behave.
Or don't. I get paid either way.
HUUUNGGRYYY!!
AGGHHH!!!
SZZKKAAA
SZZKKAA
SZZKAA

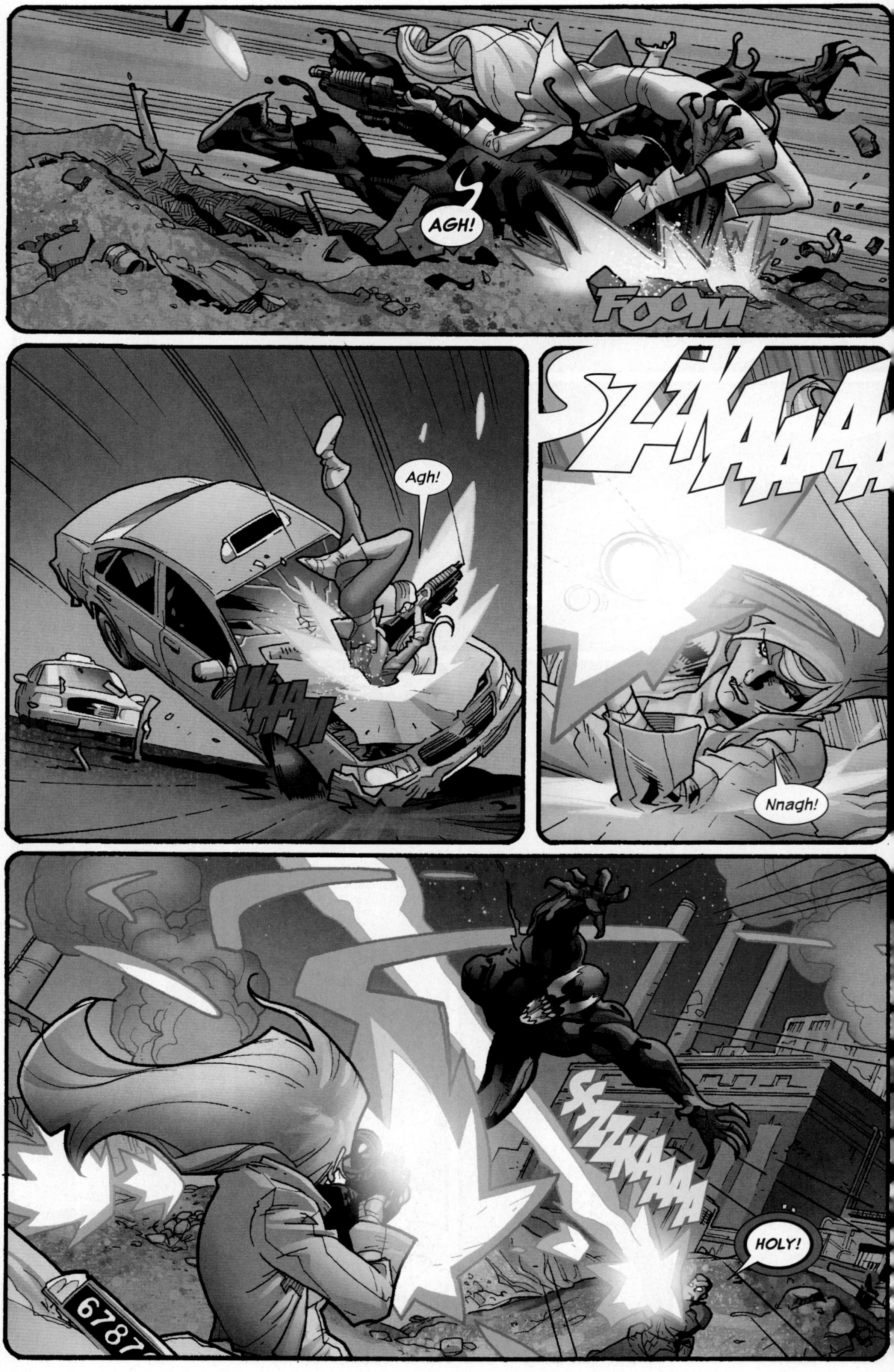
AGH!
FOOM
Agh!
WHAM
SZZKAAAA
Nnagh!
SSZZKAAAA
HOLY!
6787

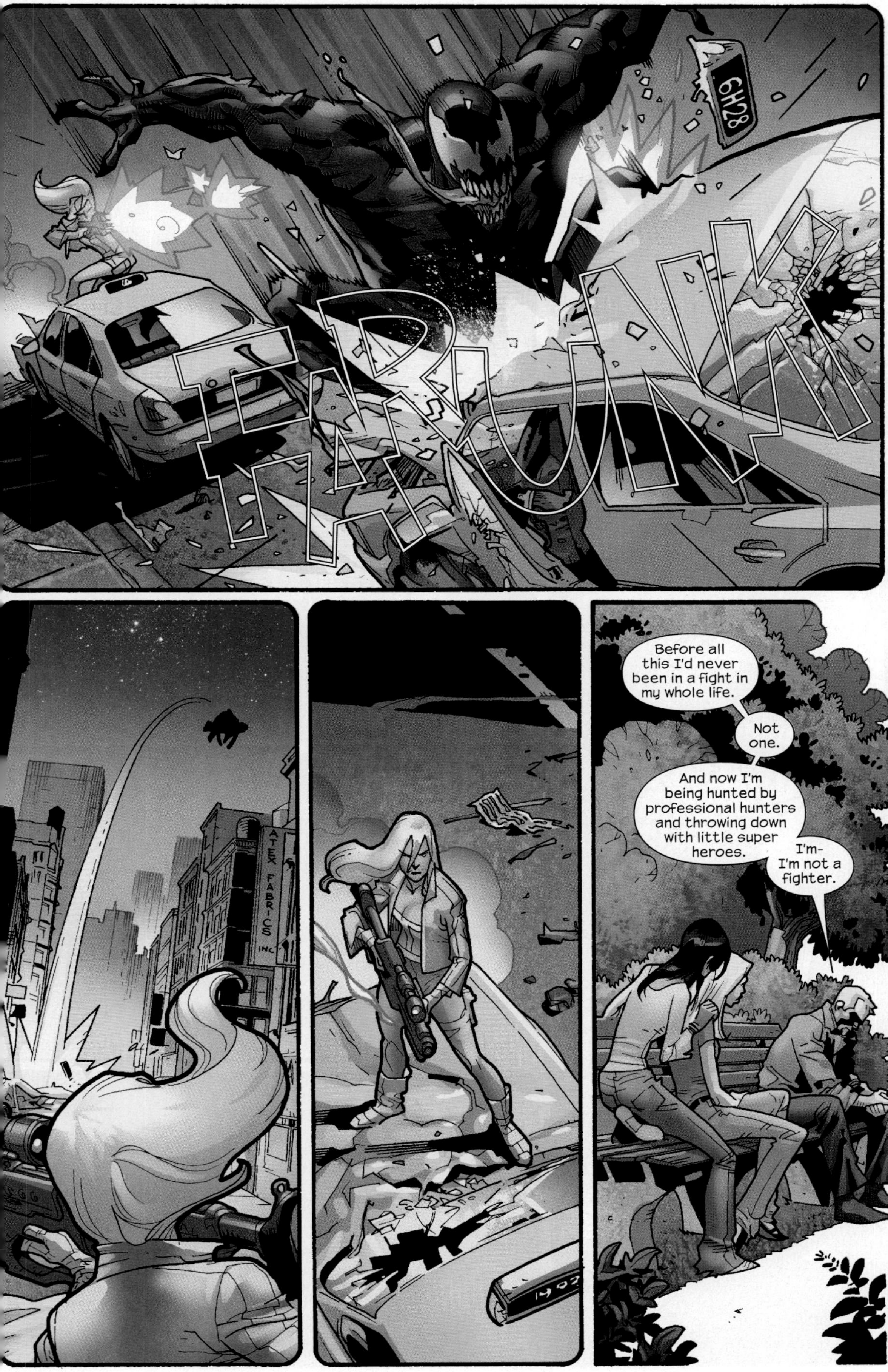
FARUNK
Before all this I'd never been in a fight in my whole life.
Not one.
And now I'm being hunted by professional hunters and throwing down with little super heroes.
I'm- I'm not a fighter.

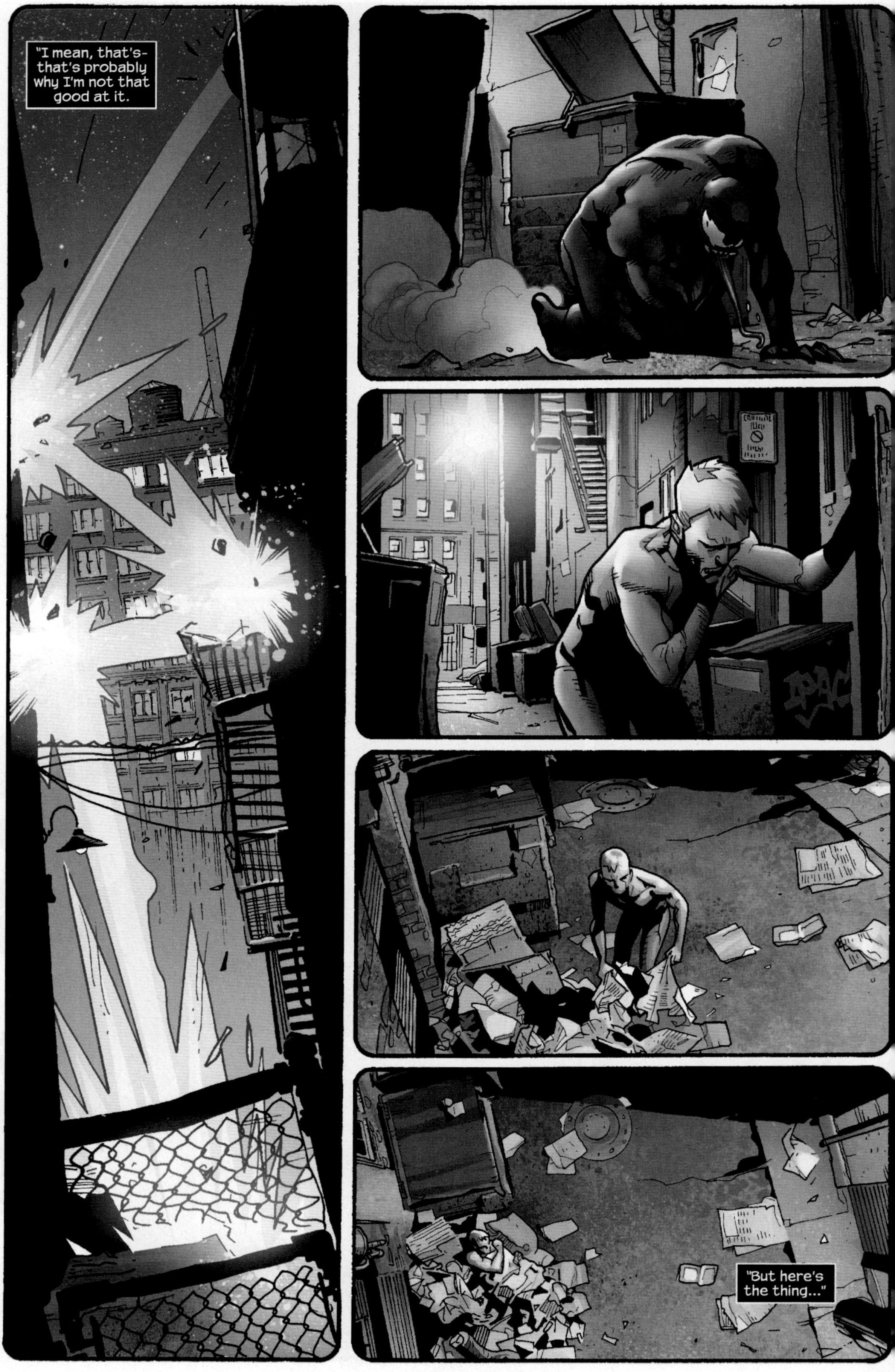
"I mean, that's-that's probably why I'm not that good at it.
"But here's the thing..."

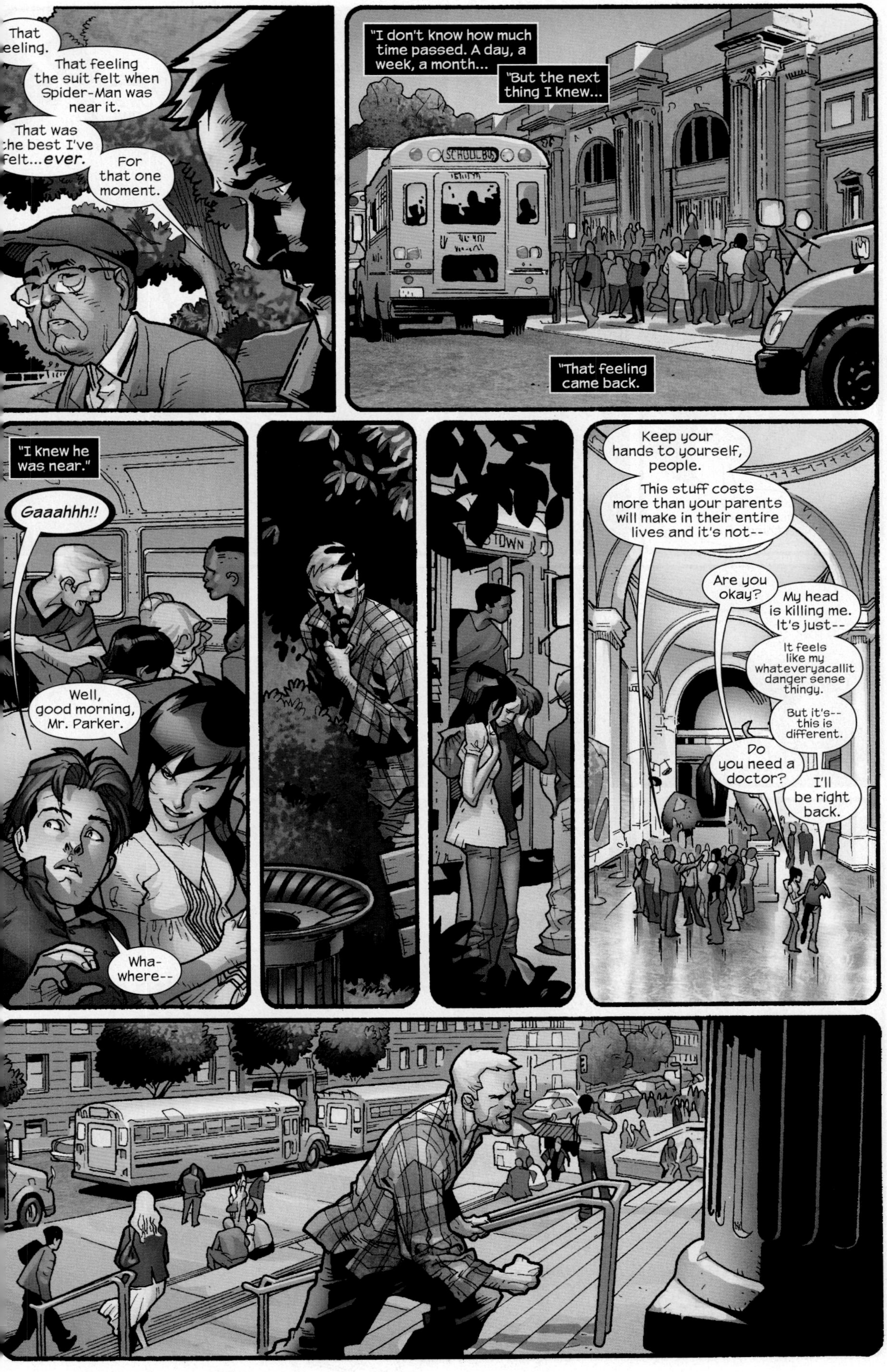

That
eeling.
That feeling the suit felt when Spider-Man was near it.
That was :he best I've felt... *ever.*
For that one moment.
"I don't know how much time passed. A day, a week, a month...
"But the next thing I knew...
"That feeling came back.
"I knew he was near."
Gaaahhh!!
Well, good morning, Mr. Parker.
Wha- where--
Keep your hands to yourself, people.
This stuff costs more than your parents will make in their entire lives and it's not--
Are you okay?
My head is killing me. It's just--
It feels like my whateveryacallit danger sense thingy.
But it's-- this is different.
Do you need a doctor?
I'll be right back.

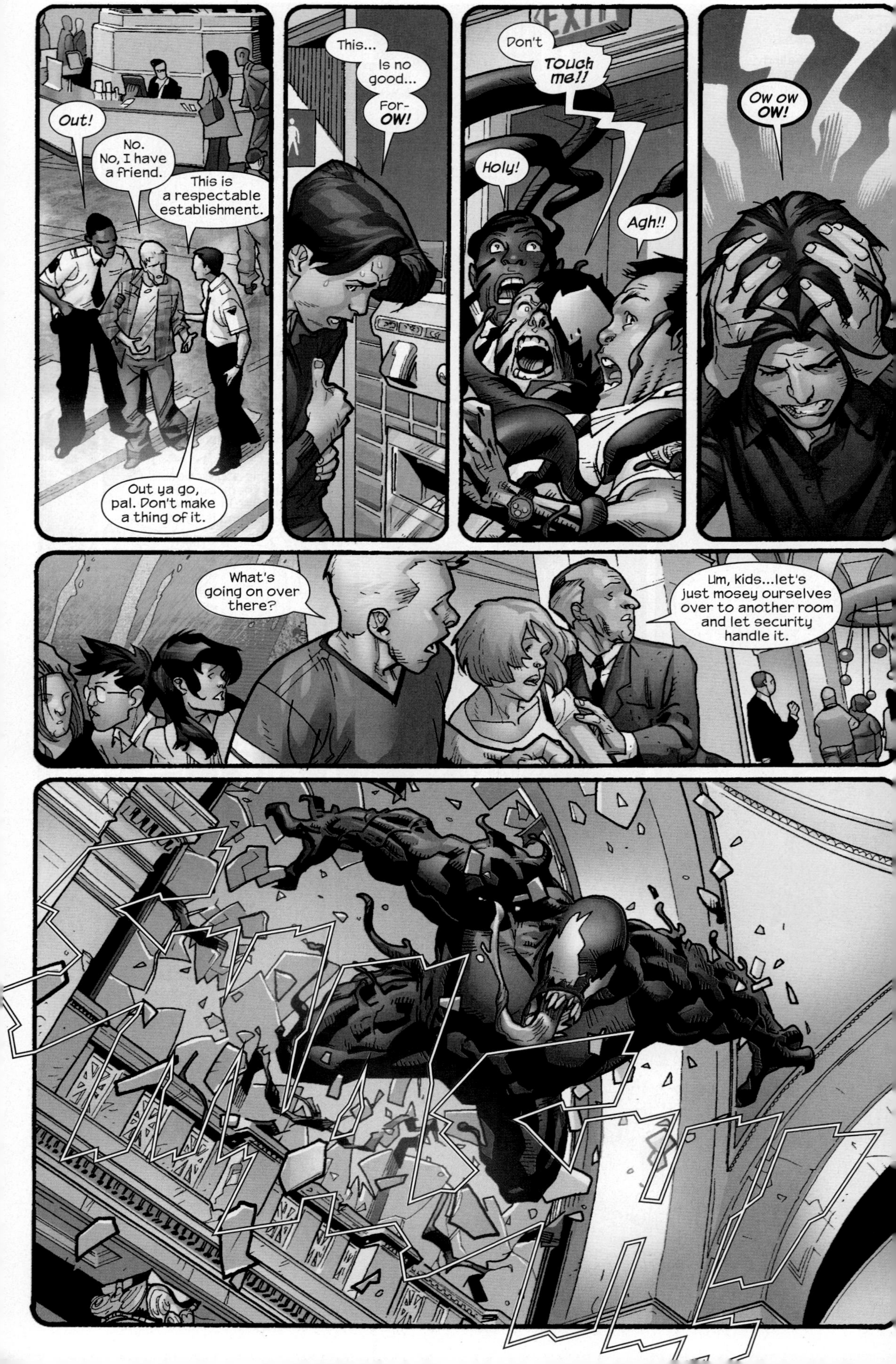
Out!
No. No, I have a friend.
This is a respectable establishment.
Out ya go, pal. Don't make a thing of it.
This...
Is no good...
For-OW!
Don't
Touch me!!
Holy!
Agh!!
Ow ow OW!
What's going on over there?
Um, kids...let's just mosey ourselves over to another room and let security handle it.

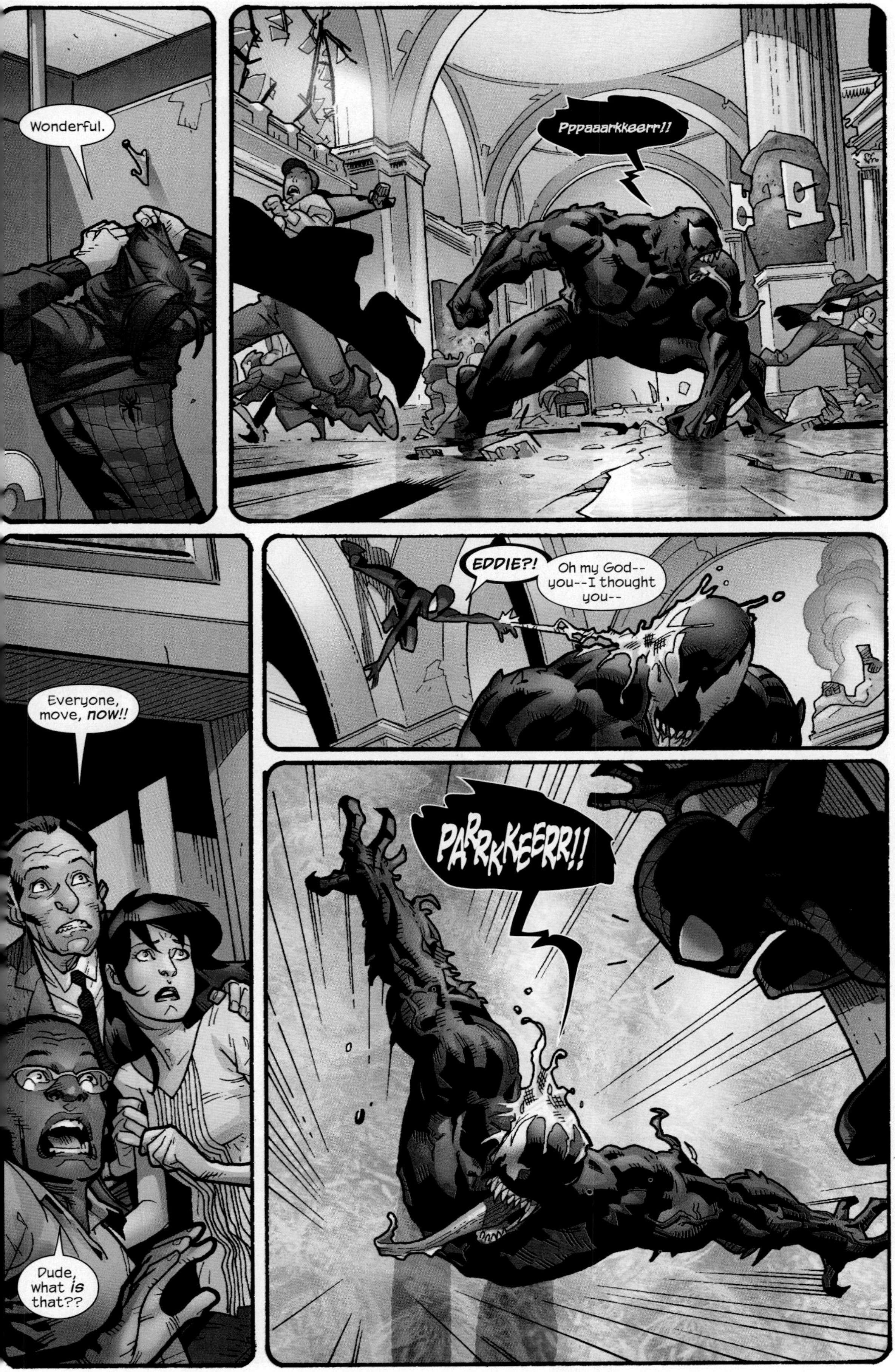
Wonderful.
Pppaaarkkeerr!!
Everyone, move, NOW!!
EDDIE?!
Oh my God--you--I thought you--
PARRKKEERR!!
Dude, what is that??

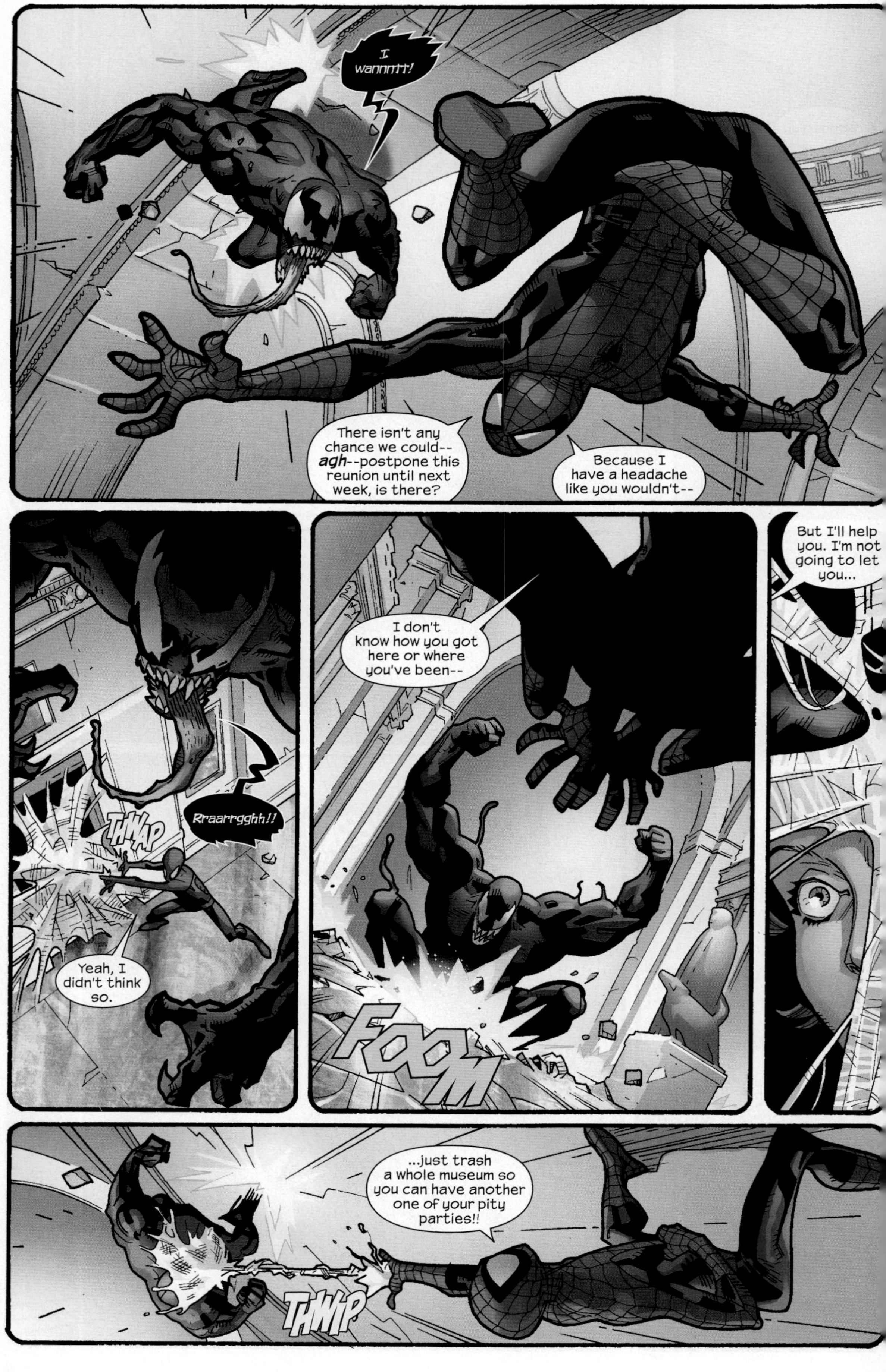
I wannnttt!
There isn't any chance we could--*agh*--postpone this reunion until next week, is there?
Because I have a headache like you wouldn't--
THWAP
Rraarrgghh!!
Yeah, I didn't think so.
I don't know how you got here or where you've been--
FOOM
But I'll help you. I'm not going to let you...
...just trash a whole museum so you can have another one of your pity parties!!
THWIP

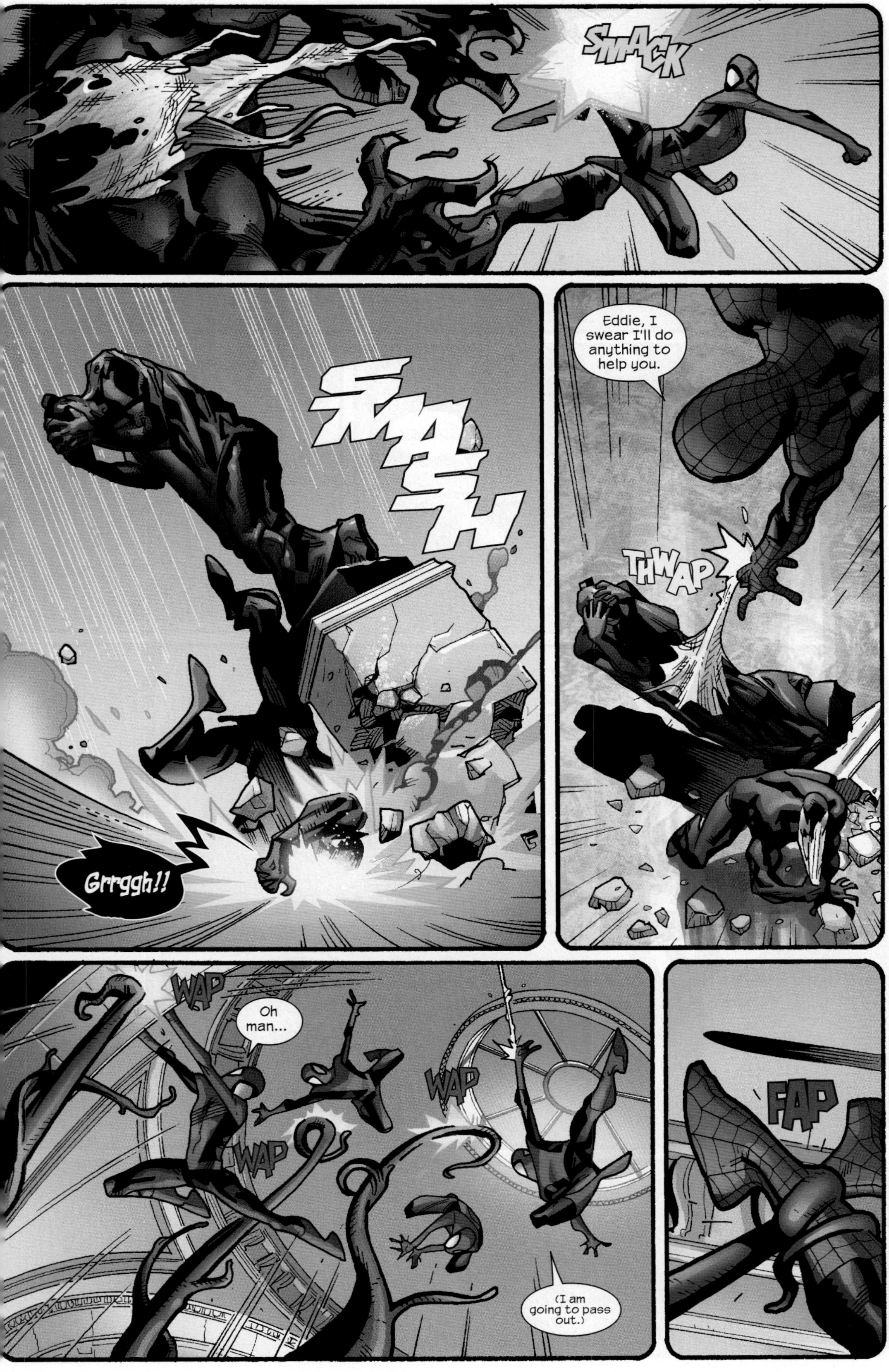
SMACK
SMASH
Grrggh!!
Eddie, I swear I'll do anything to help you.
THWAP
WAP
Oh man...
WAP
WAP
(I am going to pass out.)
FAP

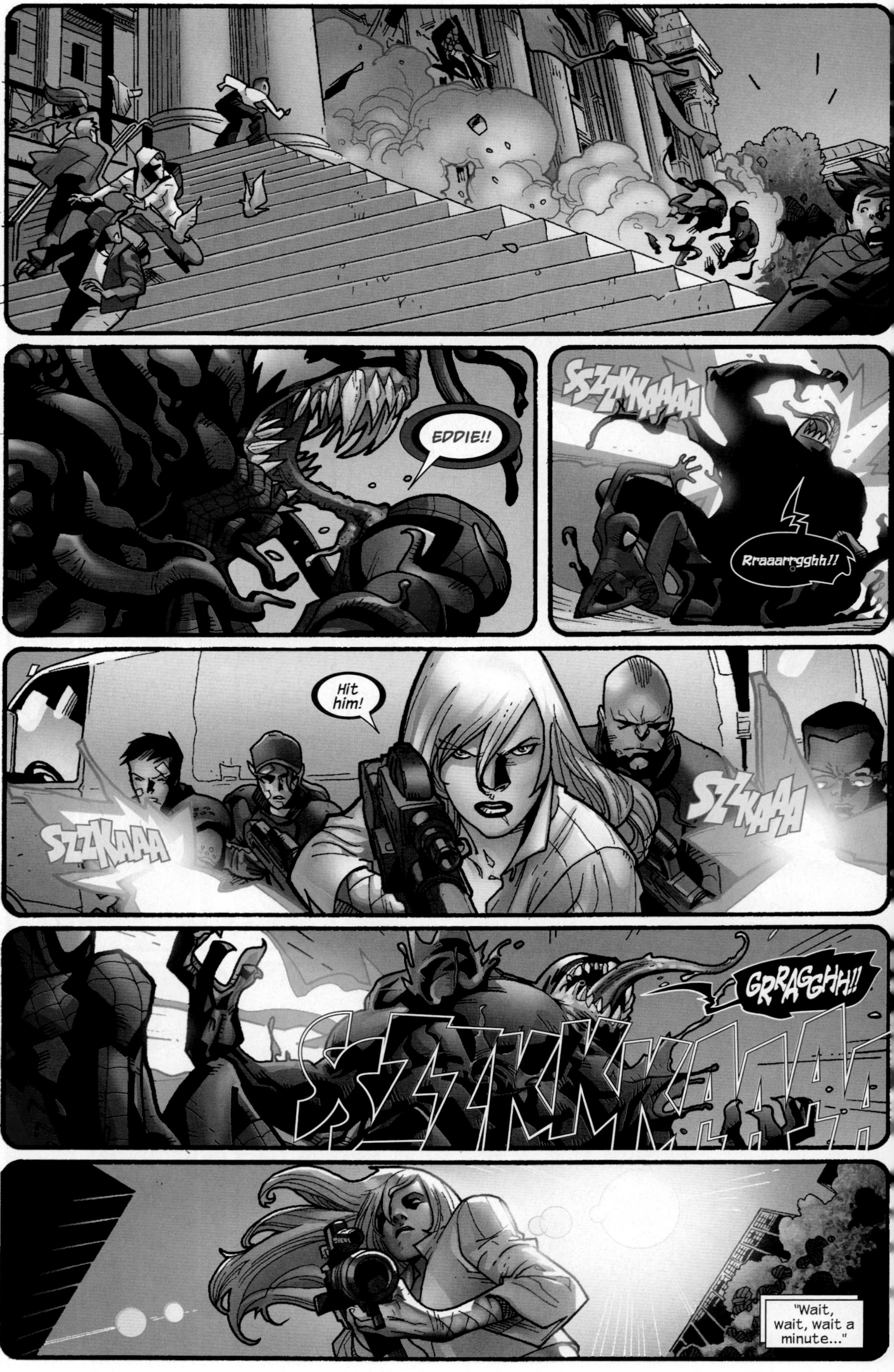
EDDIE!!
SZZKKAAAAA
Rraaarrgghh!!
Hit him!
SZZKAAA
SZKAAA
GRRAGGHH!!
SZZKKKAAAA
"Wait, wait, wait a minute..."

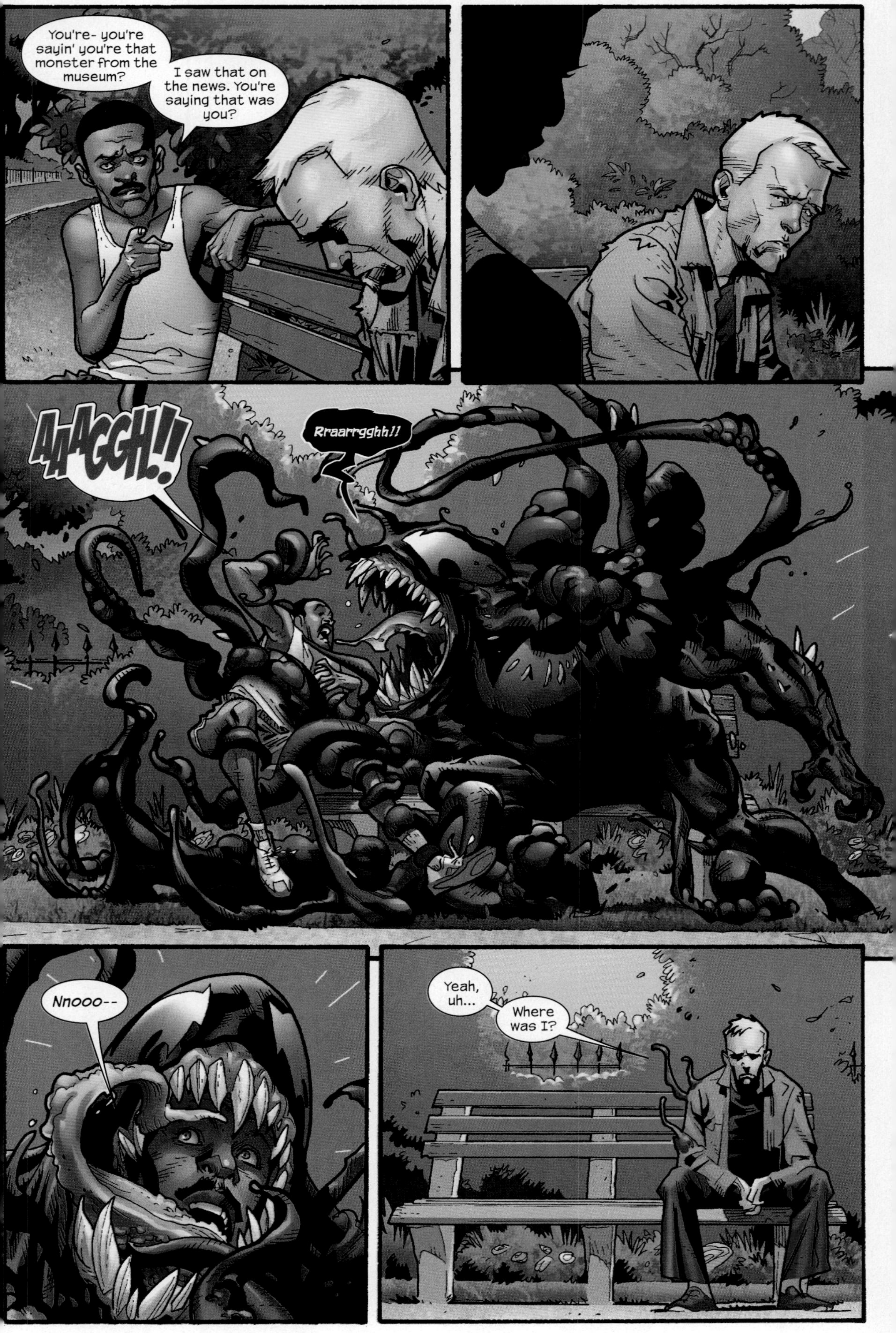

You're- you're sayin' you're that monster from the museum?
I saw that on the news. You're saying that was you?
AAAGGH!!
Rraarrgghh!!
Nnooo--
Yeah, uh...
Where was I?

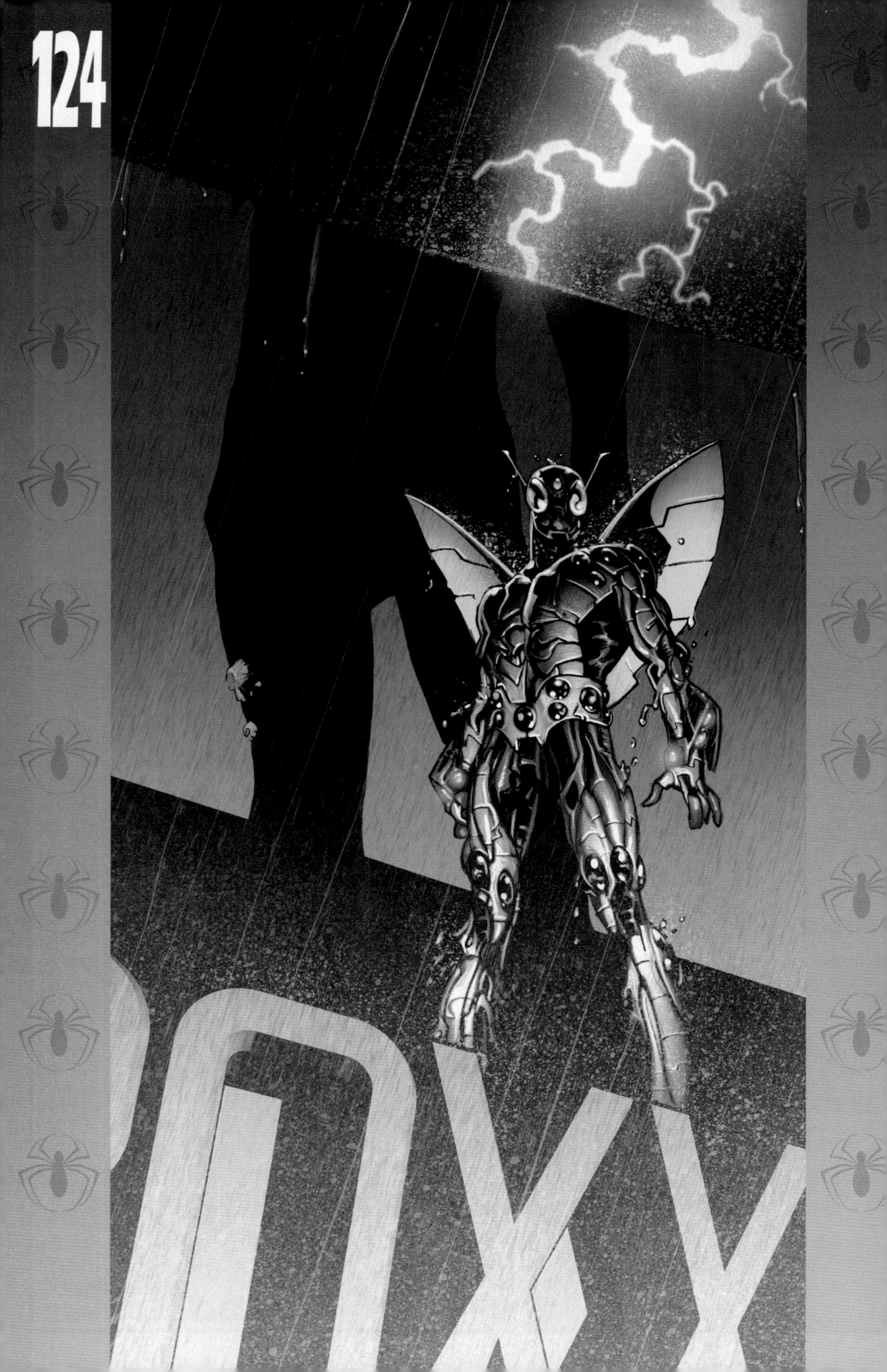
124

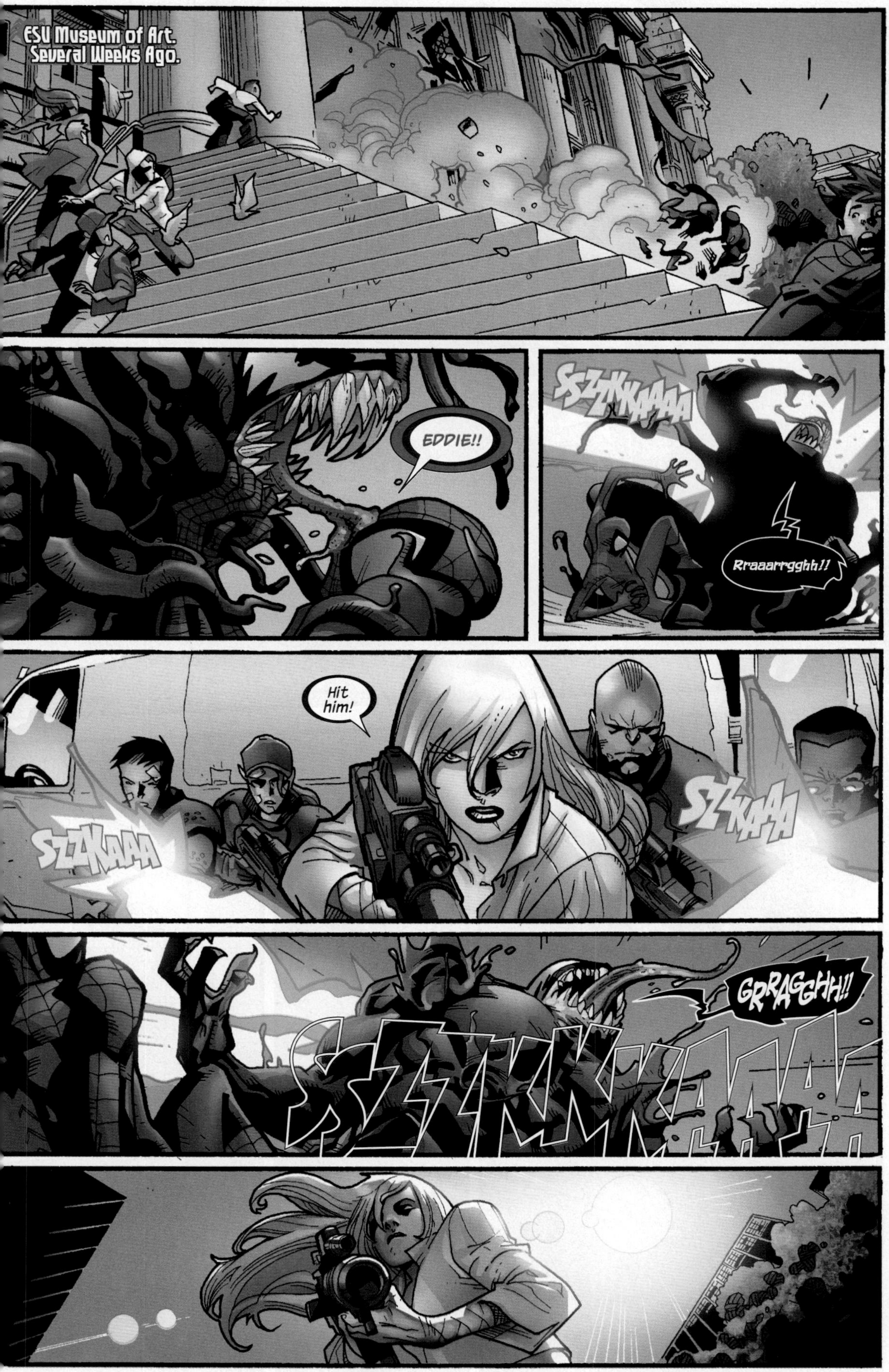
ESU Museum of Art. Several Weeks Ago.
EDDIE!!
SZZKKAAAA
Rraaarrgghh!!
Hit him!
SZZKAAA
SZZKAAA
GRRAGGHH!!
SZZKKAAAA

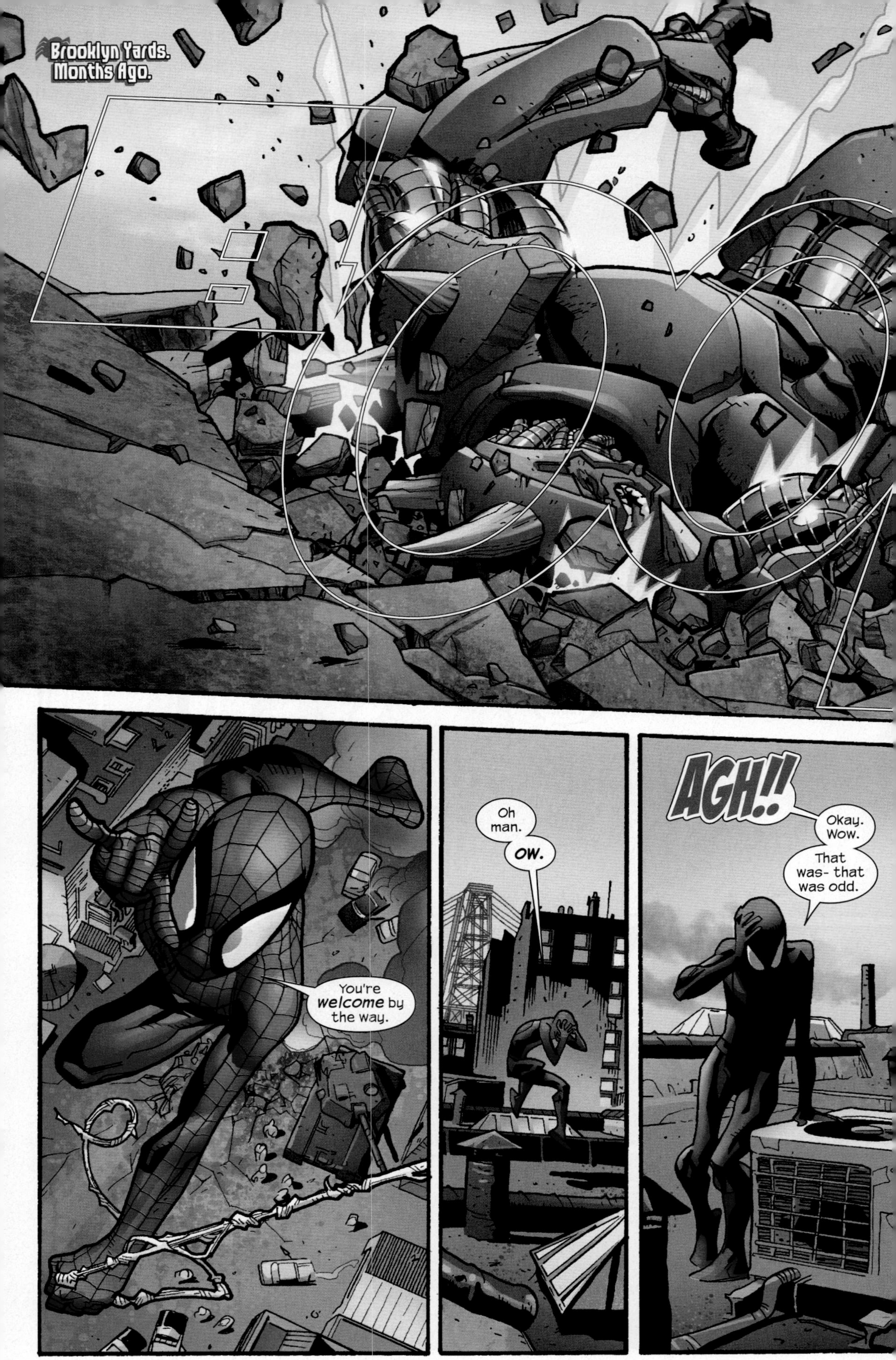
Brooklyn Yards.
Months Ago.
You're welcome by the way.
Oh man.
OW.
AGH!!
Okay. Wow.
That was- that was odd.

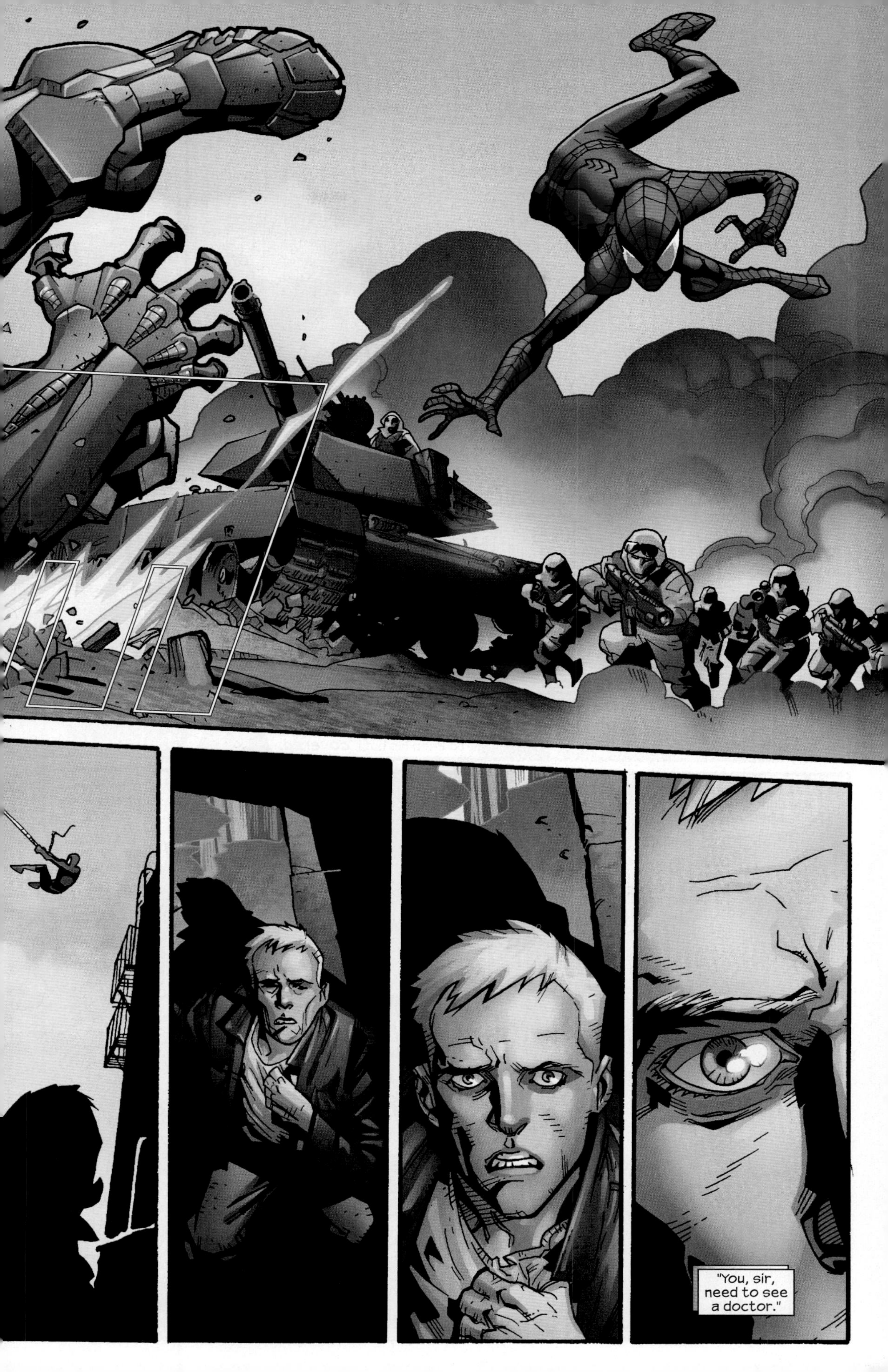
"You, sir, need to see a doctor."

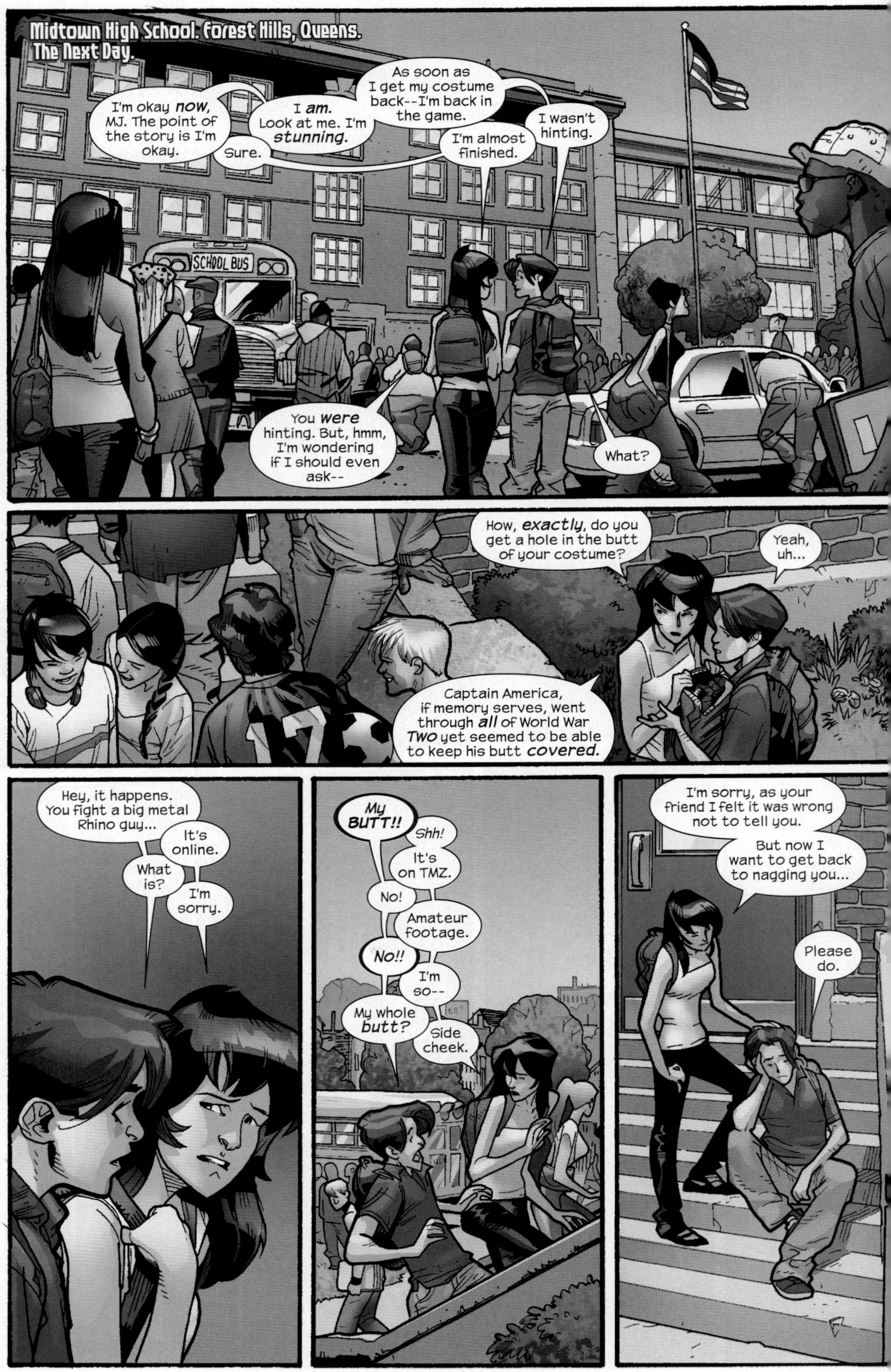
Midtown High School. Forest Hills, Queens.
The Next Day.
I'm okay now, MJ. The point of the story is I'm okay.
Sure.
I am. Look at me. I'm stunning.
As soon as I get my costume back--I'm back in the game.
I'm almost finished.
I wasn't hinting.
SCHOOL BUS
You were hinting. But, hmm, I'm wondering if I should even ask--
What?
How, exactly, do you get a hole in the butt of your costume?
Yeah, uh...
Captain America, if memory serves, went through all of World War Two yet seemed to be able to keep his butt covered.
Hey, it happens. You fight a big metal Rhino guy...
It's online.
What is?
I'm sorry.
My BUTT!!
Shh!
It's on TMZ.
No!
Amateur footage.
No!!
I'm so--
My whole butt?
Side cheek.
I'm sorry, as your friend I felt it was wrong not to tell you.
But now I want to get back to nagging you...
Please do.

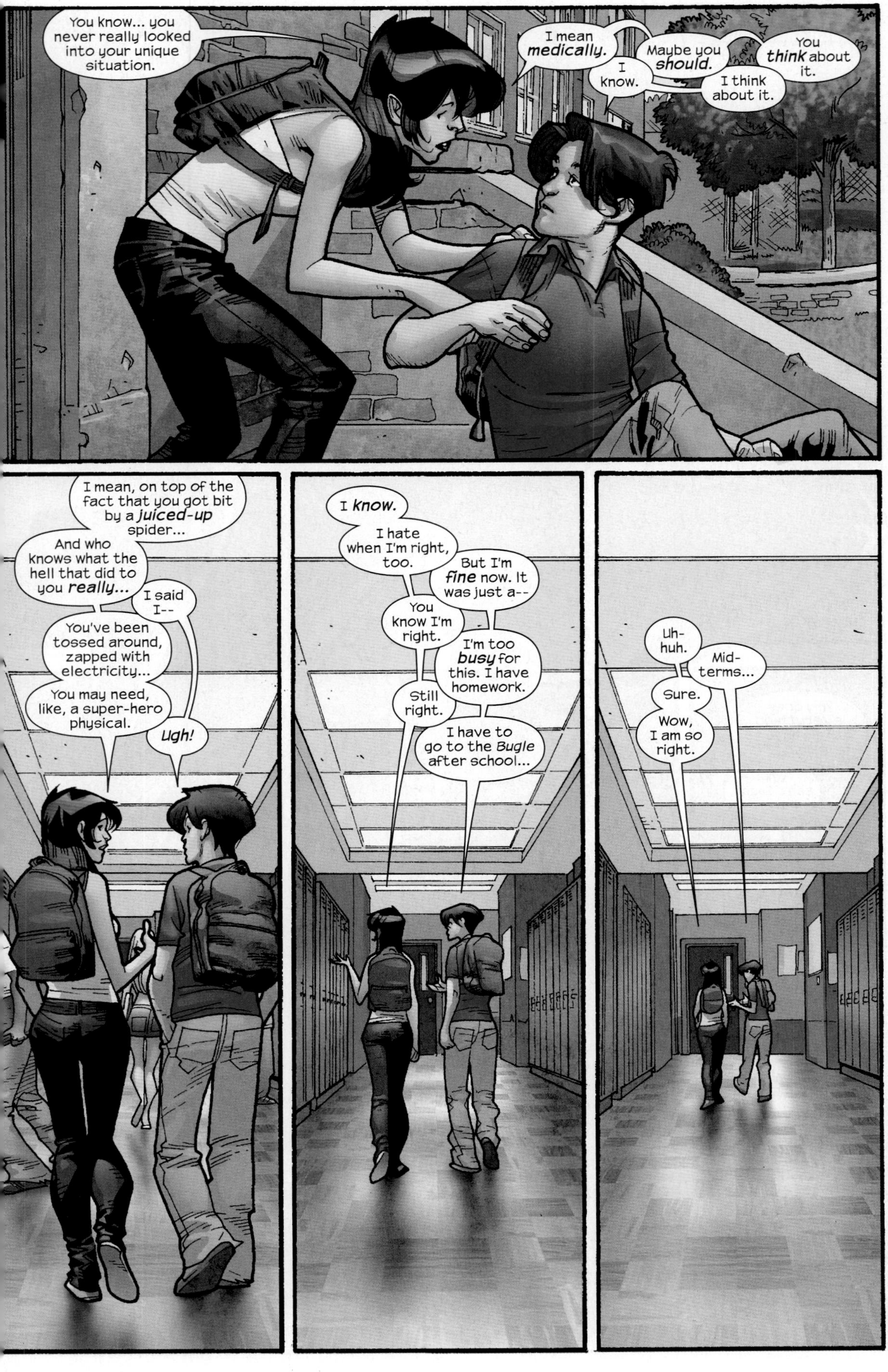
You know... you never really looked into your unique situation.
I mean medically.
I know.
Maybe you should.
I think about it.
You think about it.
I mean, on top of the fact that you got bit by a juiced-up spider...
And who knows what the hell that did to you really...
I said I--
You've been tossed around, zapped with electricity...
You may need, like, a super-hero physical.
Ugh!
I know.
I hate when I'm right, too.
But I'm fine now. It was just a--
You know I'm right.
I'm too busy for this. I have homework.
Still right.
I have to go to the Bugle after school...
Uh-huh.
Mid-terms...
Sure.
Wow, I am so right.

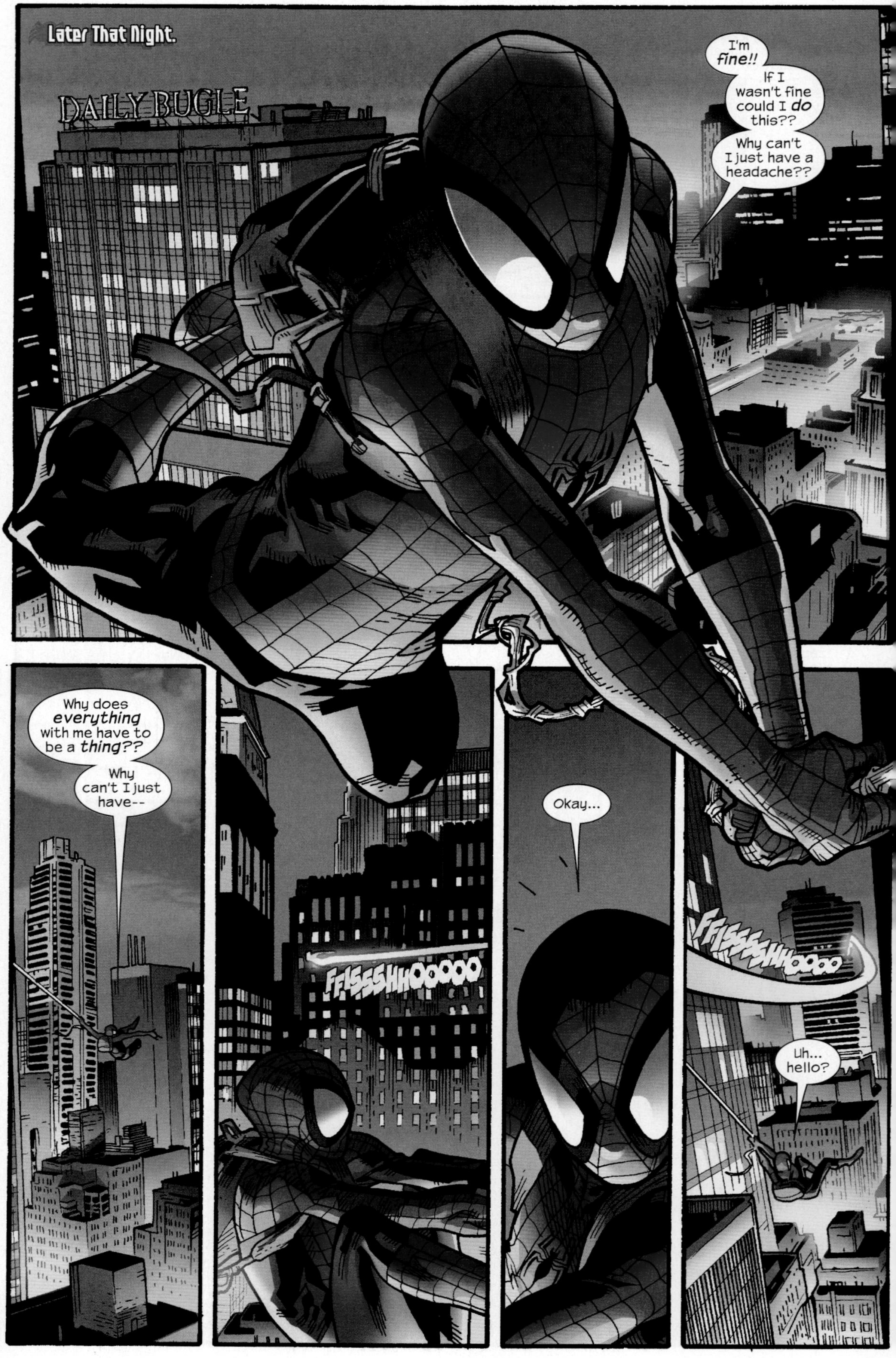

Later That Night.
DAILY BUGLE
I'm *fine!!*
If I wasn't fine could I *do* this??
Why can't I just have a headache??
Why does *everything* with me have to be a *thing??*
Why can't I just have--
FFISSSHHOOOOO
Okay...
FFISSSHHOOOO
Uh... hello?

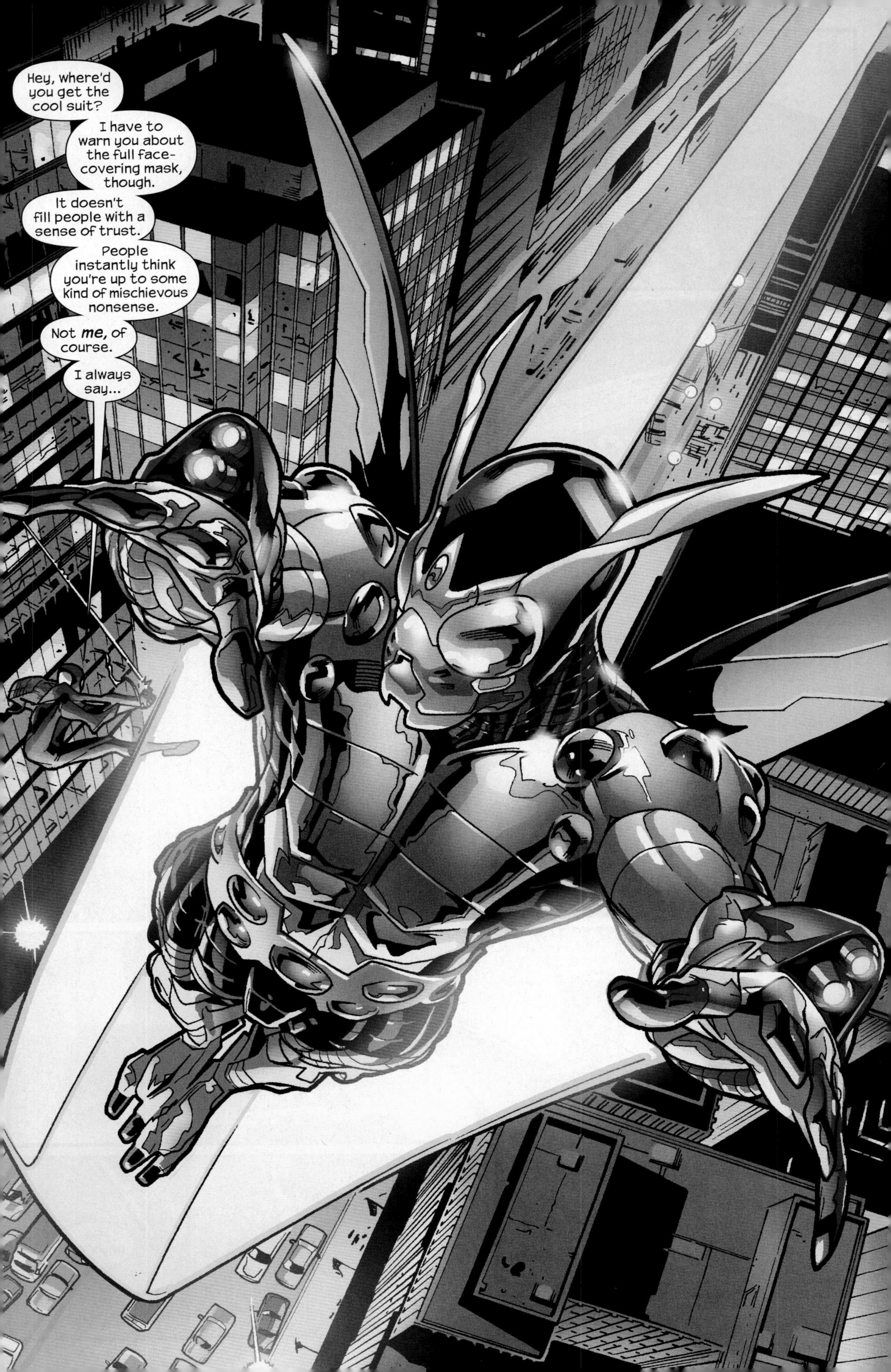
Hey, where'd you get the cool suit?
I have to warn you about the full face-covering mask, though.
It doesn't fill people with a sense of trust.
People instantly think you're up to some kind of mischievous nonsense.
Not *me,* of course.
I always say...

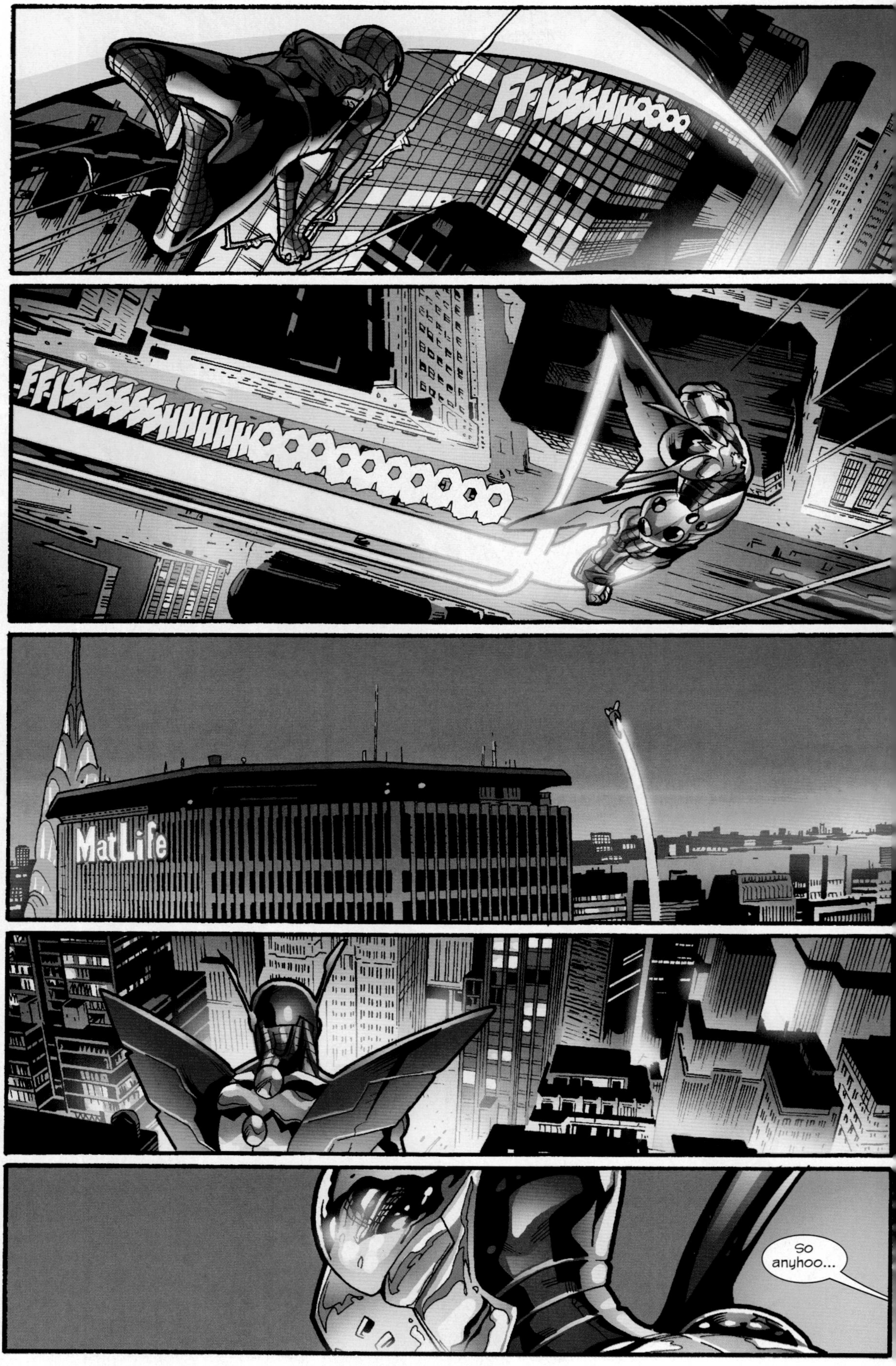
FFISSSHHOOOO
FFISSSSSSHHHHHOOOOOOOOOOOO
MatLife
So anyhoo...

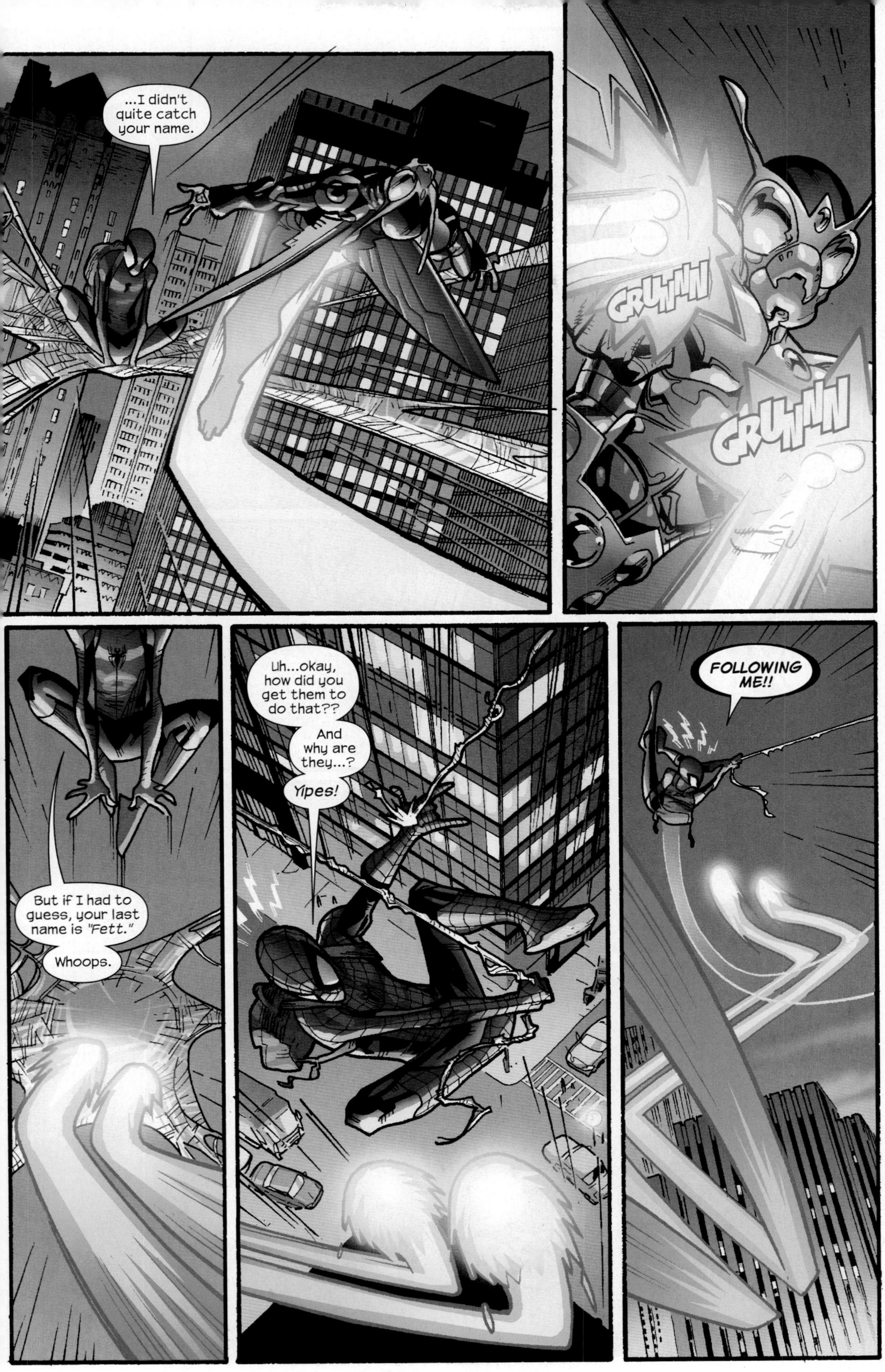
...I didn't quite catch your name.
GRUNNN
GRUNNN
But if I had to guess, your last name is "Fett."
Whoops.
Uh...okay, how did you get them to do that??
And why are they...?
Yipes!
FOLLOWING ME!!

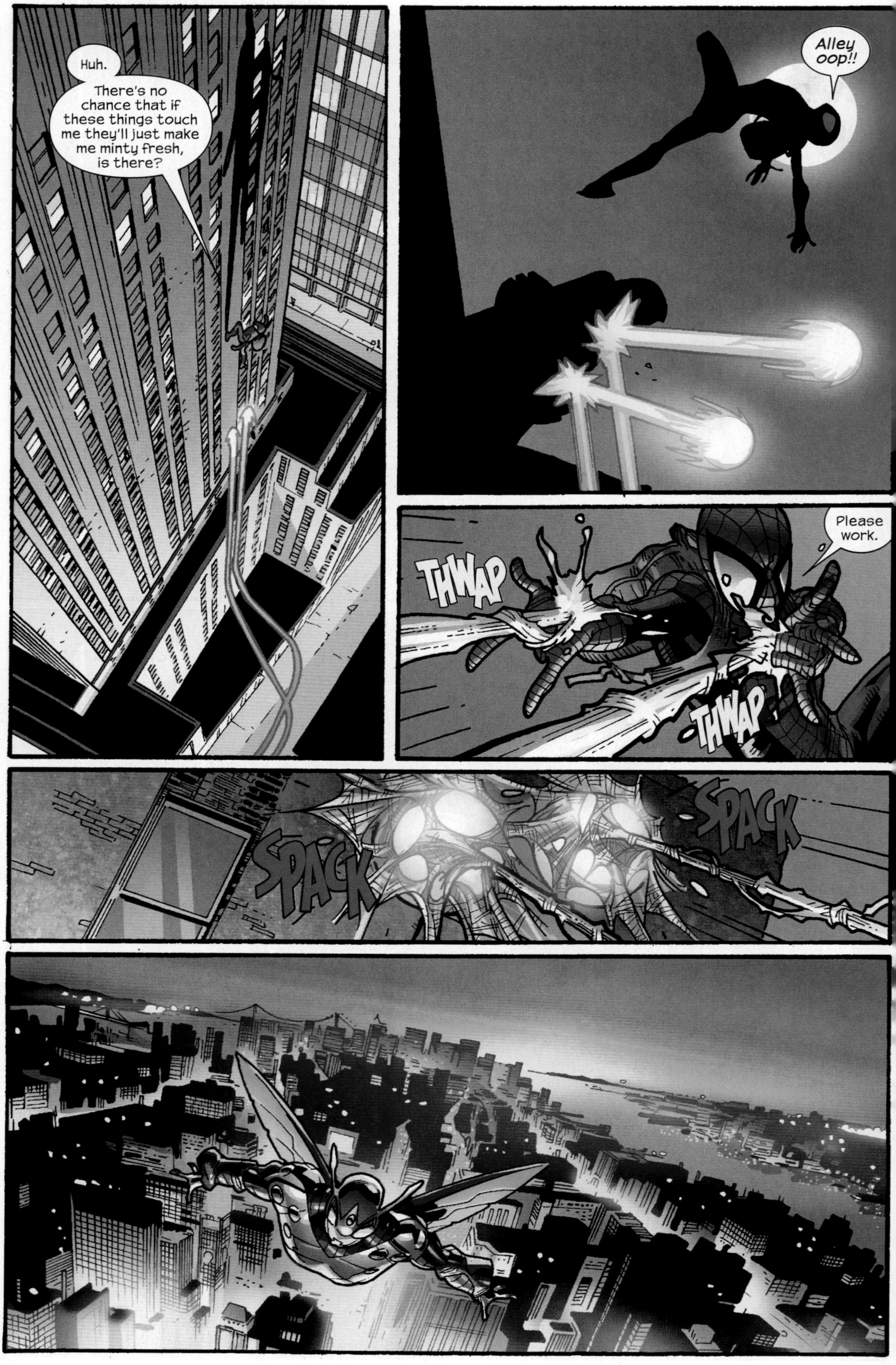
Huh.
There's no chance that if these things touch me they'll just make me minty fresh, is there?
Alley oop!!
THWAP
Please work.
THWAP
SPACK
SPACK

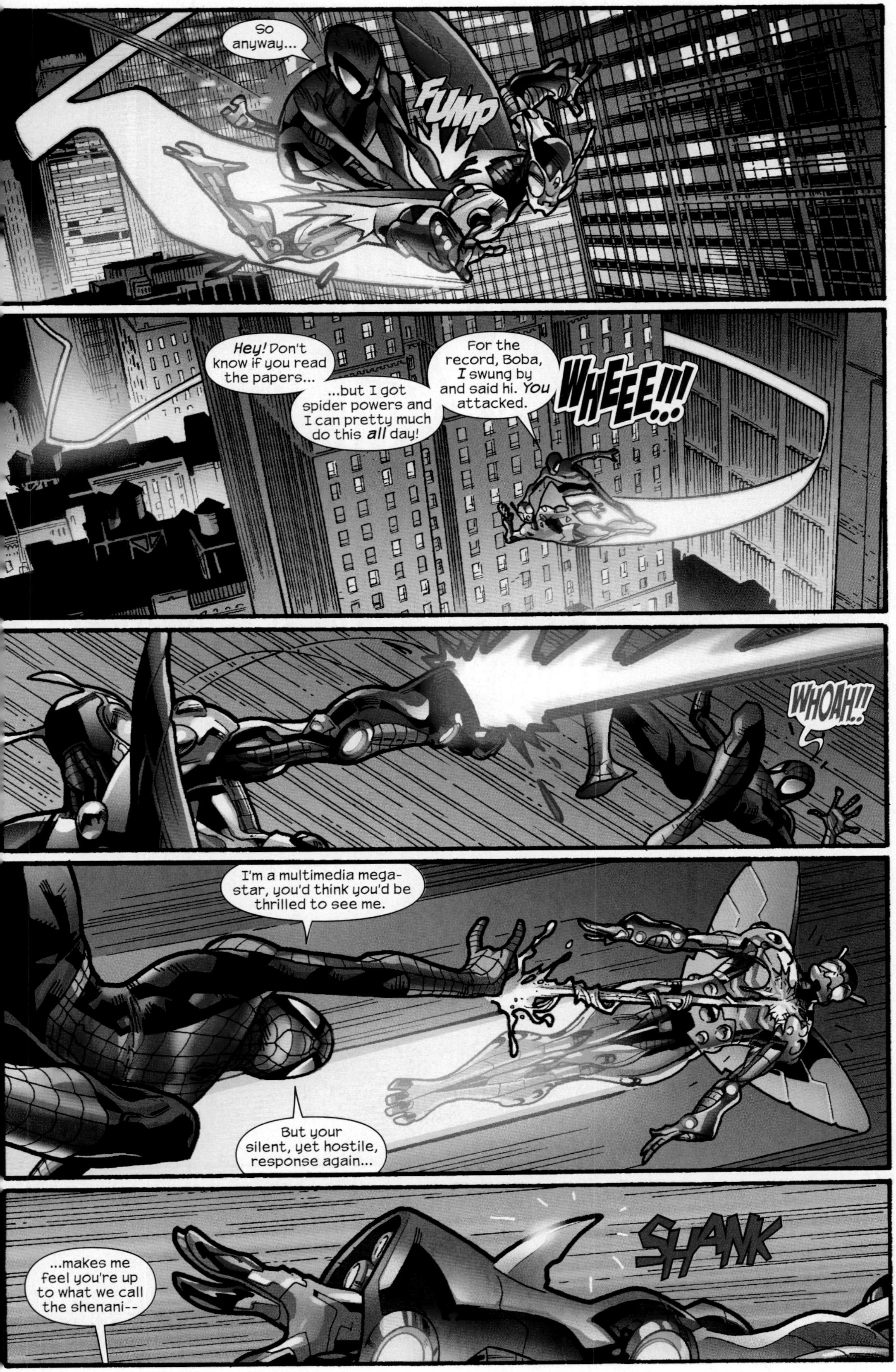

So anyway...
FUMP
Hey! Don't know if you read the papers...
...but I got spider powers and I can pretty much do this all day!
For the record, Boba, I swung by and said hi. You attacked.
WHEEE!!!
WHOAH!!
I'm a multimedia mega-star, you'd think you'd be thrilled to see me.
But your silent, yet hostile, response again...
SHANK
...makes me feel you're up to what we call the shenani--

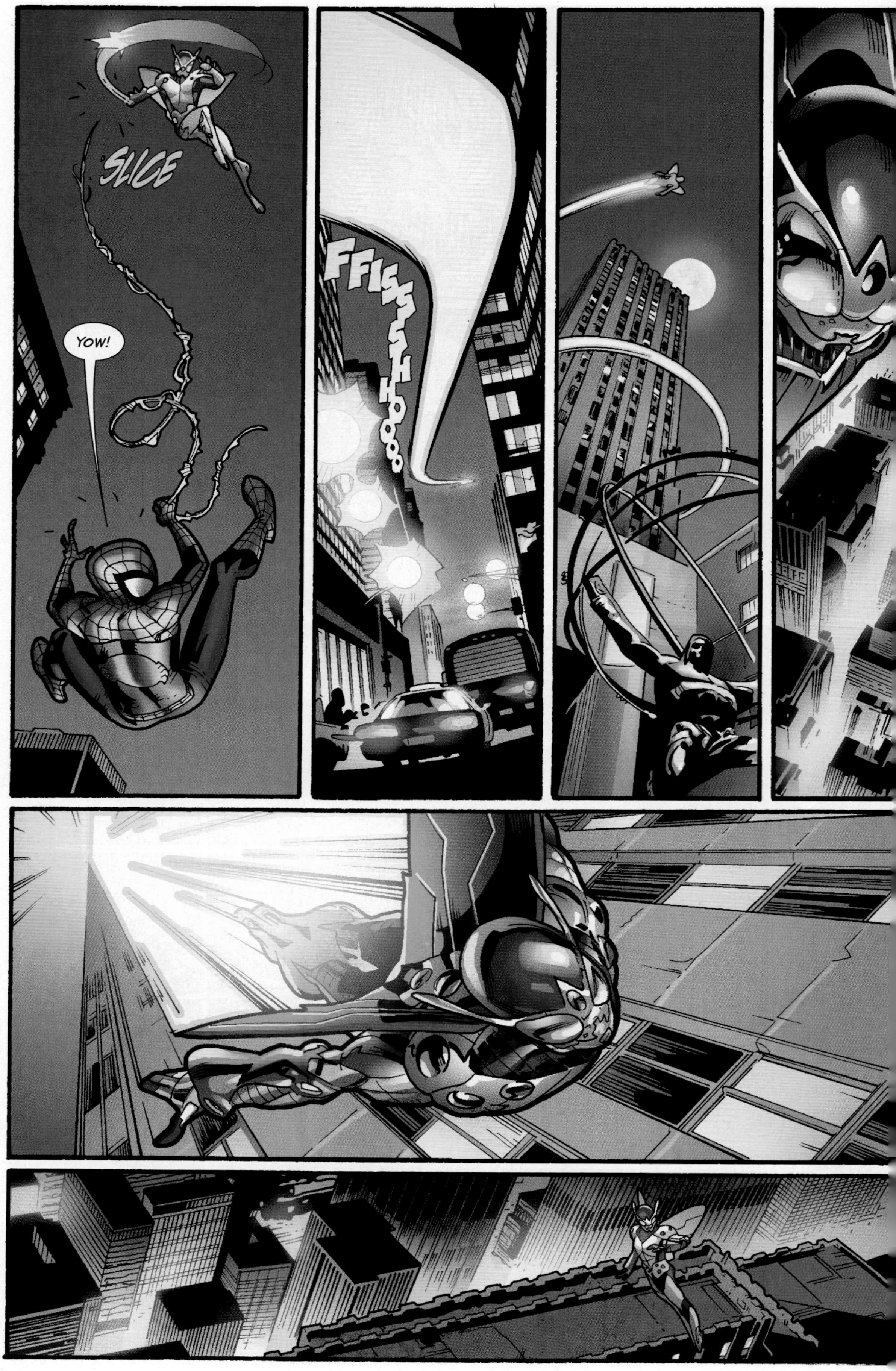
SLICE
YOW!
FFISSSHHOOOO

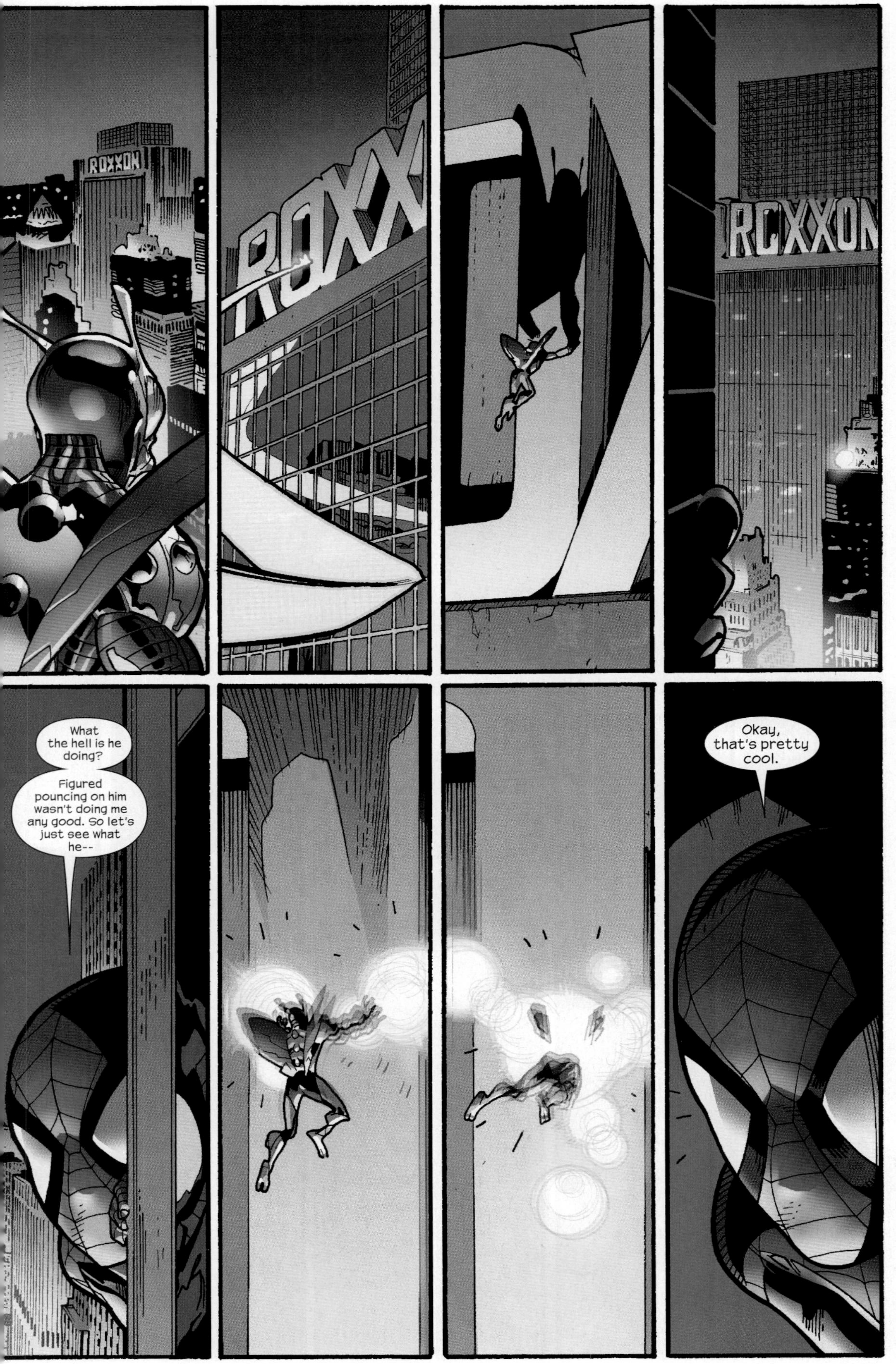
ROXXON
ROXX
RCXXON
What the hell is he doing?
Figured pouncing on him wasn't doing me any good. So let's just see what he--
Okay, that's pretty cool.

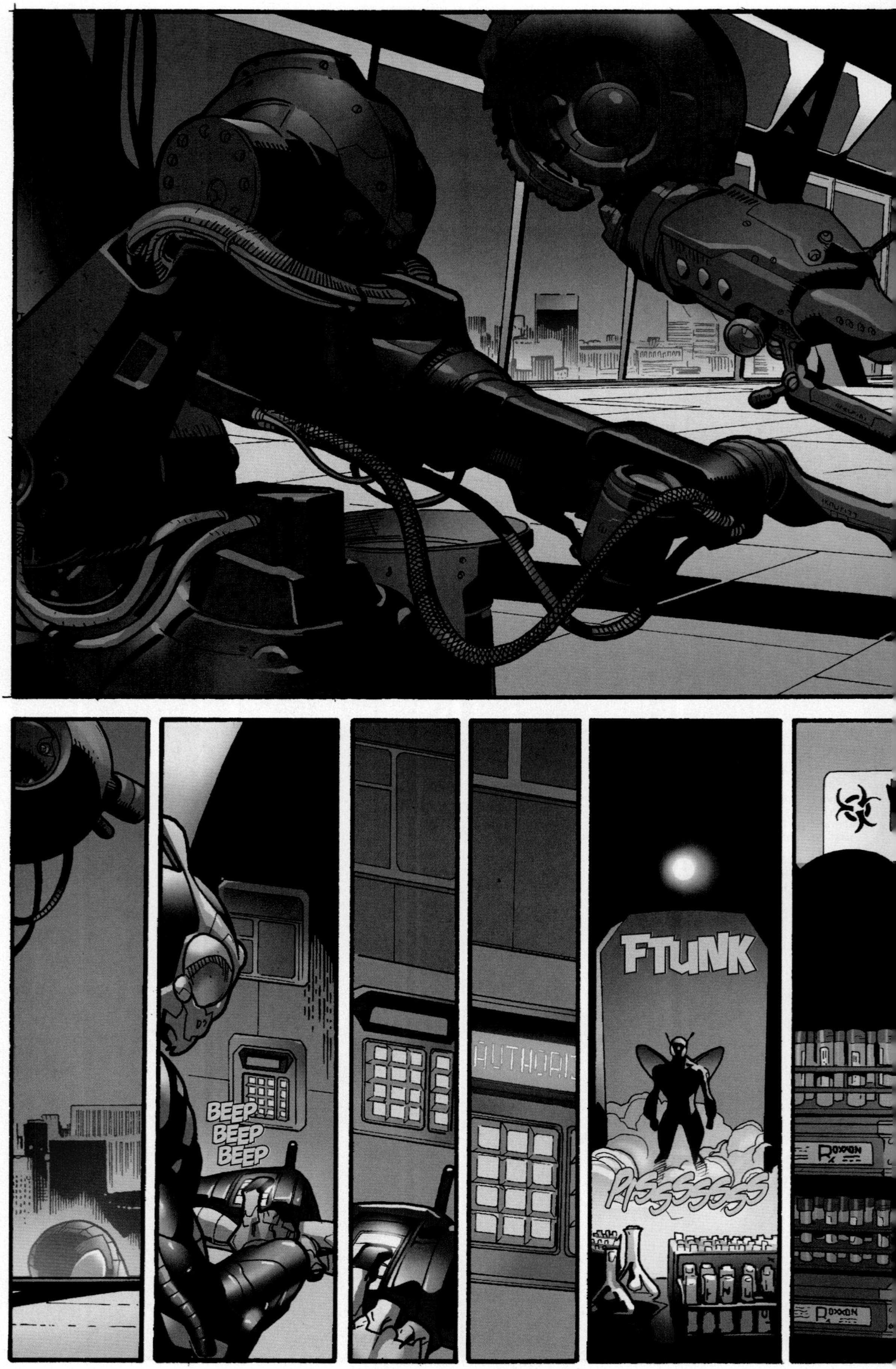

BEEP
BEEP
BEEP
AUTHORI
FTUNK
PISSSSSSS
ROXXON
ROXXON

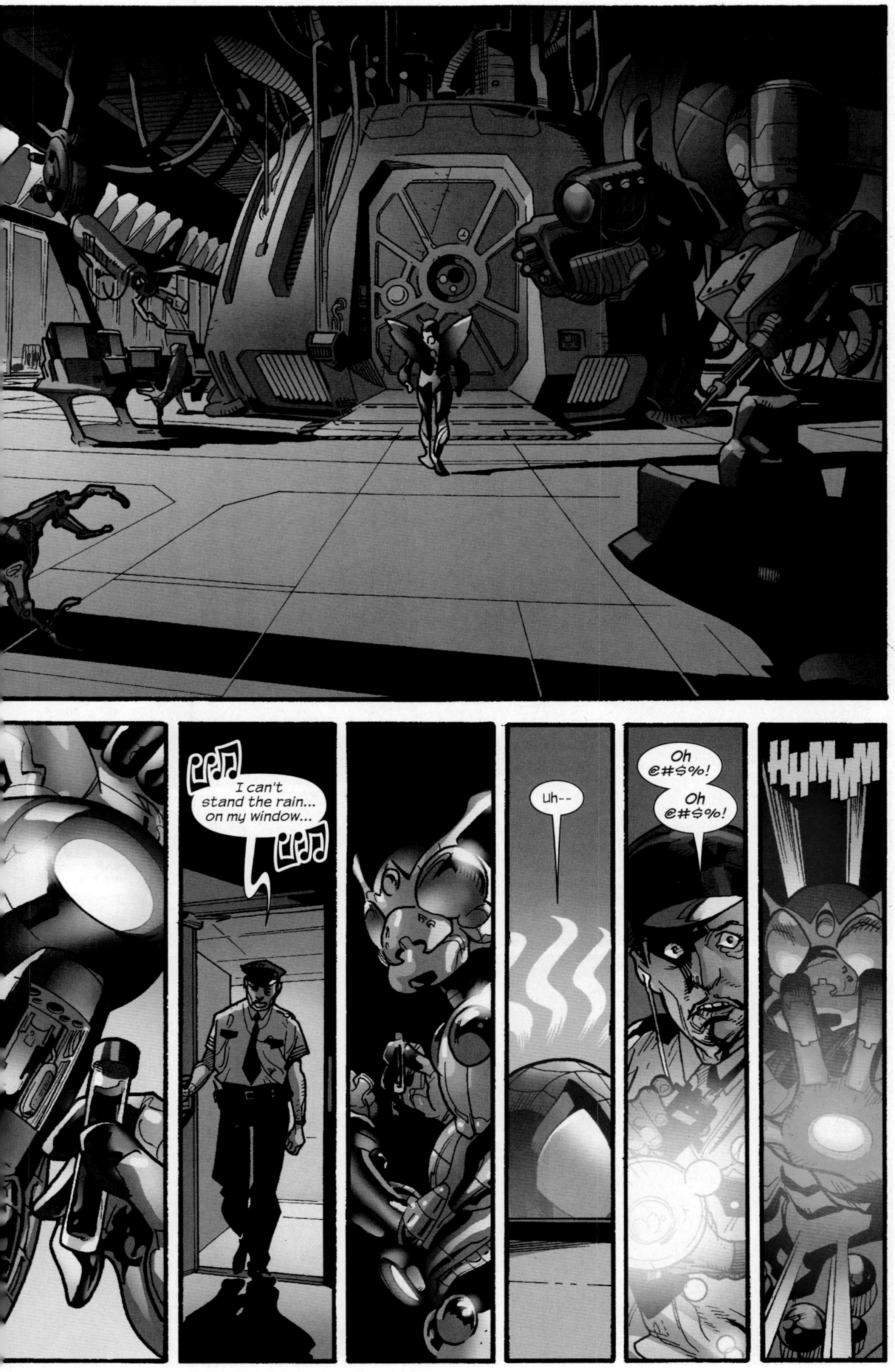

I can't stand the rain... on my window...
Uh--
Oh @#$%!
Oh @#$%!
HHMMMM

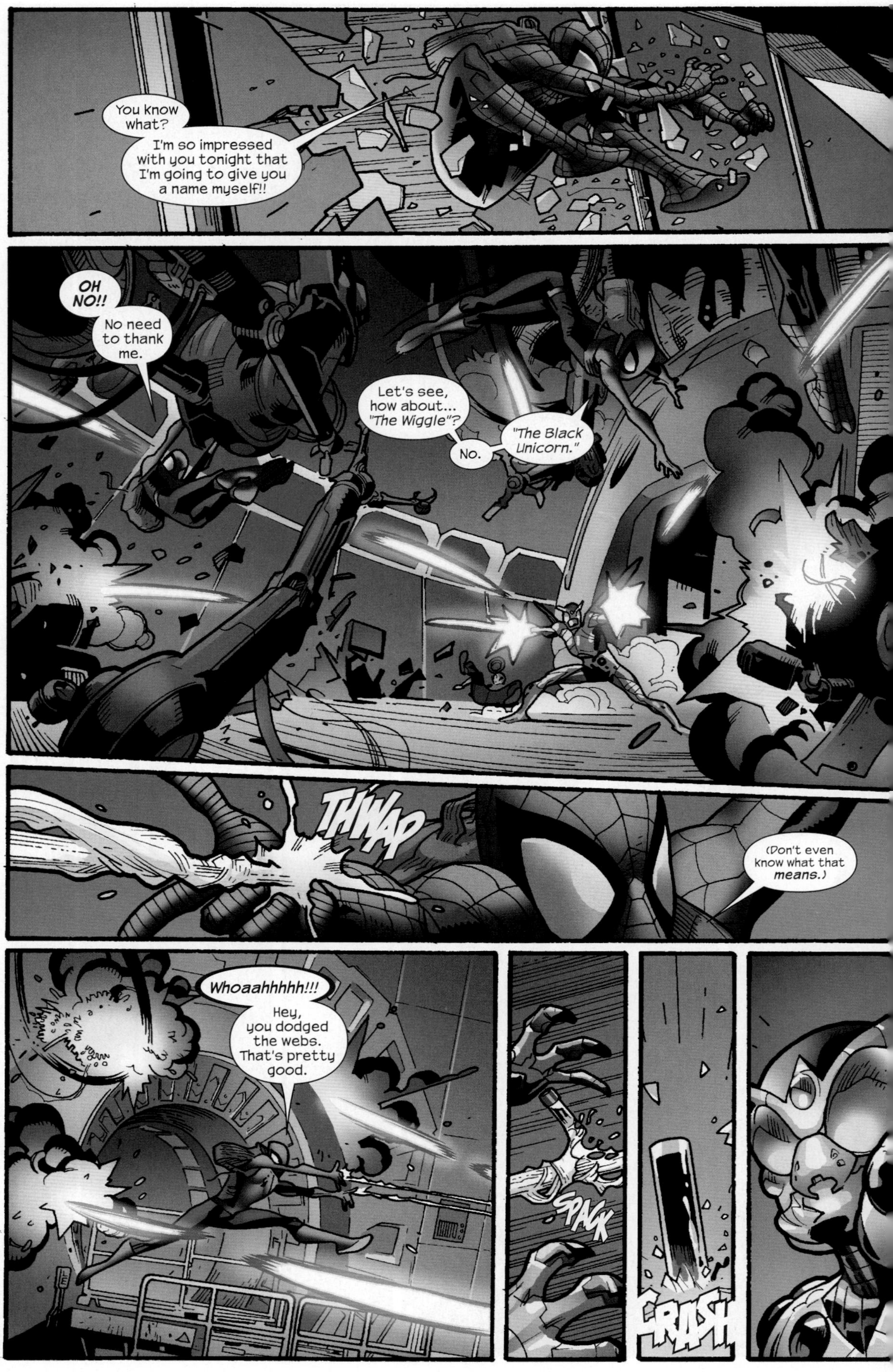

You know what?
I'm so impressed with you tonight that I'm going to give you a name myself!!
OH NO!!
No need to thank me.
Let's see, how about... "The Wiggle"?
No.
"The Black Unicorn."
THWAP
(Don't even know what that means.)
Whoaahhhhh!!!
Hey, you dodged the webs. That's pretty good.
SPACK
CRASH

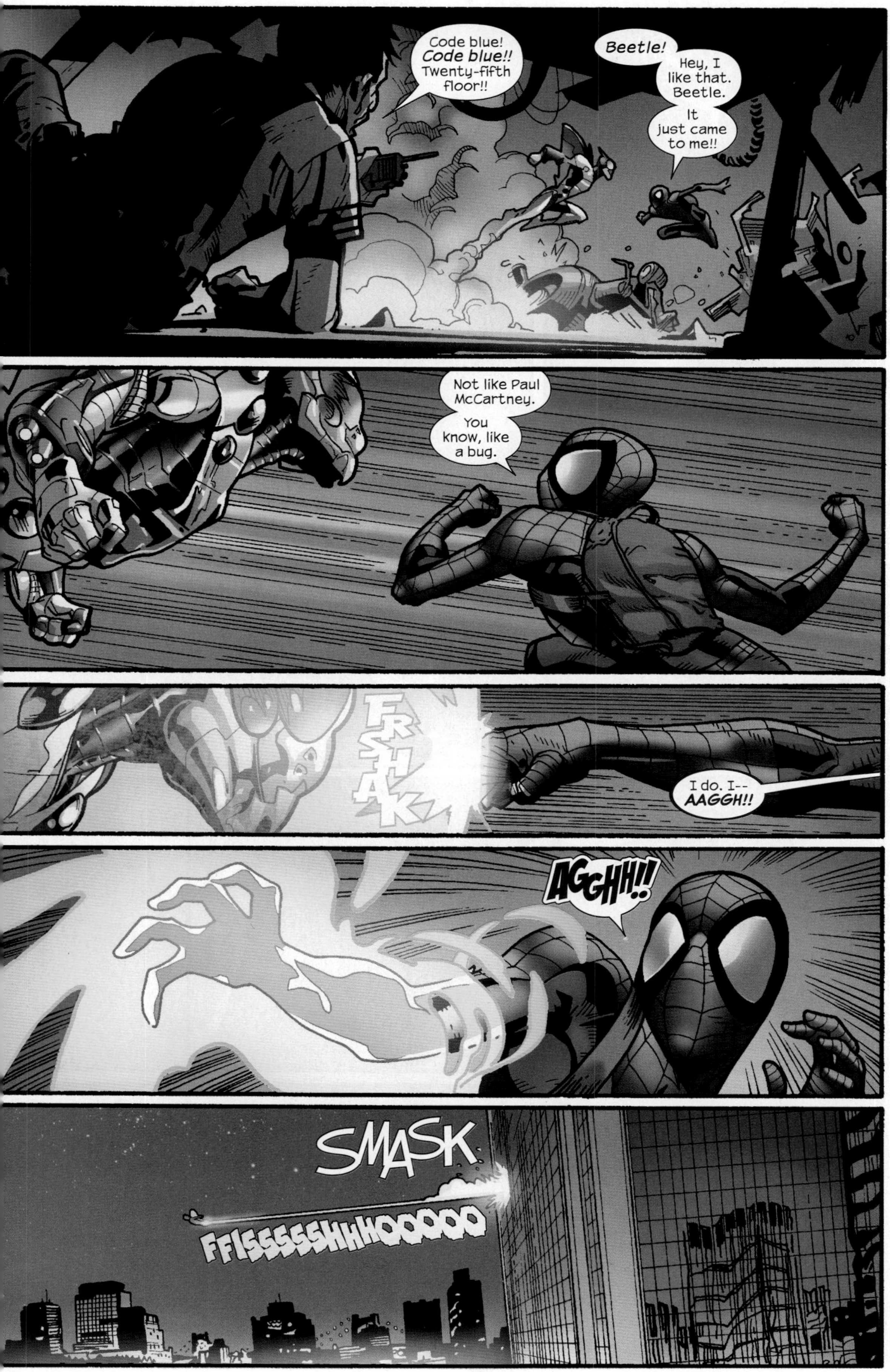
Code blue! *Code blue!!* Twenty-fifth floor!!
Beetle!
Hey, I like that. Beetle.
It just came to me!!
Not like Paul McCartney.
You know, like a bug.
FRSHAK
I do. I-- **AAGGH!!**
AGGHH!!
SMASK
FFISSSSSHHHOOOOO

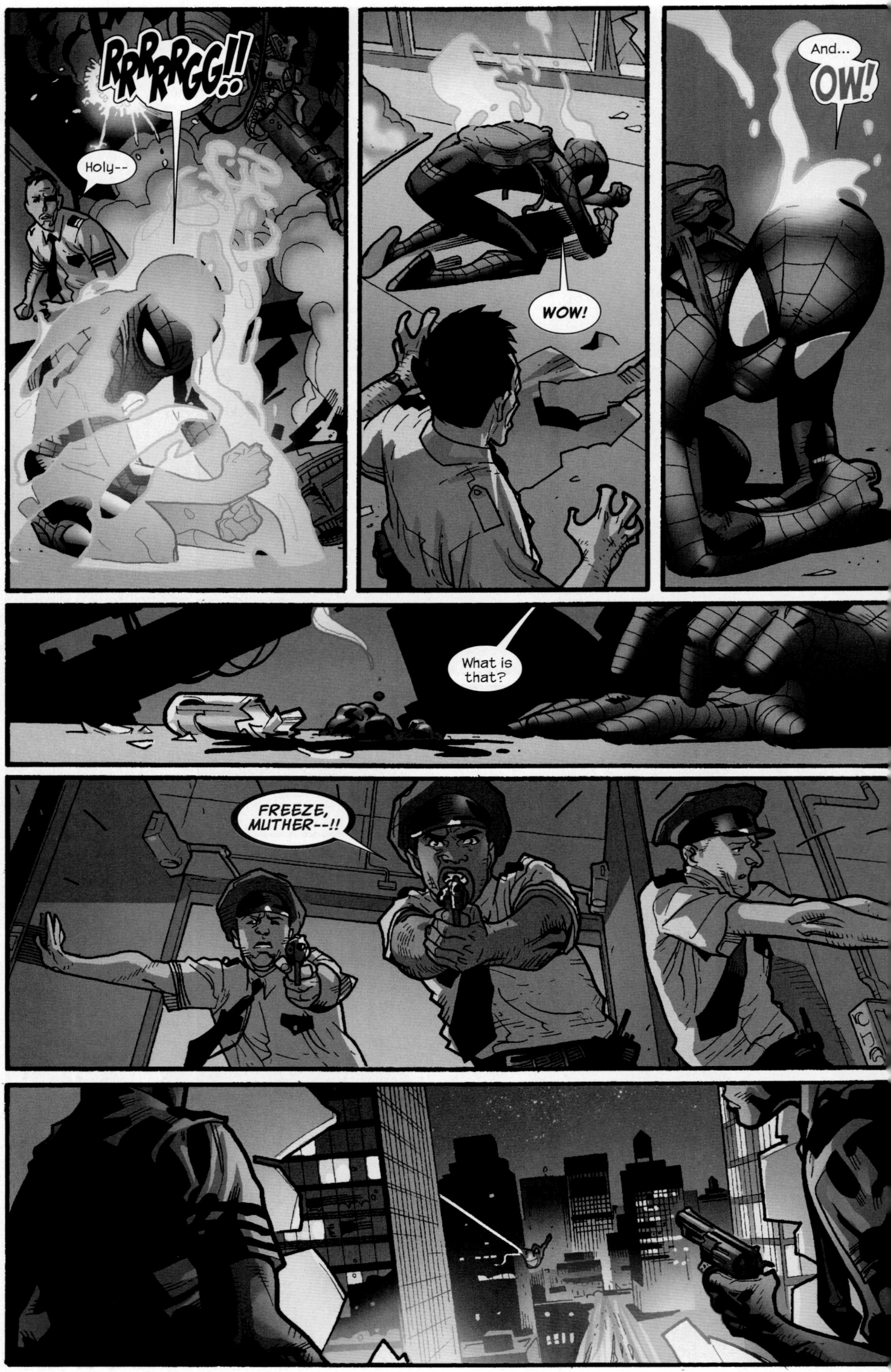
RRRRRGG!!
Holy--
WOW!
And...
OW!
What is that?
FREEZE, MUTHER--!!

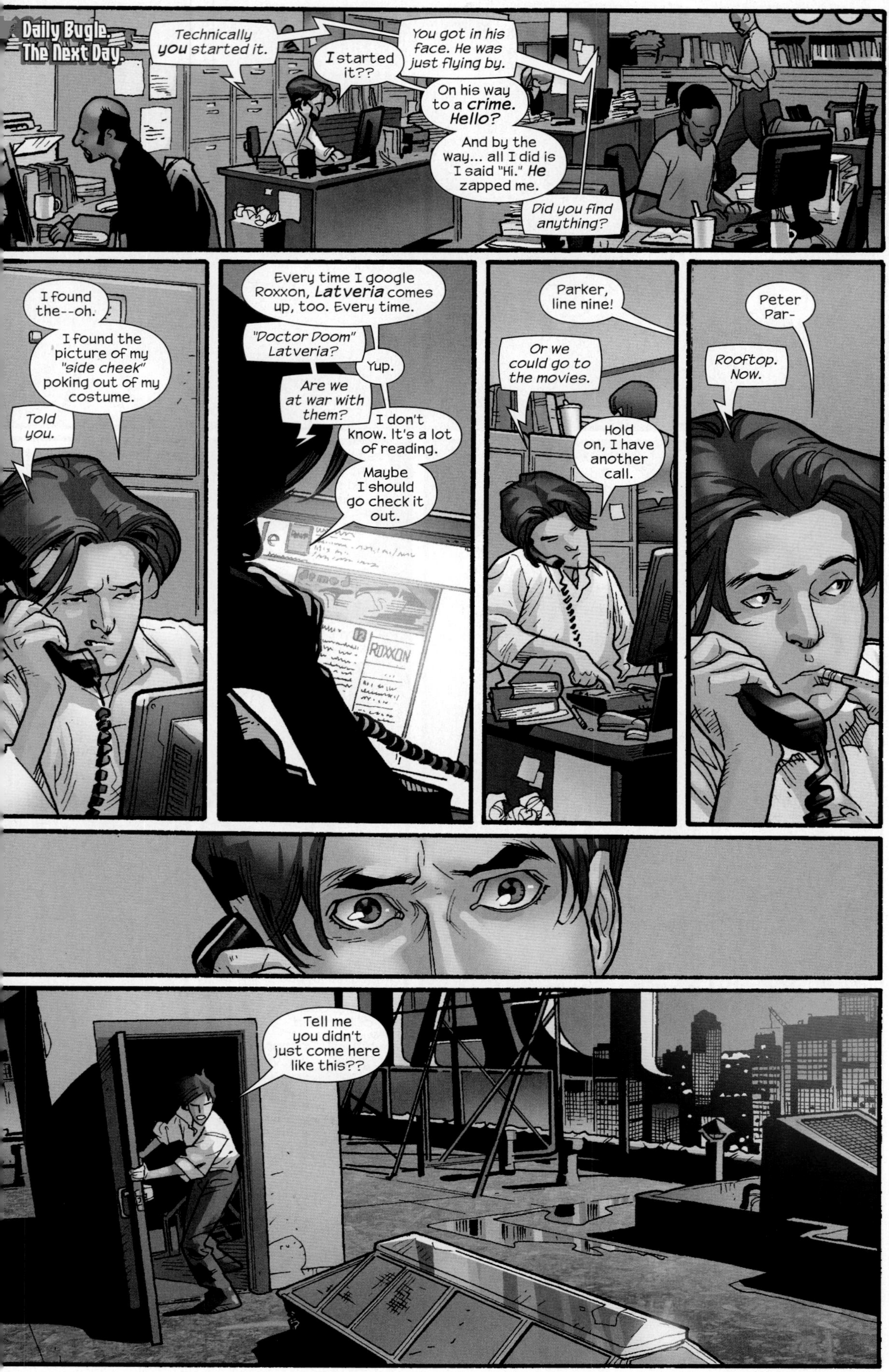
Daily Bugle. The Next Day.
Technically you started it.
I started it??
You got in his face. He was just flying by.
On his way to a crime. Hello?
And by the way... all I did is I said "Hi." He zapped me.
Did you find anything?
I found the--oh.
I found the picture of my "side cheek" poking out of my costume.
Told you.
Every time I google Roxxon, Latveria comes up, too. Every time.
"Doctor Doom" Latveria?
Yup.
Are we at war with them?
I don't know. It's a lot of reading.
Maybe I should go check it out.
ROXXON
Parker, line nine!
Or we could go to the movies.
Hold on, I have another call.
Peter Par-
Rooftop. Now.
Tell me you didn't just come here like this??

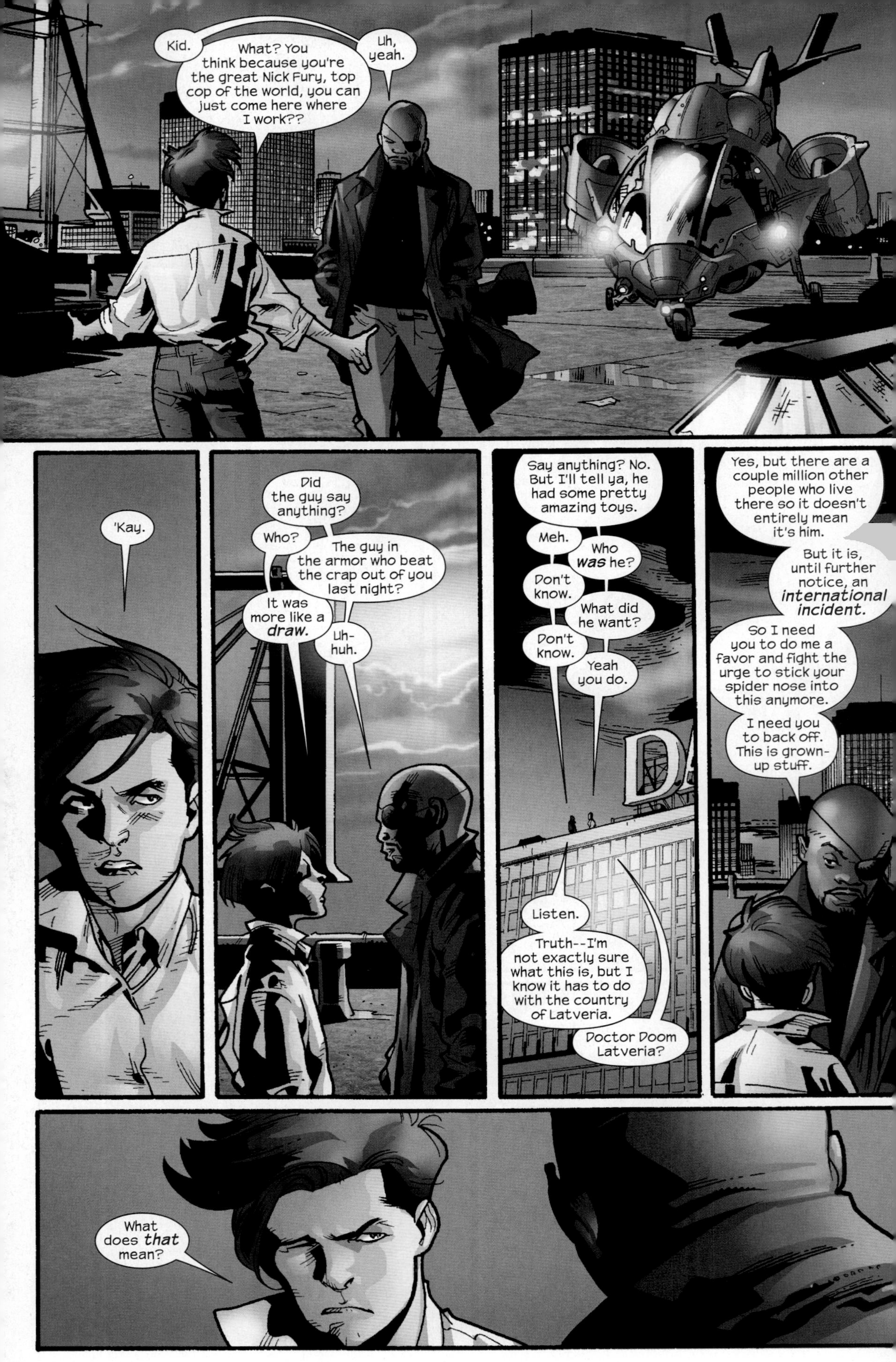
Kid.
What? You think because you're the great Nick Fury, top cop of the world, you can just come here where I work??
Uh, yeah.
'Kay.
Did the guy say anything?
Who?
The guy in the armor who beat the crap out of you last night?
It was more like a *draw.*
Uh-huh.
Say anything? No. But I'll tell ya, he had some pretty amazing toys.
Meh.
Who *was* he?
Don't know.
What did he want?
Don't know.
Yeah you do.
Listen.
Truth--I'm not exactly sure what this is, but I know it has to do with the country of Latveria.
Doctor Doom Latveria?
Yes, but there are a couple million other people who live there so it doesn't entirely mean it's him.
But it is, until further notice, an ***international incident.***
So I need you to do me a favor and fight the urge to stick your spider nose into this anymore.
I need you to back off. This is grown-up stuff.
What does *that* mean?

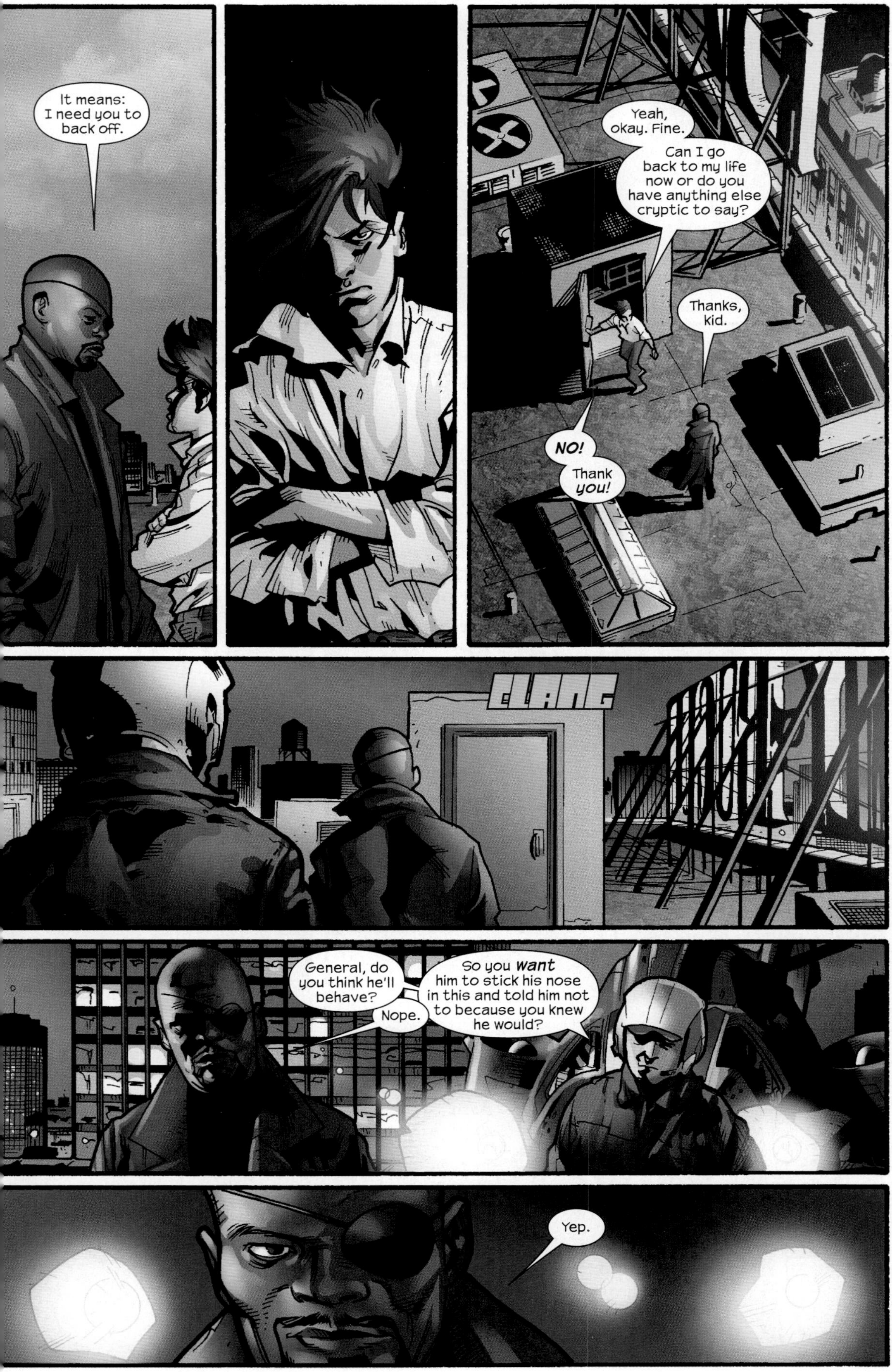

It means: I need you to back off.
Yeah, okay. Fine.
Can I go back to my life now or do you have anything else cryptic to say?
Thanks, kid.
NO!
Thank you!
CLANG
General, do you think he'll behave?
Nope.
So you want him to stick his nose in this and told him not to because you knew he would?
Yep.

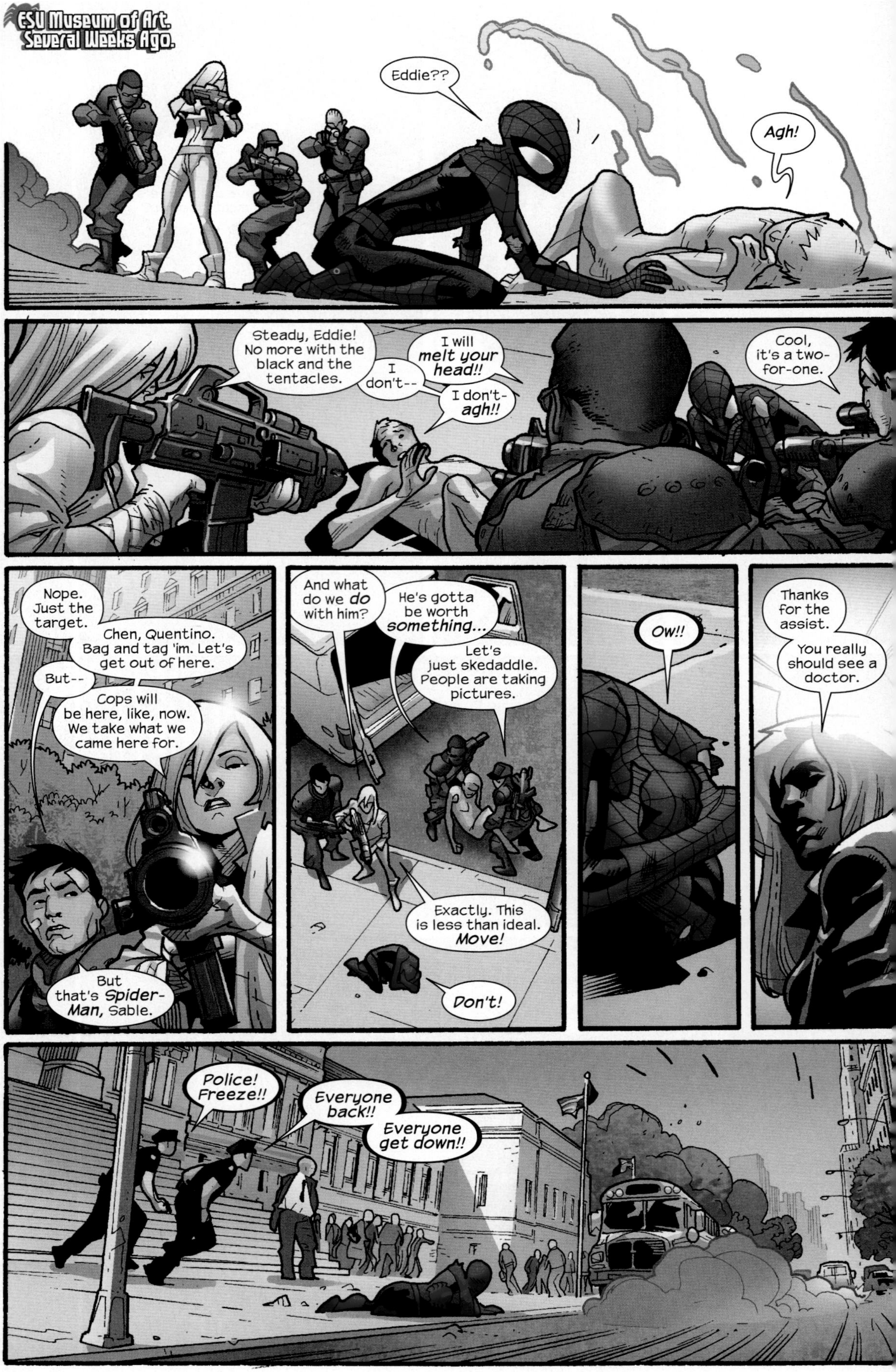

ESU Museum of Art. Several Weeks Ago.
Eddie??
Agh!
Steady, Eddie! No more with the black and the tentacles.
I don't--
I will melt your head!!
I don't-agh!!
Cool, it's a two-for-one.
Nope. Just the target.
Chen, Quentino. Bag and tag 'im. Let's get out of here.
But--
Cops will be here, like, now. We take what we came here for.
But that's Spider-Man, Sable.
And what do we do with him?
He's gotta be worth something...
Let's just skedaddle. People are taking pictures.
Exactly. This is less than ideal. Move!
Don't!
Ow!!
Thanks for the assist.
You really should see a doctor.
Police! Freeze!!
Everyone back!!
Everyone get down!!

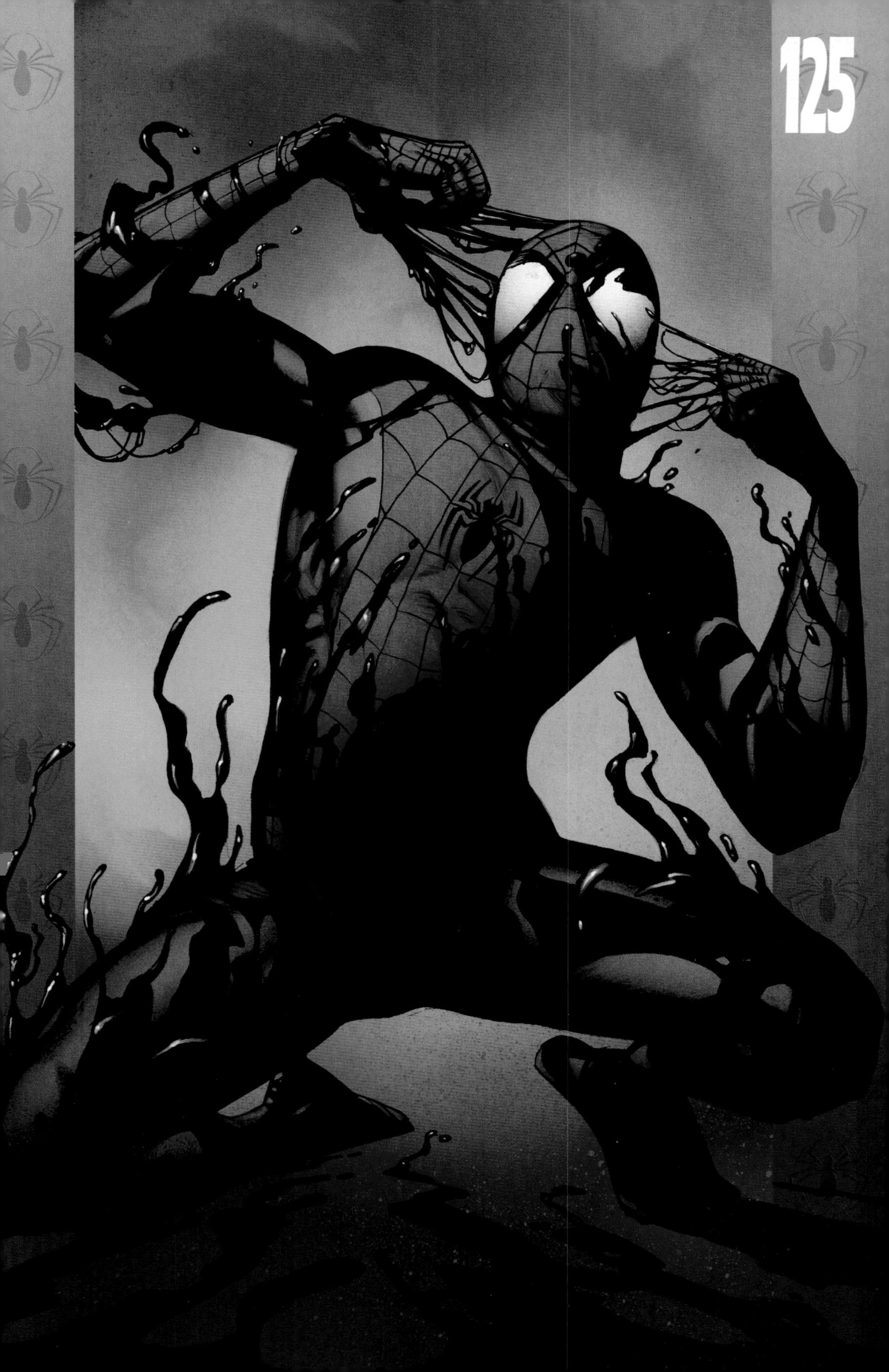
125

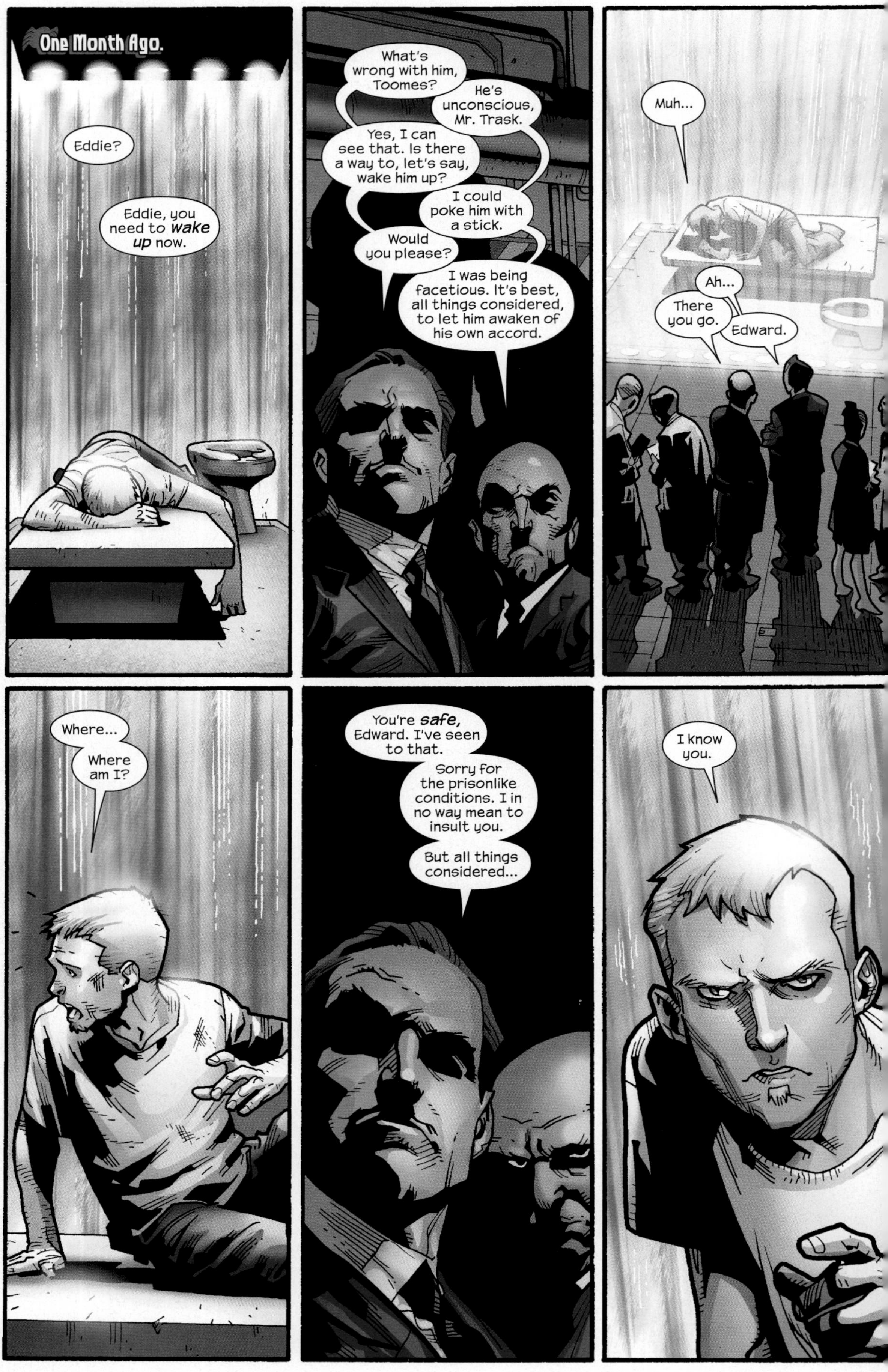
One Month Ago.
Eddie?
Eddie, you need to *wake up* now.
What's wrong with him, Toomes?
He's unconscious, Mr. Trask.
Yes, I can see that. Is there a way to, let's say, wake him up?
I could poke him with a stick.
Would you please?
I was being facetious. It's best, all things considered, to let him awaken of his own accord.
Muh...
Ah...
There you go.
Edward.
Where...
Where am I?
You're *safe,* Edward. I've seen to that.
Sorry for the prisonlike conditions. I in no way mean to insult you.
But all things considered...
I know you.

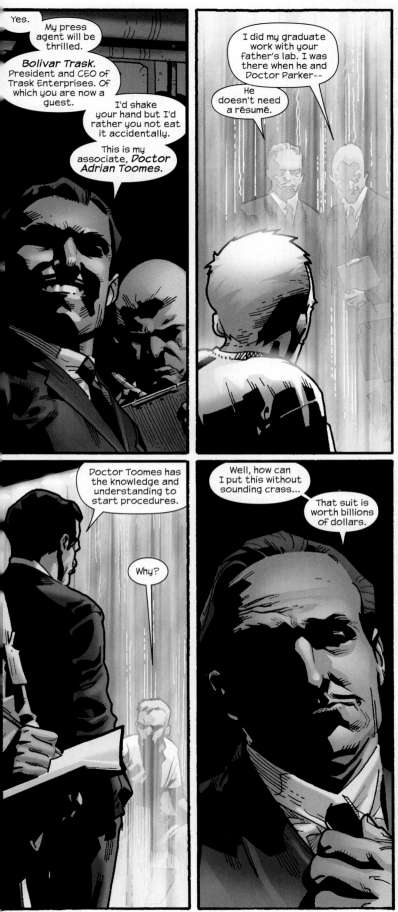

Yes. My press agent will be thrilled.

Bolivar Trask. President and CEO of Trask Enterprises. Of which you are now a guest.

I'd shake your hand but I'd rather you not eat it accidentally.

This is my associate, *Doctor Adrian Toomes.*

I did my graduate work with your father's lab. I was there when he and Doctor Parker--

He doesn't need a résumé.

Let's get down to business, shall we, Edward?

We have gone to great *lengths* to get you here. To help you.

We *know* you can't control yourself anymore. We know it's not your fault what has happened to you.

We know that *the suit,* as we'll call it, has attached to you, and is feeding on you.

It's a parasitic organism.

And we're going to help you get rid of it.

We're going to *help* you get your life back.

Doctor Toomes has the knowledge and understanding to start procedures.

Why?

Well, how can I put this without sounding crass...

That suit is worth billions of dollars.

It was my father's.

Ooh. Actually...

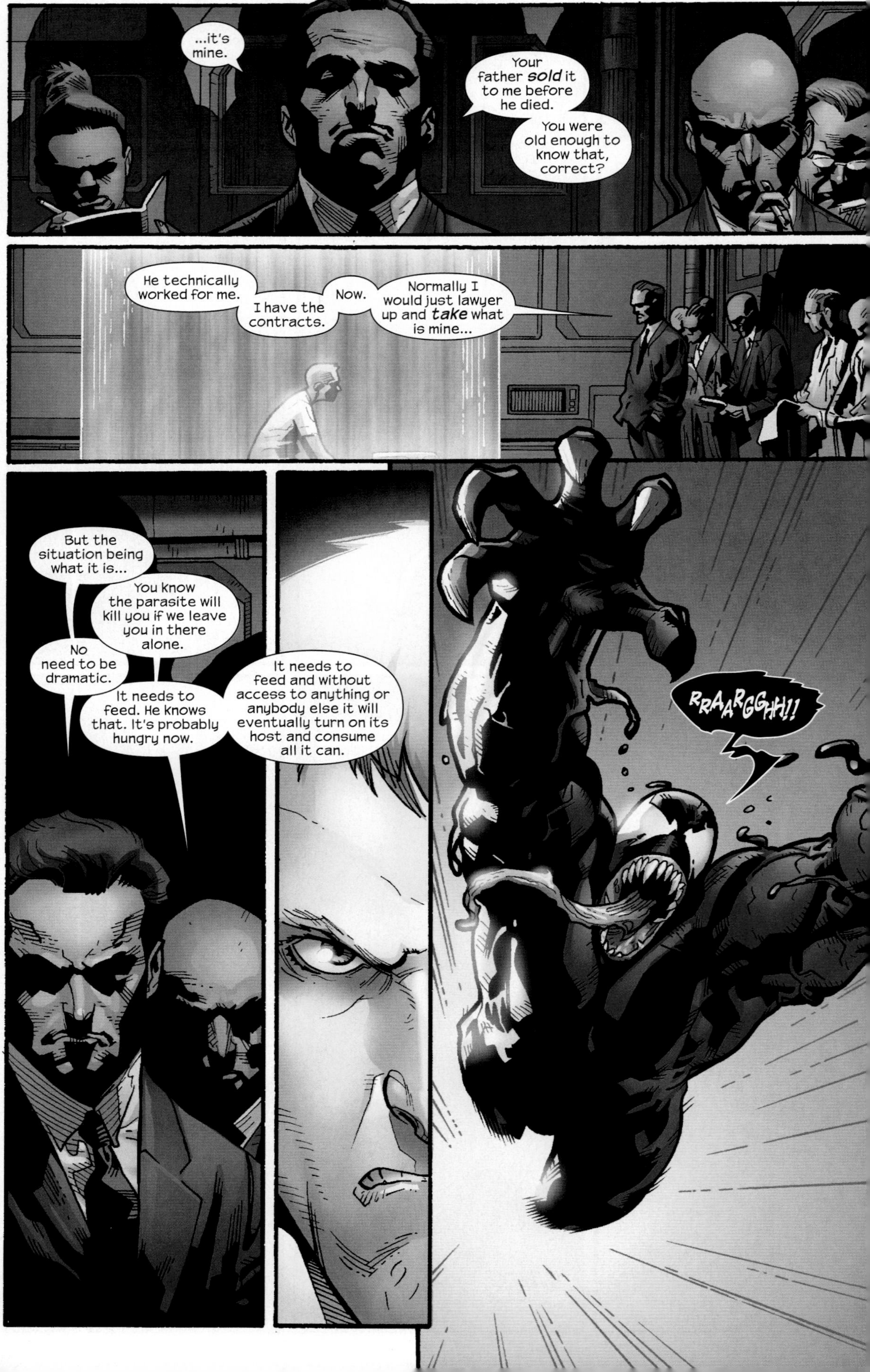
...it's mine.
Your father *sold* it to me before he died.
You were old enough to know that, correct?
He technically worked for me.
I have the contracts.
Now.
Normally I would just lawyer up and *take* what is mine...
But the situation being what it is...
You know the parasite will kill you if we leave you in there alone.
No need to be dramatic.
It needs to feed. He knows that. It's probably hungry now.
It needs to feed and without access to anything or anybody else it will eventually turn on its host and consume all it can.
RRAARGGHH!!

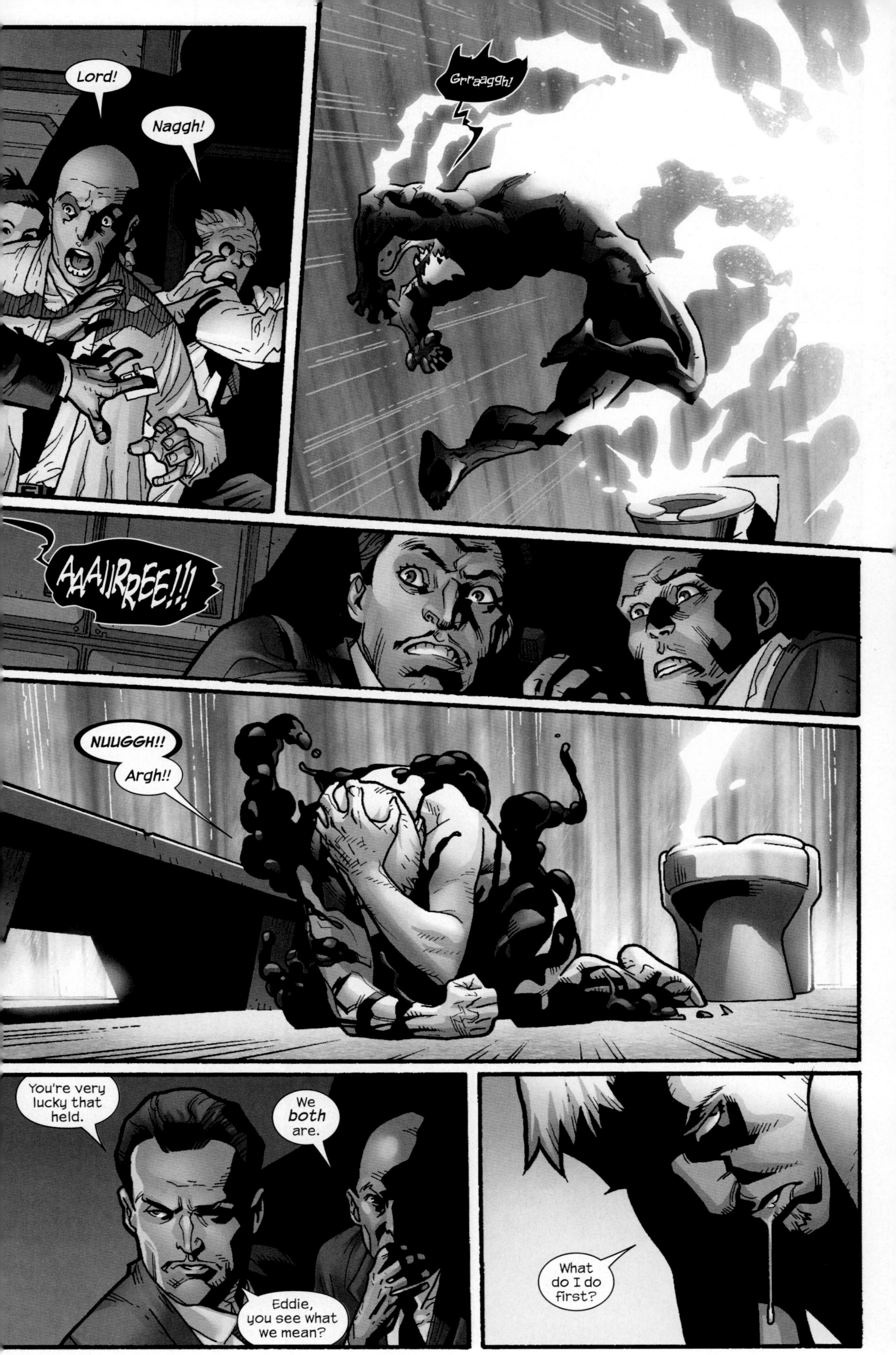

Lord!
Naggh!
Grraaggh!
AAAIIRREE!!!
NUUGGH!!
Argh!!
You're very lucky that held.
We *both* are.
Eddie, you see what we mean?
What do I do first?

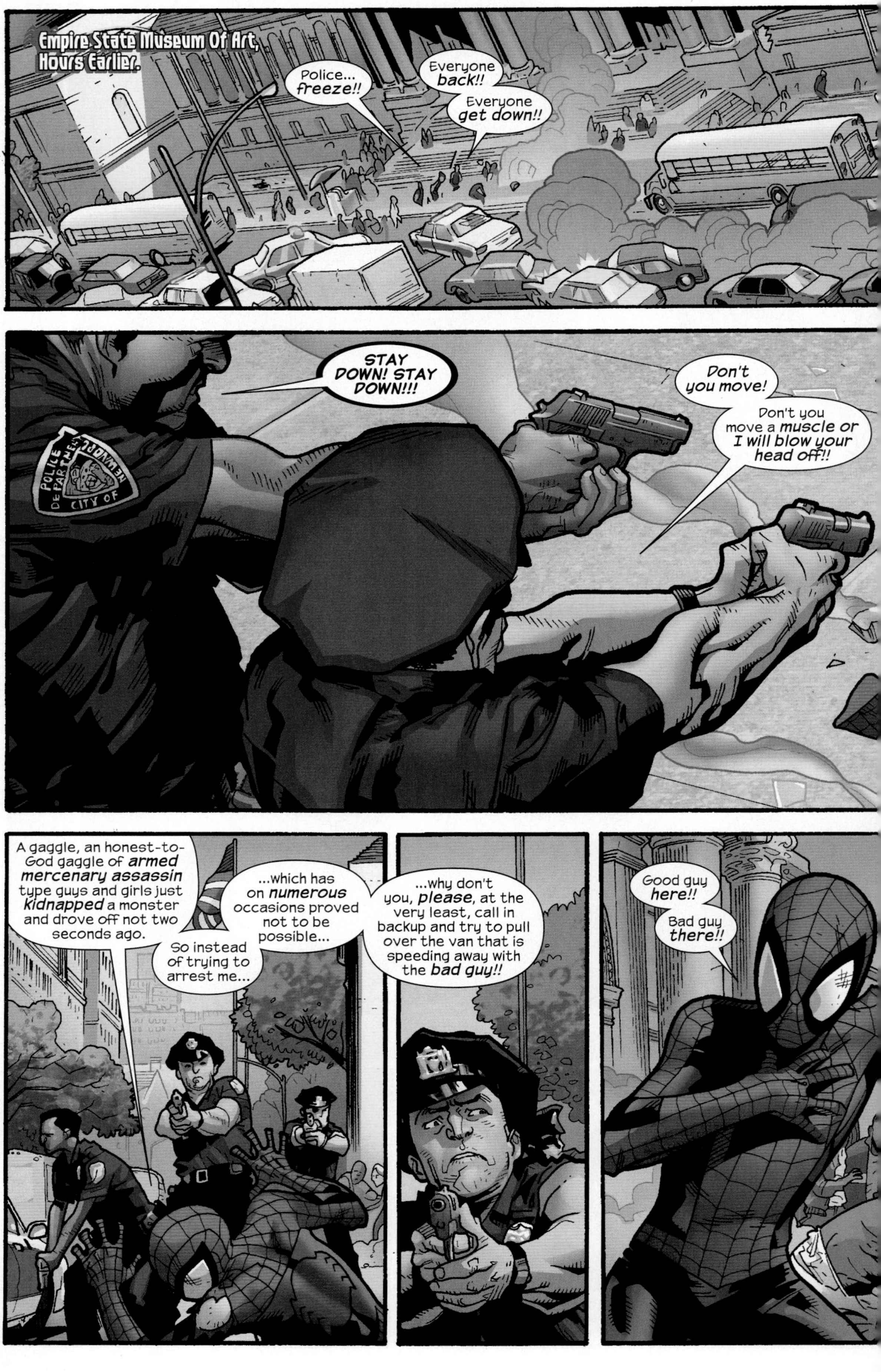
Empire State Museum Of Art, Hours Earlier.
Police... freeze!!
Everyone back!!
Everyone get down!!
STAY DOWN! STAY DOWN!!!
Don't you move!
Don't you move a muscle or I will blow your head off!!
POLICE DEPARTMENT CITY OF NEW YORK
A gaggle, an honest-to-God gaggle of armed mercenary assassin type guys and girls just kidnapped a monster and drove off not two seconds ago.
So instead of trying to arrest me...
...which has on numerous occasions proved not to be possible...
...why don't you, please, at the very least, call in backup and try to pull over the van that is speeding away with the bad guy!!
Good guy here!!
Bad guy there!!

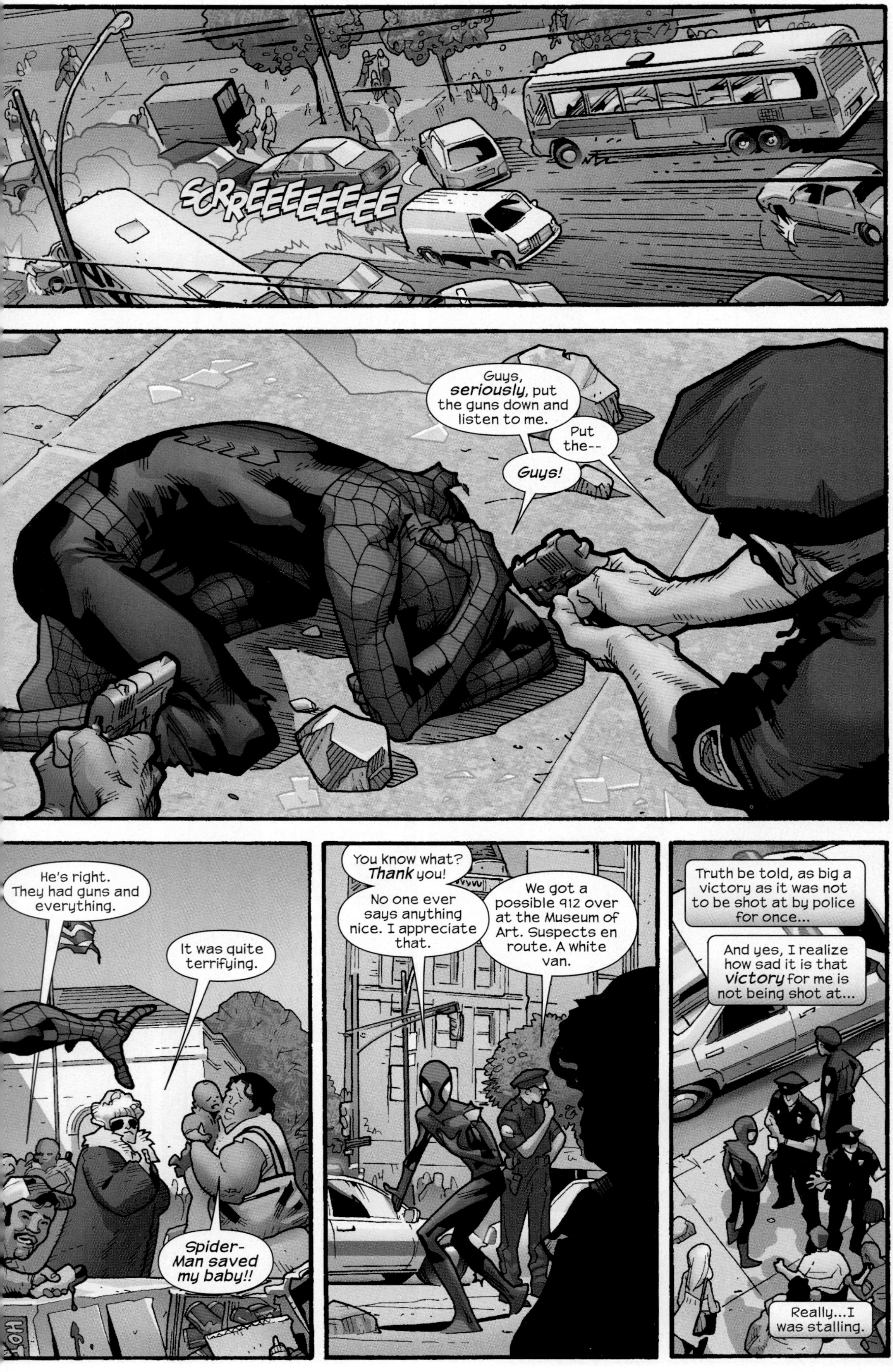
SCRREEEEEEEEE
Guys, seriously, put the guns down and listen to me.
Put the--
Guys!
He's right. They had guns and everything.
It was quite terrifying.
Spider-Man saved my baby!!
You know what? Thank you!
No one ever says anything nice. I appreciate that.
We got a possible 912 over at the Museum of Art. Suspects en route. A white van.
Truth be told, as big a victory as it was not to be shot at by police for once...
And yes, I realize how sad it is that victory for me is not being shot at...
Really...I was stalling.

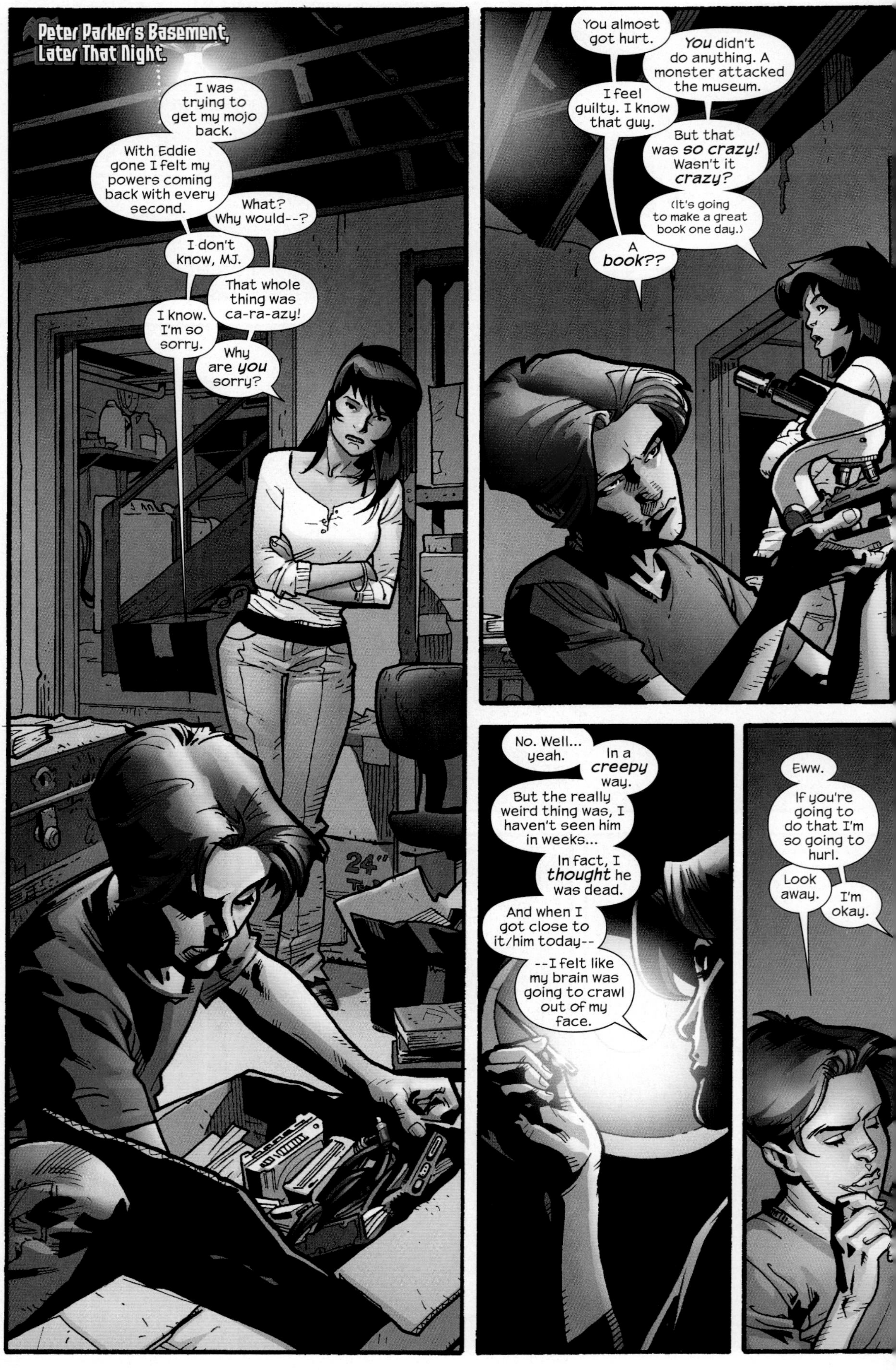

Peter Parker's Basement, Later That Night.
I was trying to get my mojo back.
With Eddie gone I felt my powers coming back with every second.
What? Why would--?
I don't know, MJ.
That whole thing was ca-ra-azy!
I know. I'm so sorry.
Why are you sorry?
You almost got hurt.
You didn't do anything. A monster attacked the museum.
I feel guilty. I know that guy.
But that was so crazy! Wasn't it crazy?
(It's going to make a great book one day.)
A book??
No. Well... yeah.
In a creepy way.
But the really weird thing was, I haven't seen him in weeks...
In fact, I thought he was dead.
And when I got close to it/him today--
--I felt like my brain was going to crawl out of my face.
Eww.
If you're going to do that I'm so going to hurl.
Look away.
I'm okay.

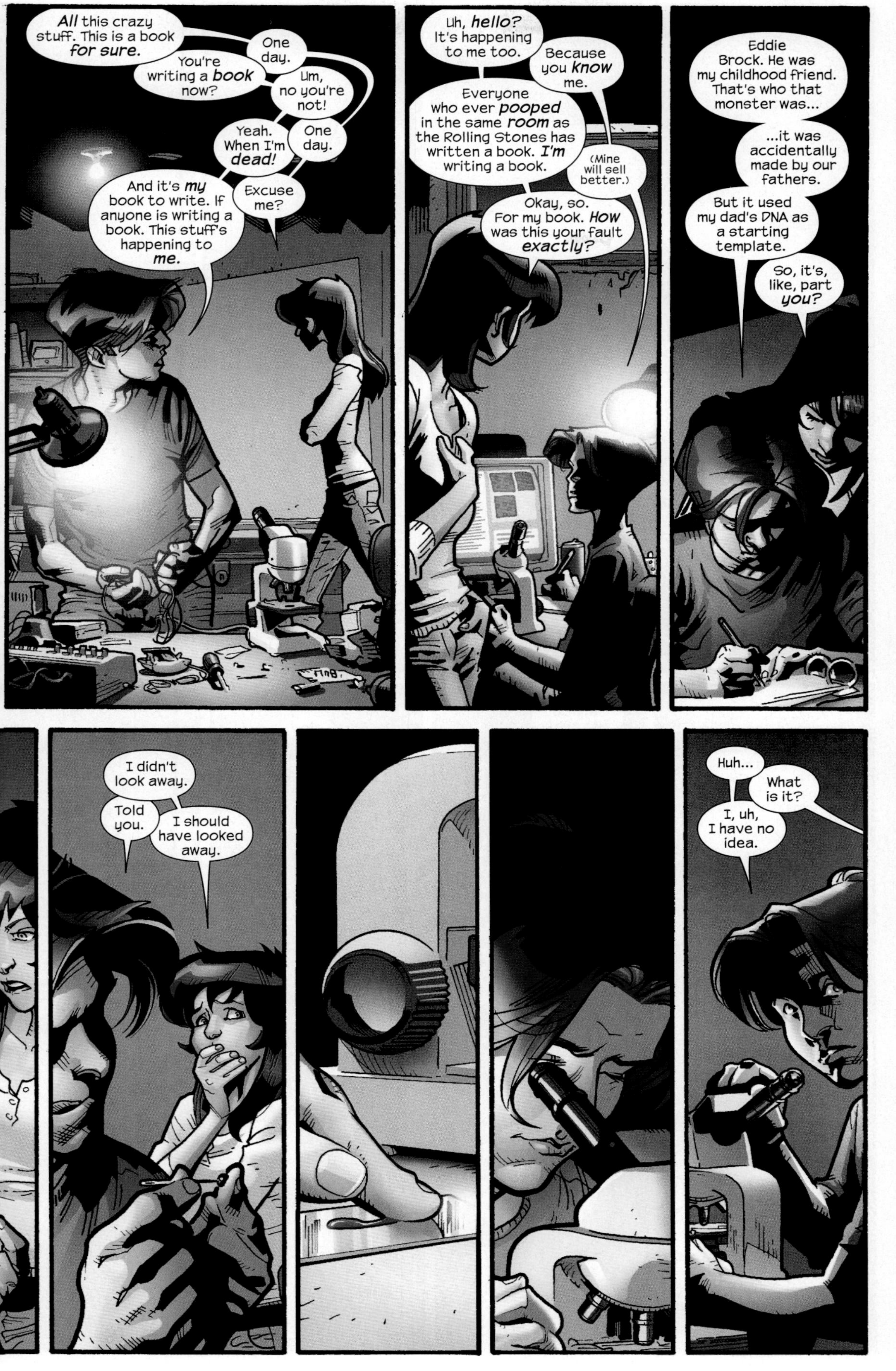
All this crazy stuff. This is a book for sure.
One day.
You're writing a book now?
Um, no you're not!
Yeah. When I'm dead!
One day.
And it's my book to write. If anyone is writing a book. This stuff's happening to me.
Excuse me?
Uh, hello? It's happening to me too.
Because you know me.
Everyone who ever pooped in the same room as the Rolling Stones has written a book. I'm writing a book.
(Mine will sell better.)
Okay, so. For my book. How was this your fault exactly?
Eddie Brock. He was my childhood friend. That's who that monster was...
...it was accidentally made by our fathers.
But it used my dad's DNA as a starting template.
So, it's, like, part you?
I didn't look away.
Told you.
I should have looked away.
Huh...
What is it?
I, uh, I have no idea.

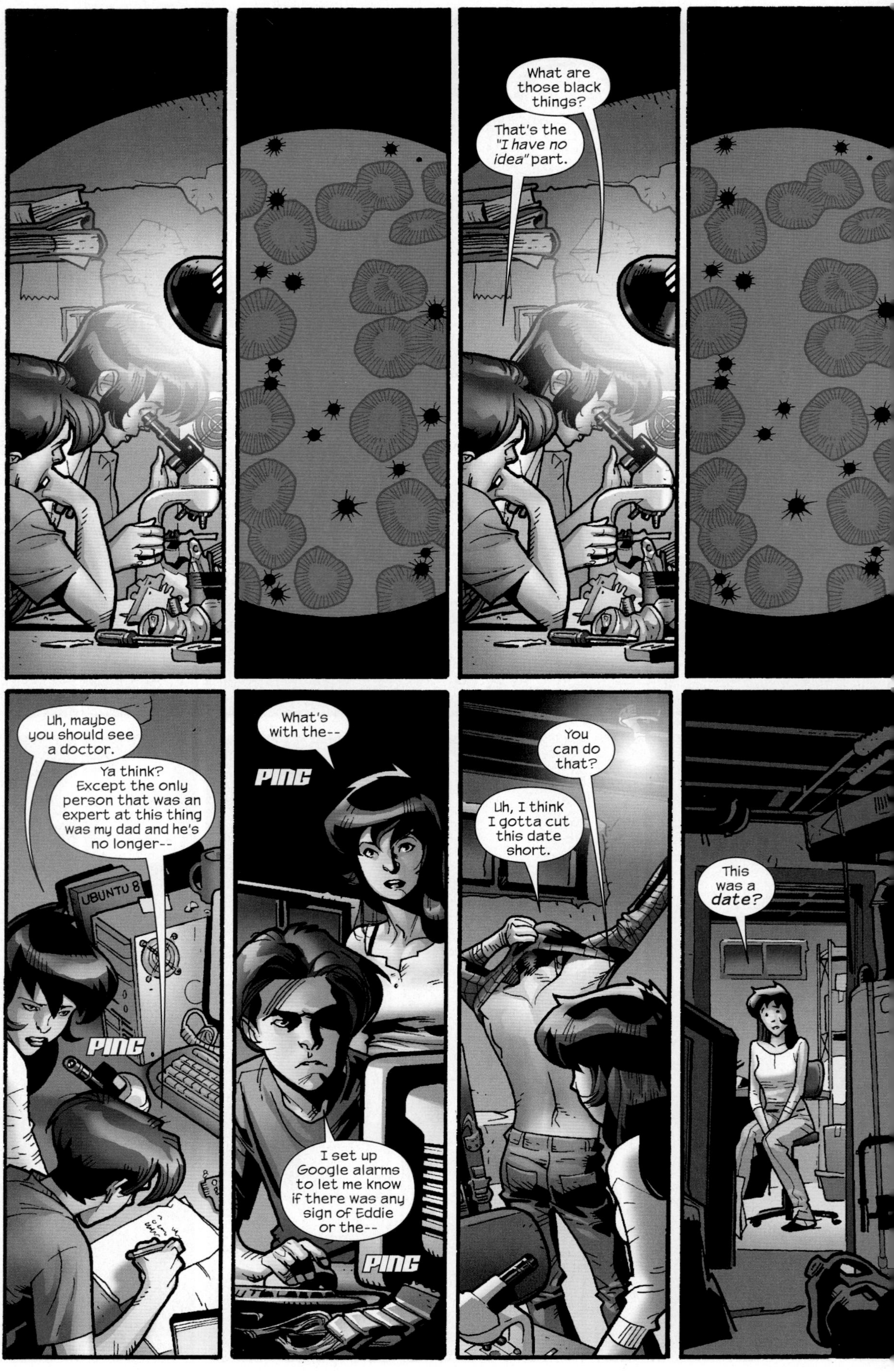
What are those black things?
That's the "I have no idea" part.
Uh, maybe you should see a doctor.
Ya think? Except the only person that was an expert at this thing was my dad and he's no longer--
UBUNTU 8
PING
What's with the--
PING
I set up Google alarms to let me know if there was any sign of Eddie or the--
PING
You can do that?
Uh, I think I gotta cut this date short.
This was a *date?*

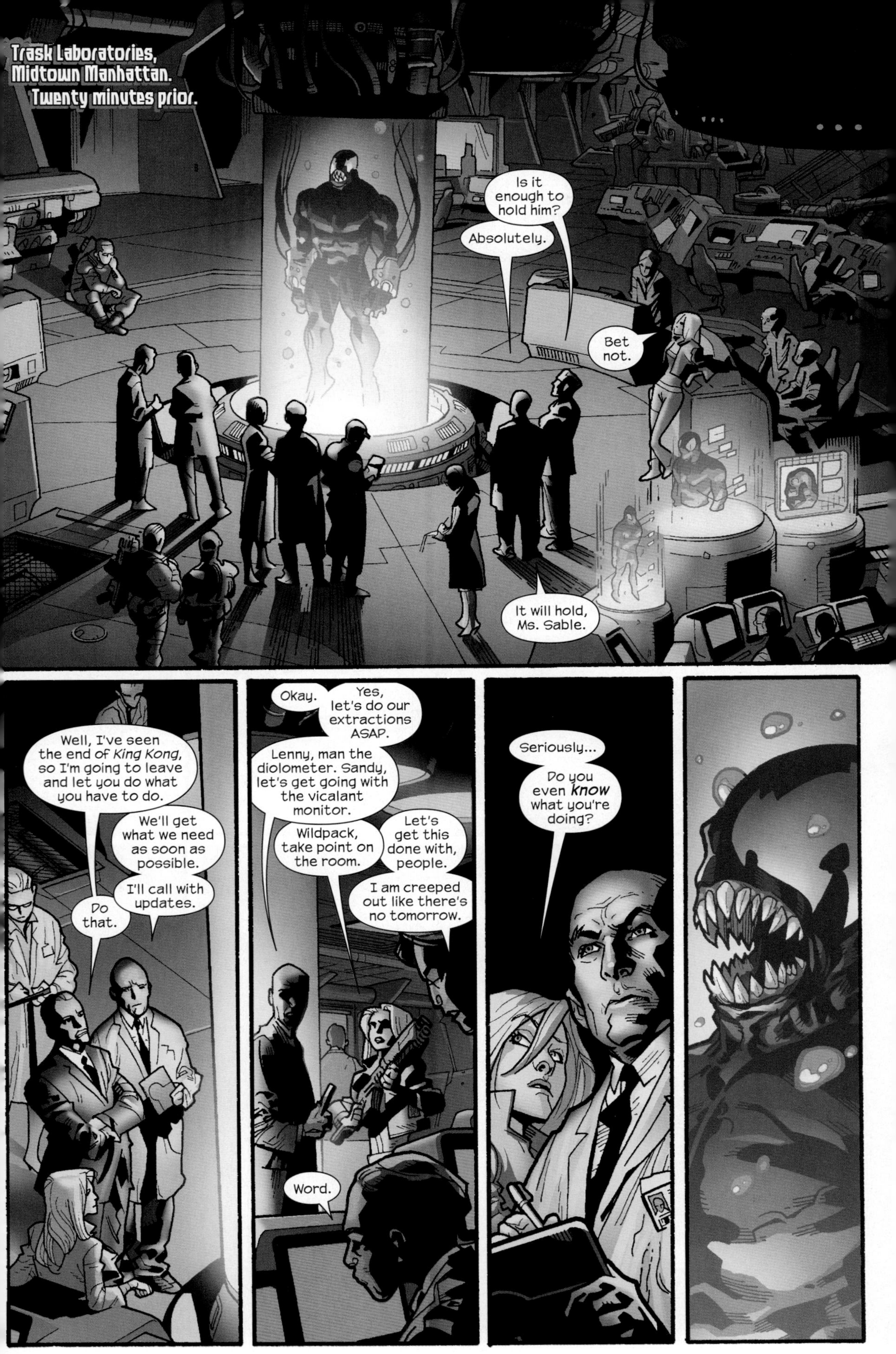
Trask Laboratories, Midtown Manhattan. Twenty minutes prior.
Is it enough to hold him?
Absolutely.
Bet not.
It will hold, Ms. Sable.
Well, I've seen the end of *King Kong*, so I'm going to leave and let you do what you have to do.
We'll get what we need as soon as possible.
I'll call with updates.
Do that.
Okay.
Yes, let's do our extractions ASAP.
Lenny, man the diolometer. Sandy, let's get going with the vicalant monitor.
Wildpack, take point on the room.
Let's get this done with, people.
I am creeped out like there's no tomorrow.
Word.
Seriously...
Do you even ***know*** what you're doing?

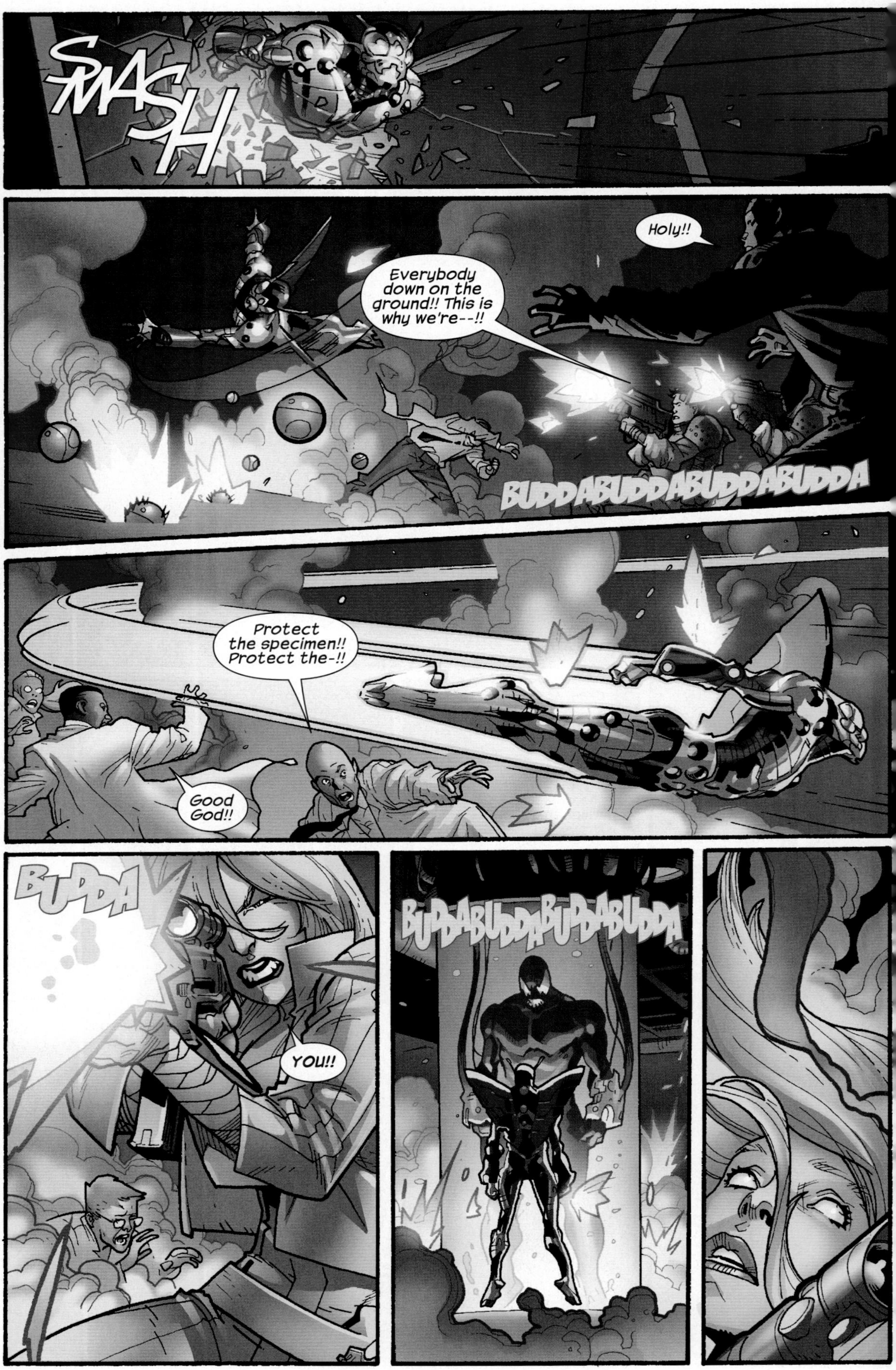
SMASH
Holy!!
Everybody down on the ground!! This is why we're--!!
BUDDABUDDABUDDABUDDA
Protect the specimen!! Protect the-!!
Good God!!
BUDDA
YOU!!
BUDDABUDDABUDDABUDDA

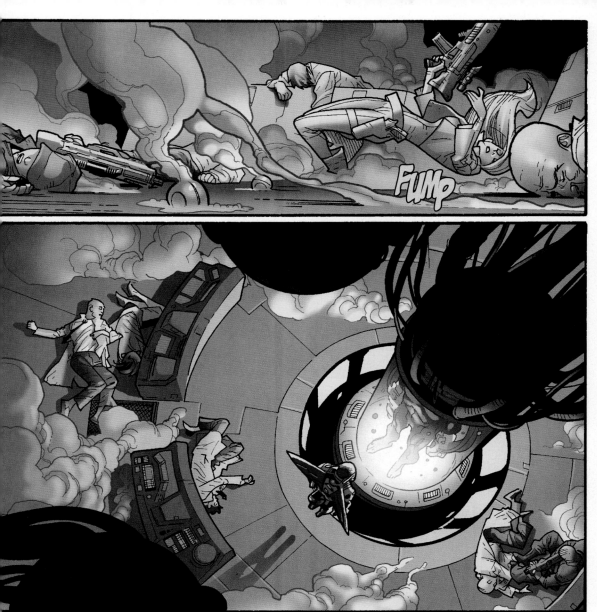

FUMP

GLEE
GLEE

STASIS FIELD
SUSPENDED.

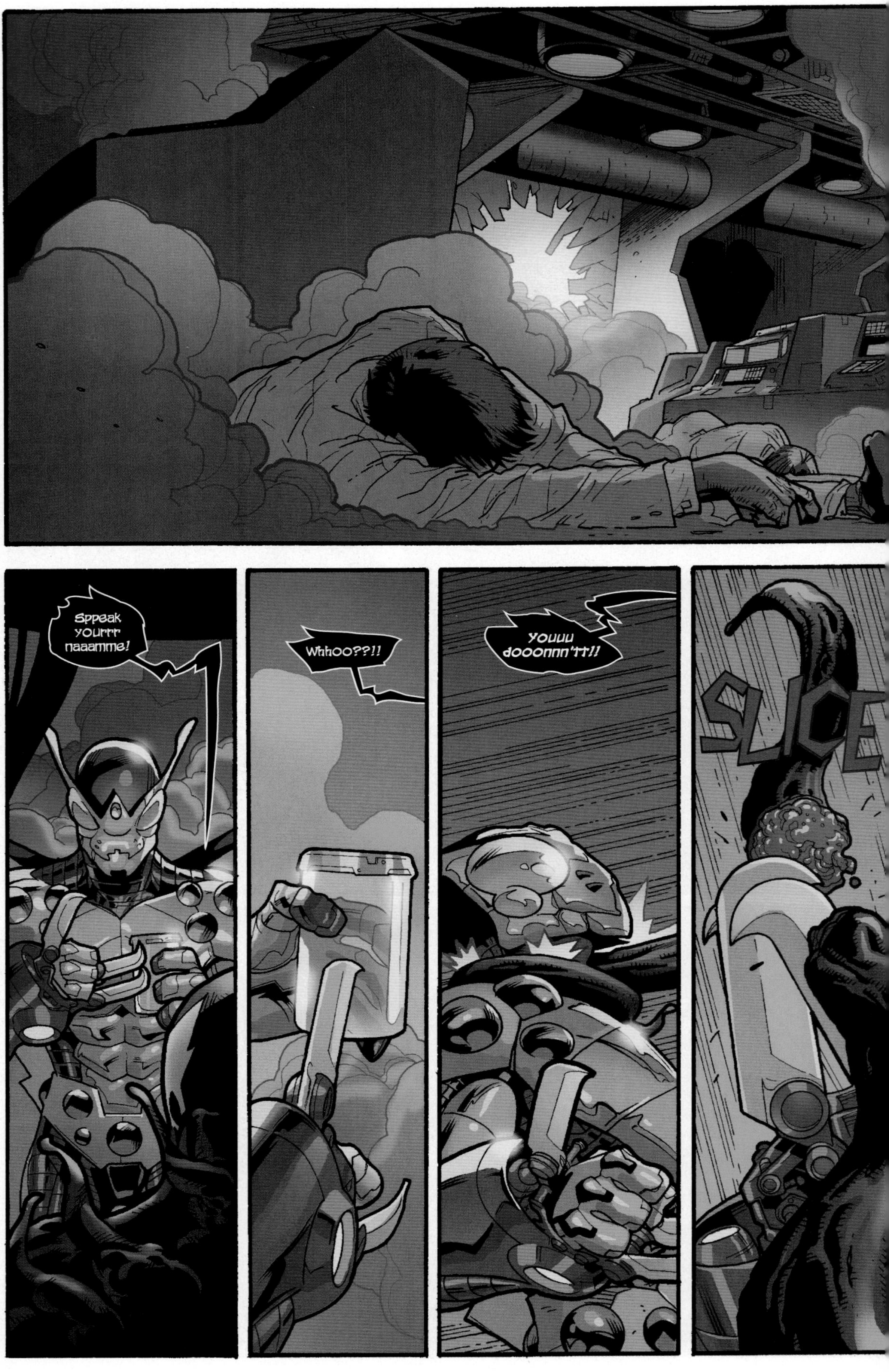
Sppeak yourrr naaamme!
Whhoo??!!
Youuu dooonnn'tt!!
SLICE

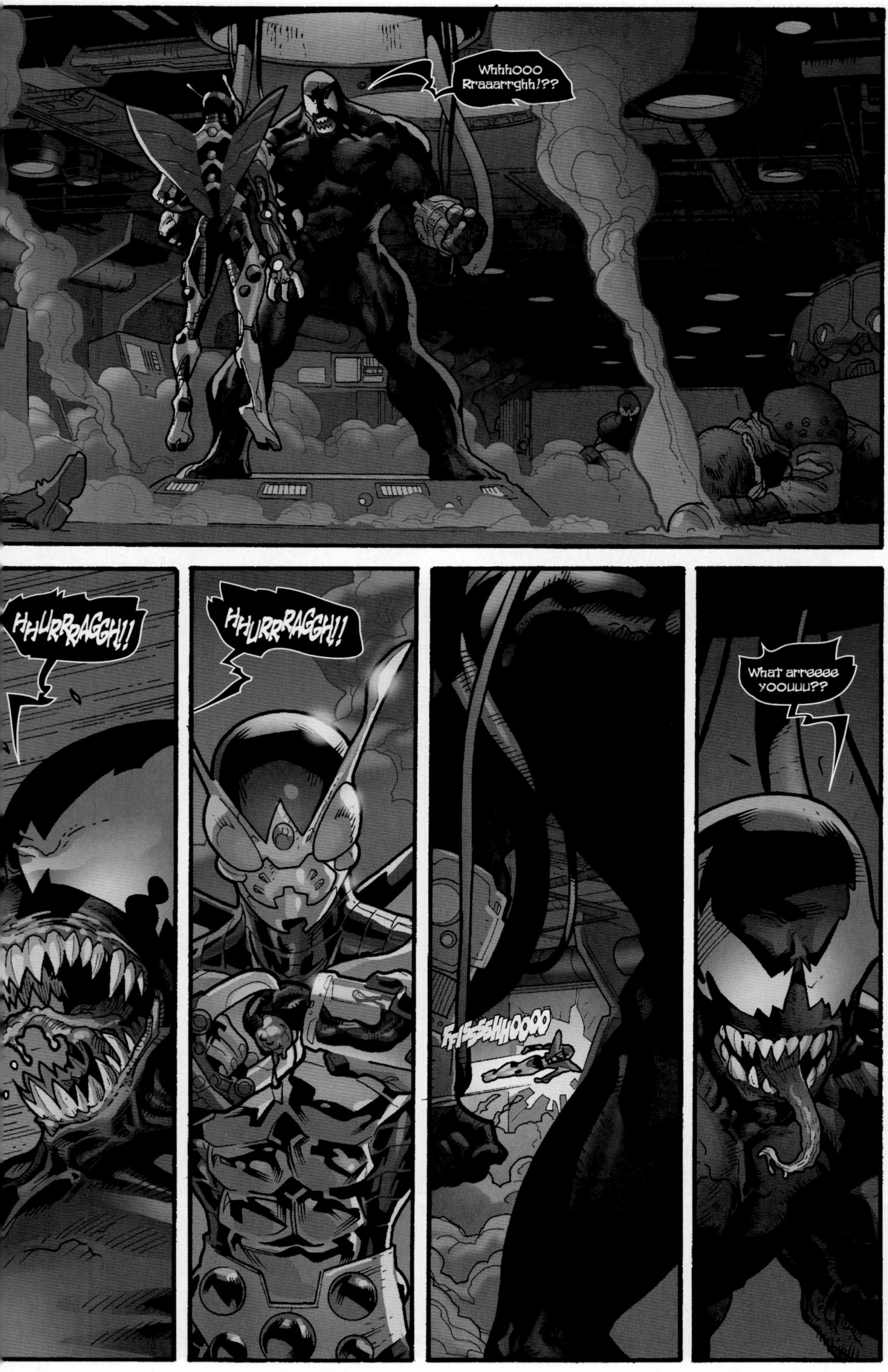
Whhhooo Rraaarrghh!??
HHURRRAGGH!!
HHURRRAGGH!!
FFISSSHHOOOO
What arreeee yoouuu??

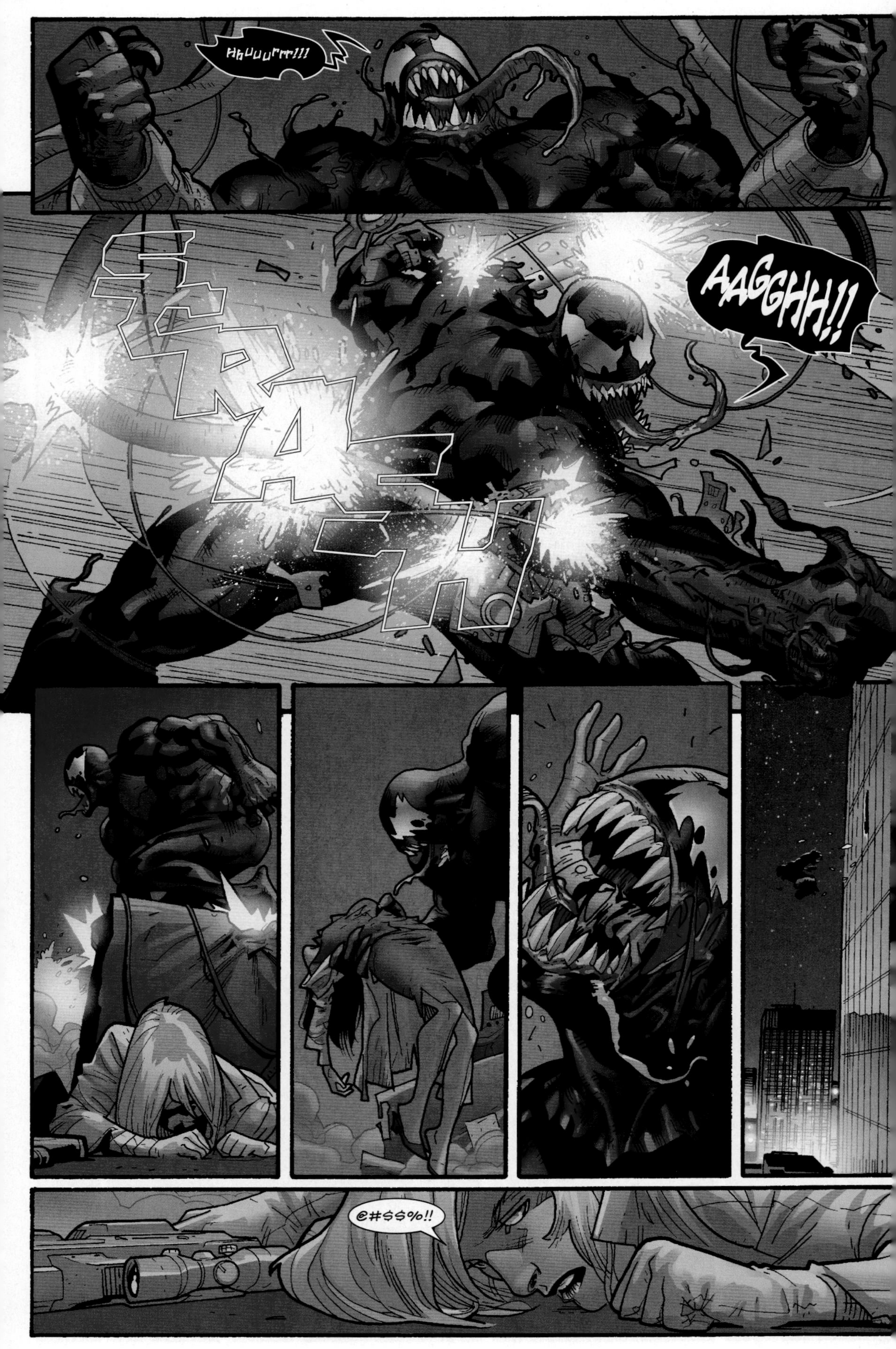
Hhuuurrr!!!
AAGGHH!!
@#$$%!!

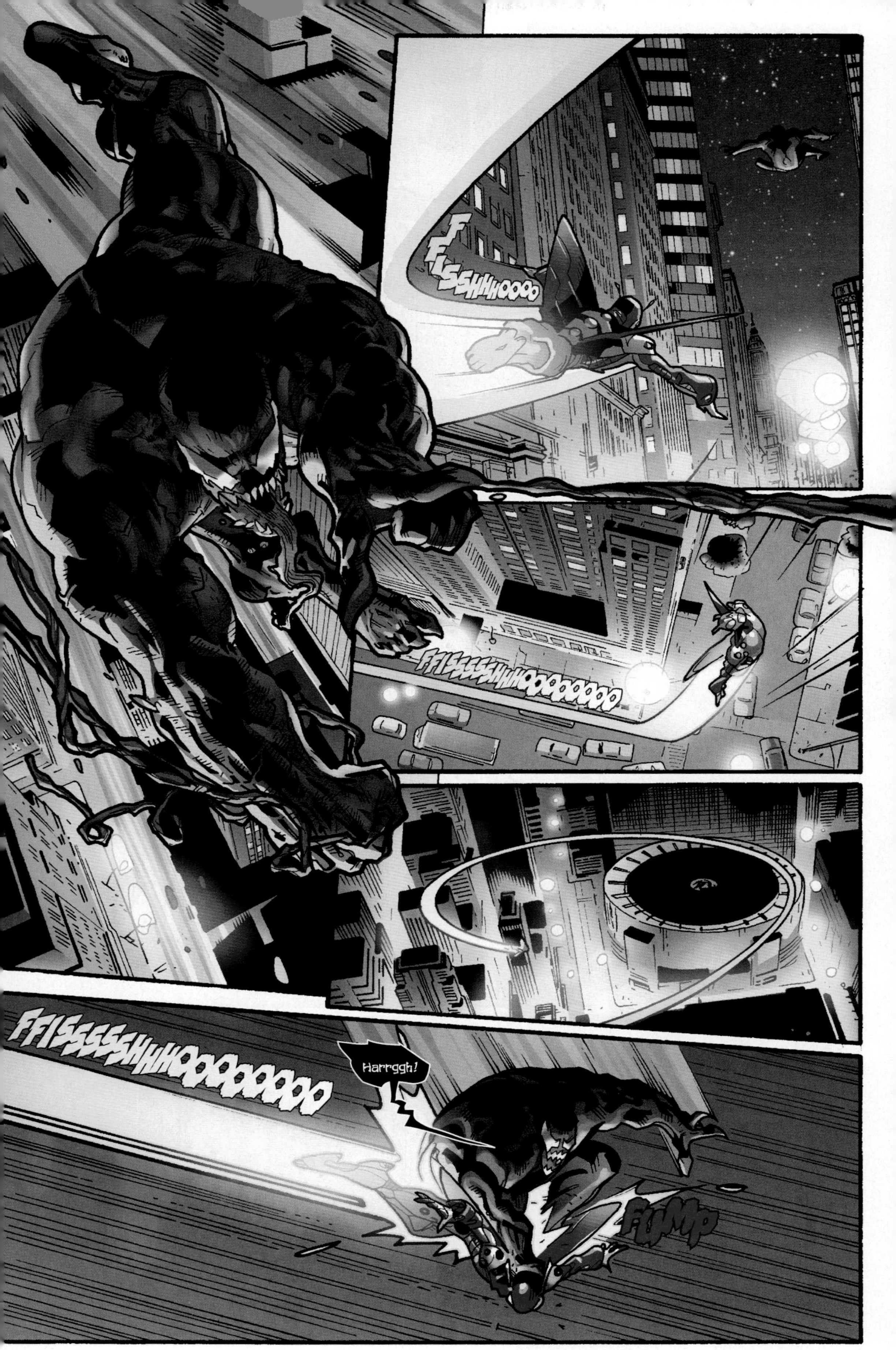
FFISSHHHOOOO
FFISSSSSHHHOOOOOOOOO
FFISSSSSSHHHOOOOOOOOOO
Harrggh!
FLUMP

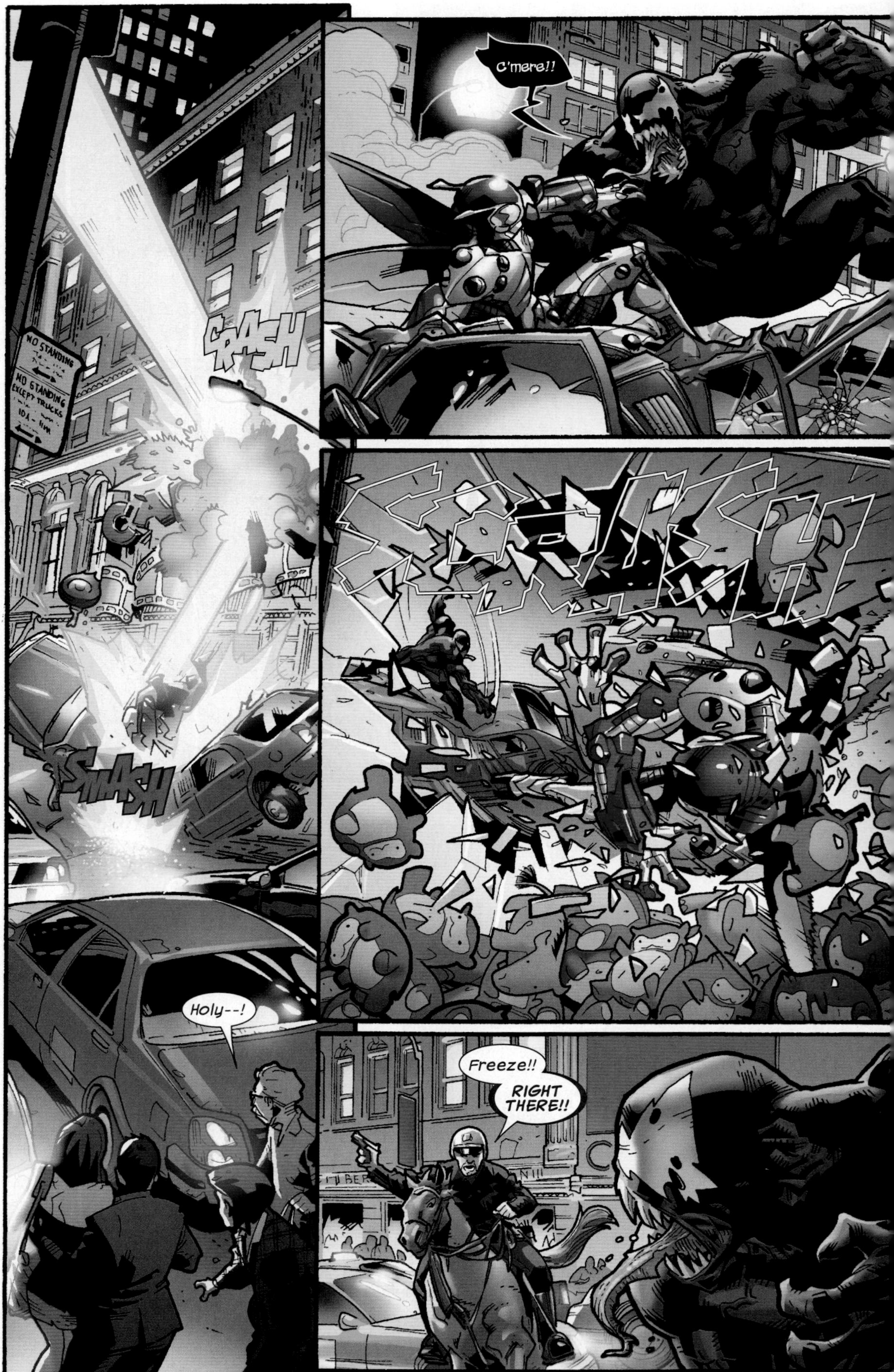

C'mere!!
CRASH
NO STANDING
NO STANDING EXCEPT TRUCKS
SMASH
CRASH
Holy--!
Freeze!!
RIGHT THERE!!

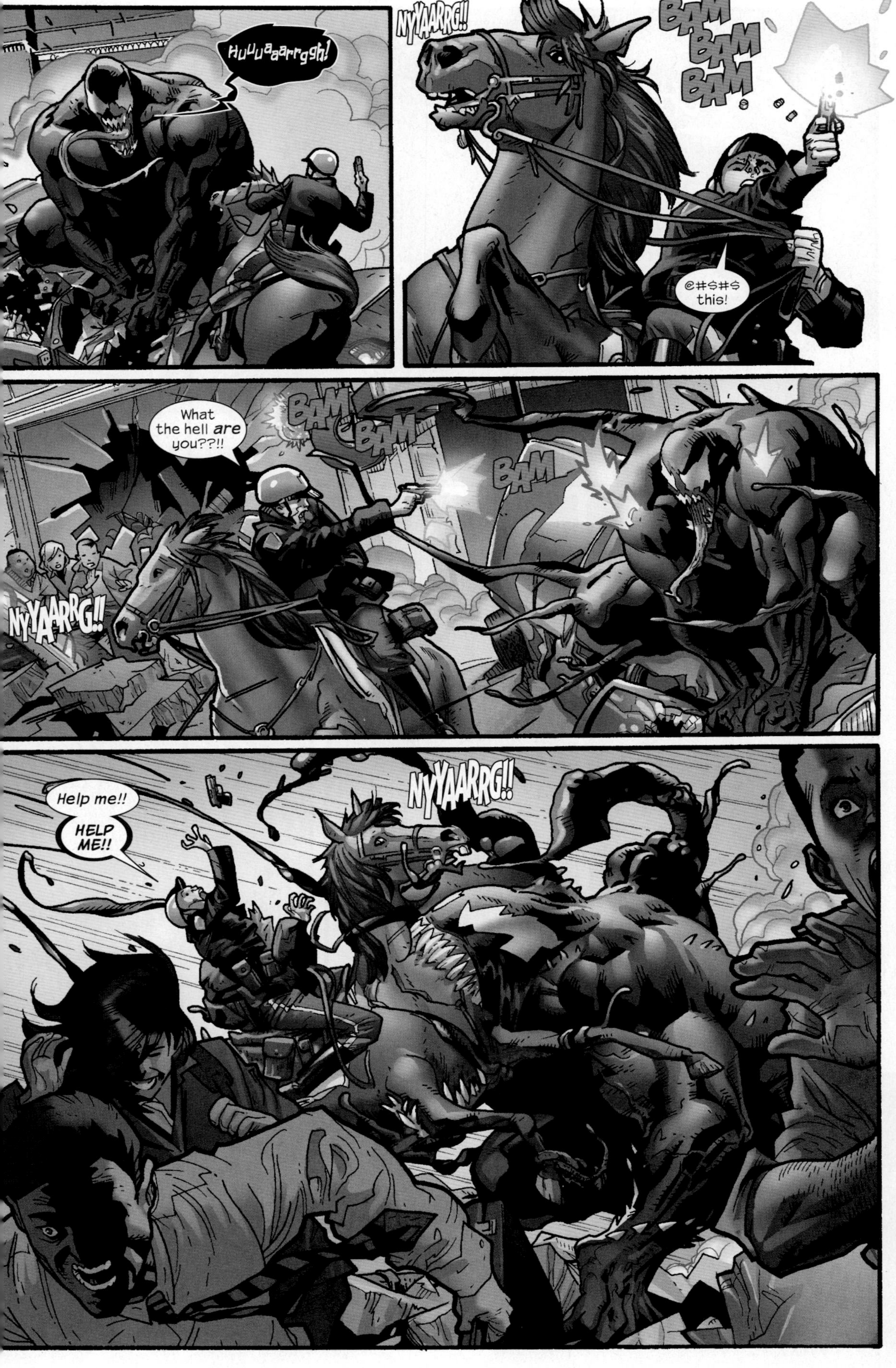
Huuuaaarrggh!
NYYAARRG!!
BAM BAM BAM
@#$#$ this!
What the hell are you??!!
BAM
BAM
BAM
NYYAARRG!!
Help me!!
HELP ME!!
NYYAARRG!!

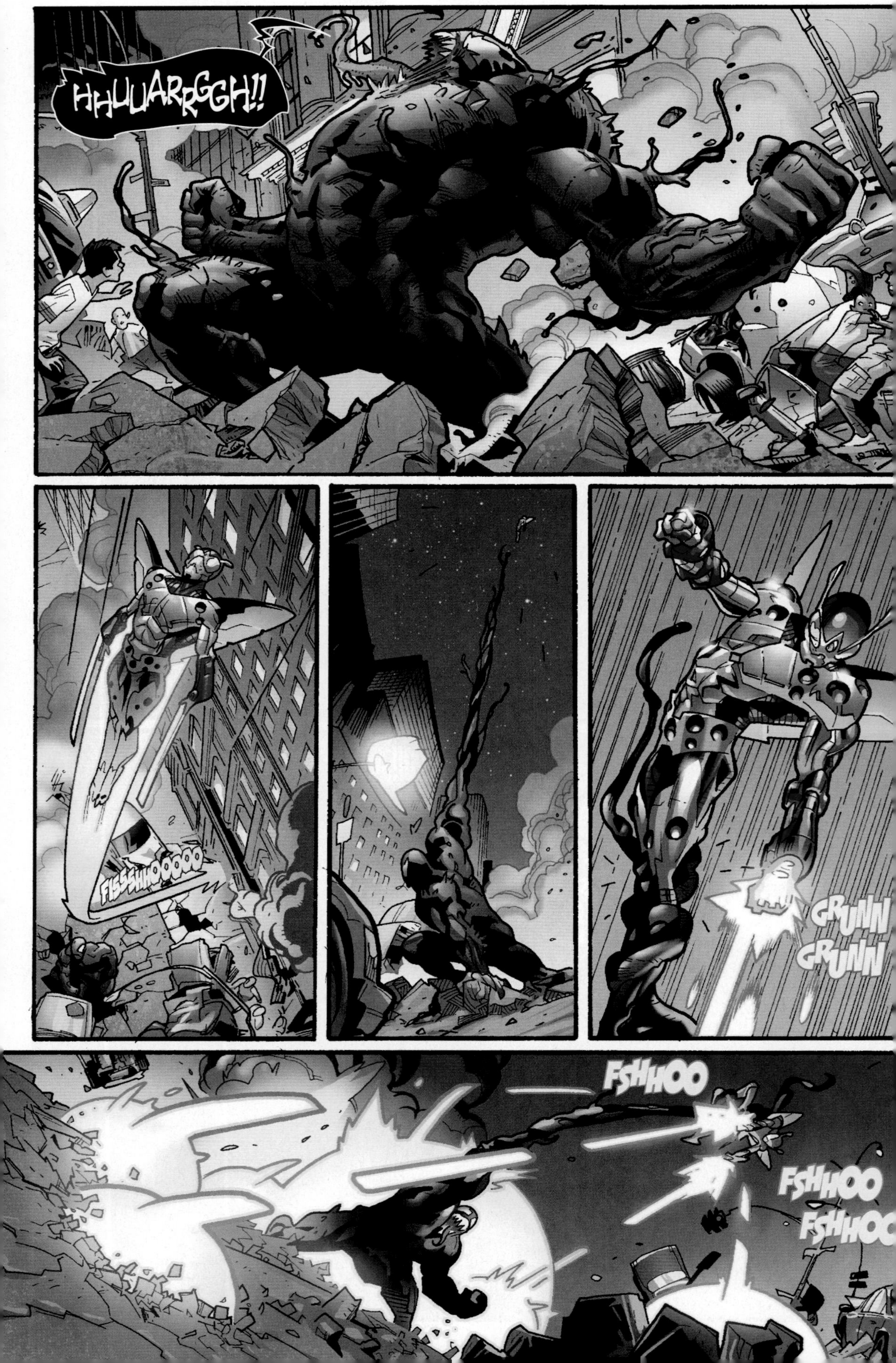
HHUUARRGGH!!
FISSSHHOOOOO
GRUNN
GRUNN
FSHHOO
FSHHOO
FSHHOO

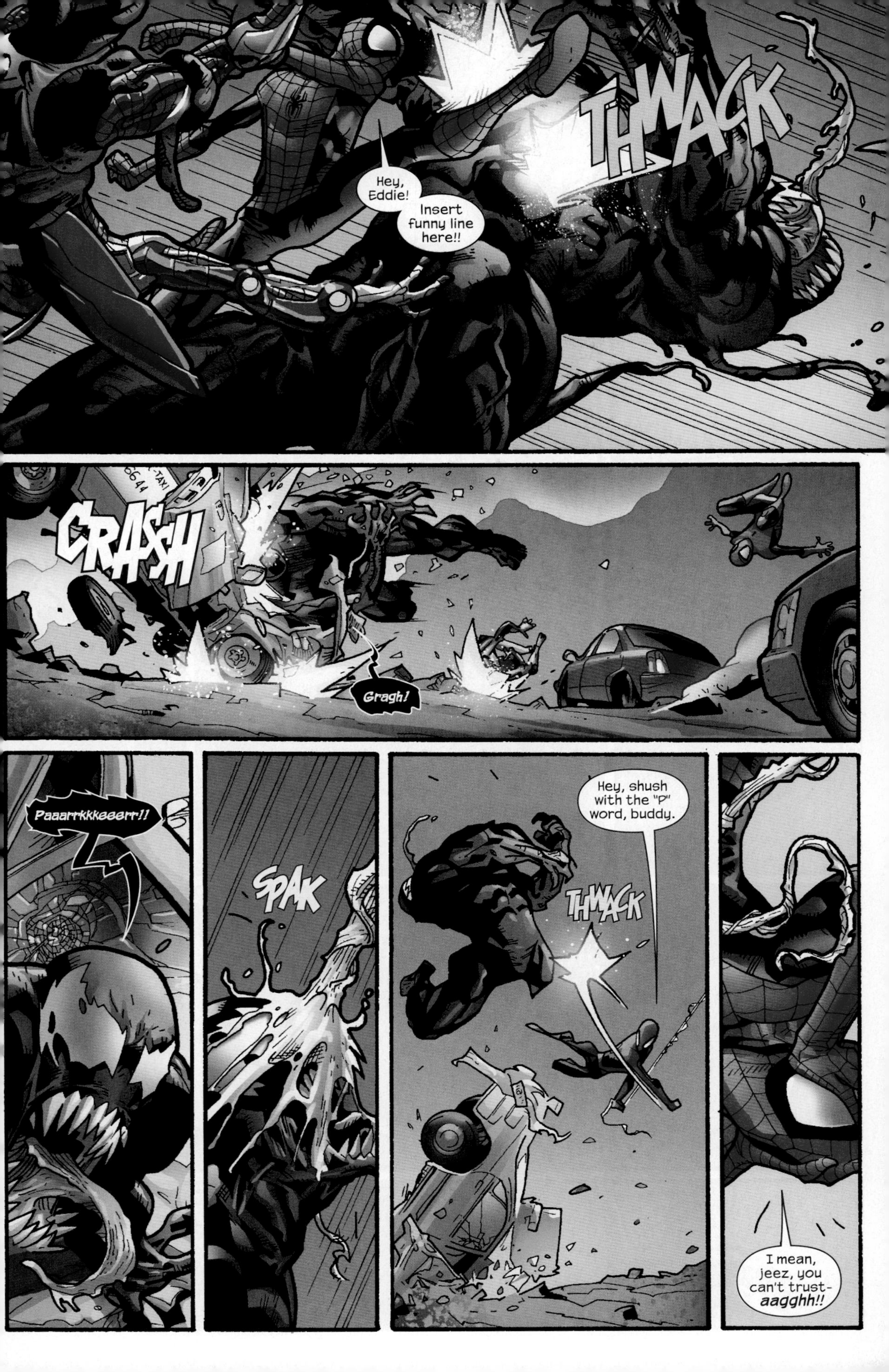
THWACK
Hey, Eddie!
Insert funny line here!!
CRASH
Gragh!
Paaarrrkkkeerrr!!
SPAK
Hey, shush with the "P" word, buddy.
THWACK
I mean, jeez, you can't trust-
aagghh!!

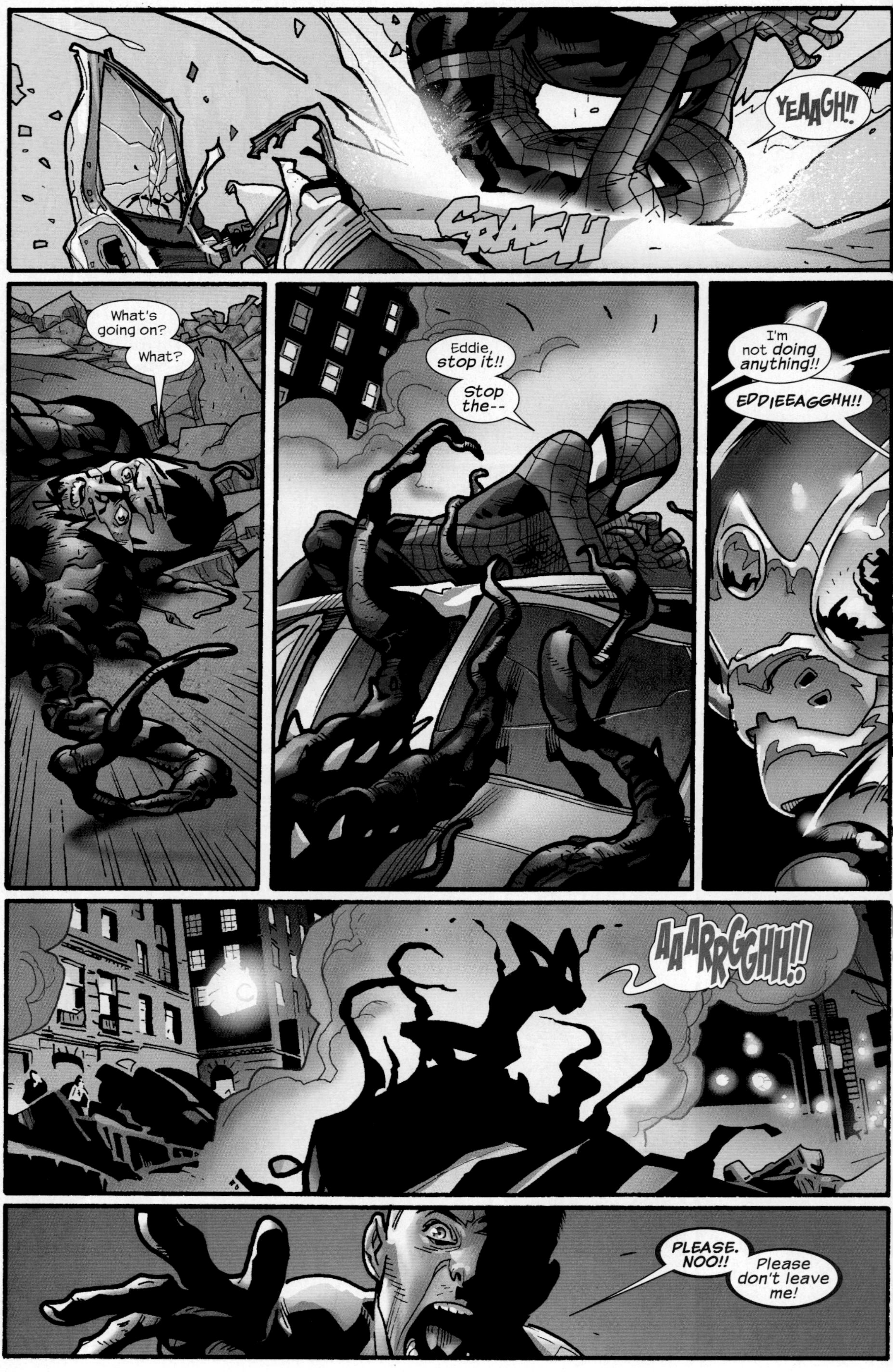
YEAAGH!!
CRASH
What's going on?
What?
Eddie, stop it!!
Stop the--
I'm not doing anything!!
EDDIEEAGGHH!!
AAARRGGHH!!
PLEASE. NOO!!
Please don't leave me!

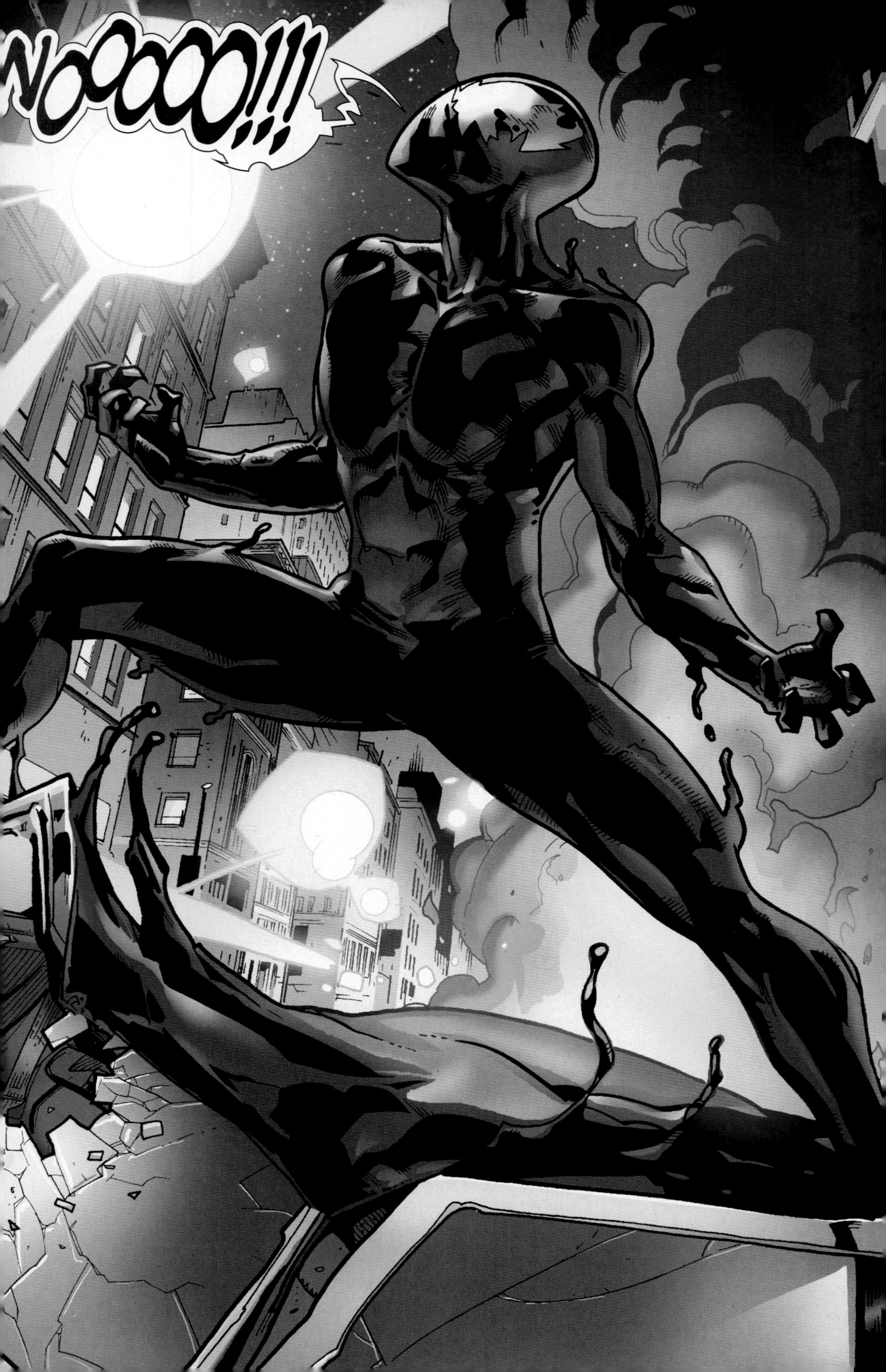
NOOOOO!!!

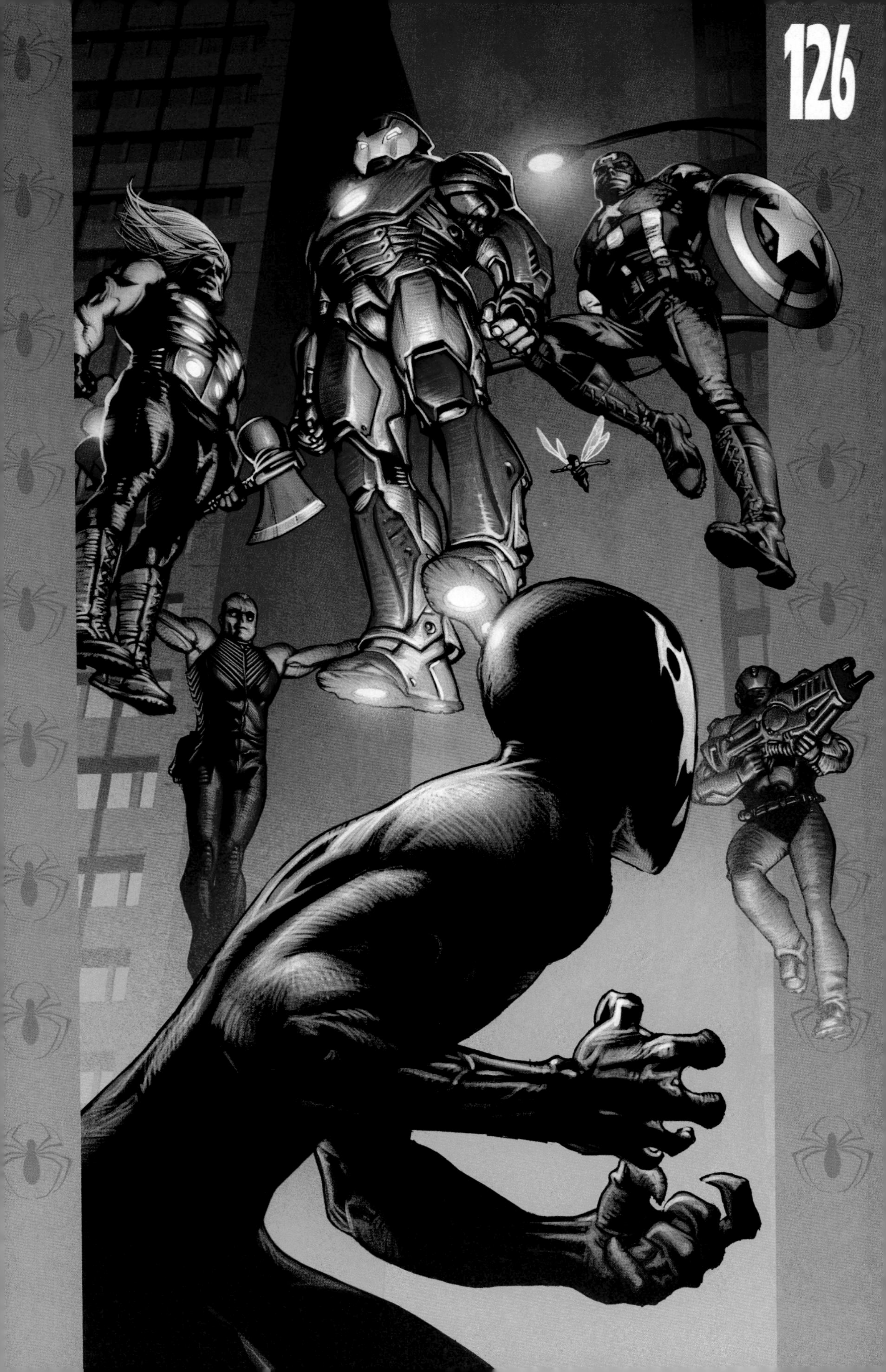
126

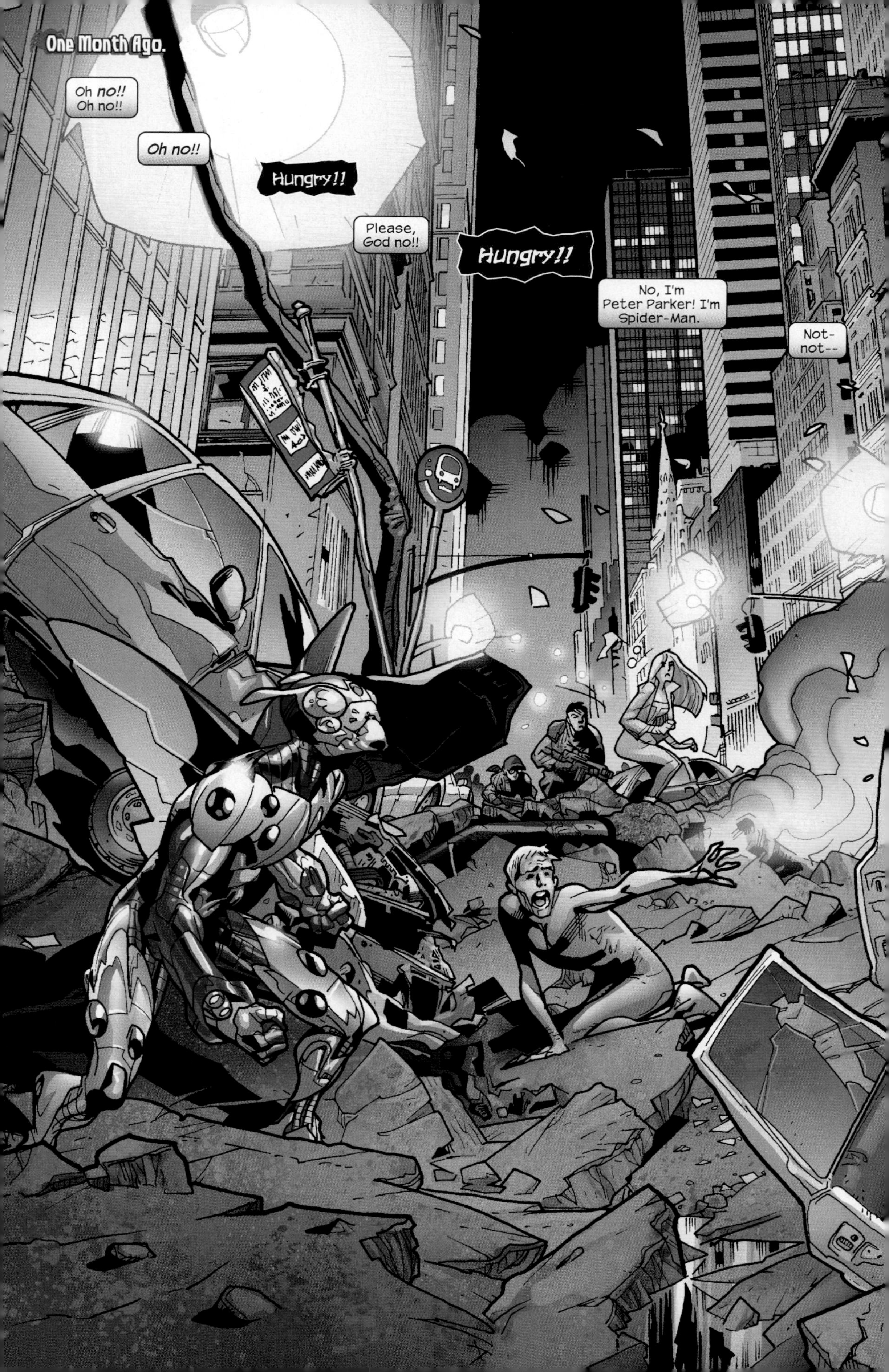

One Month Ago.
Oh no!! Oh no!!
Oh no!!
Hungry!!
Please, God no!!
Hungry!!
No, I'm Peter Parker! I'm Spider-Man.
Not- not--

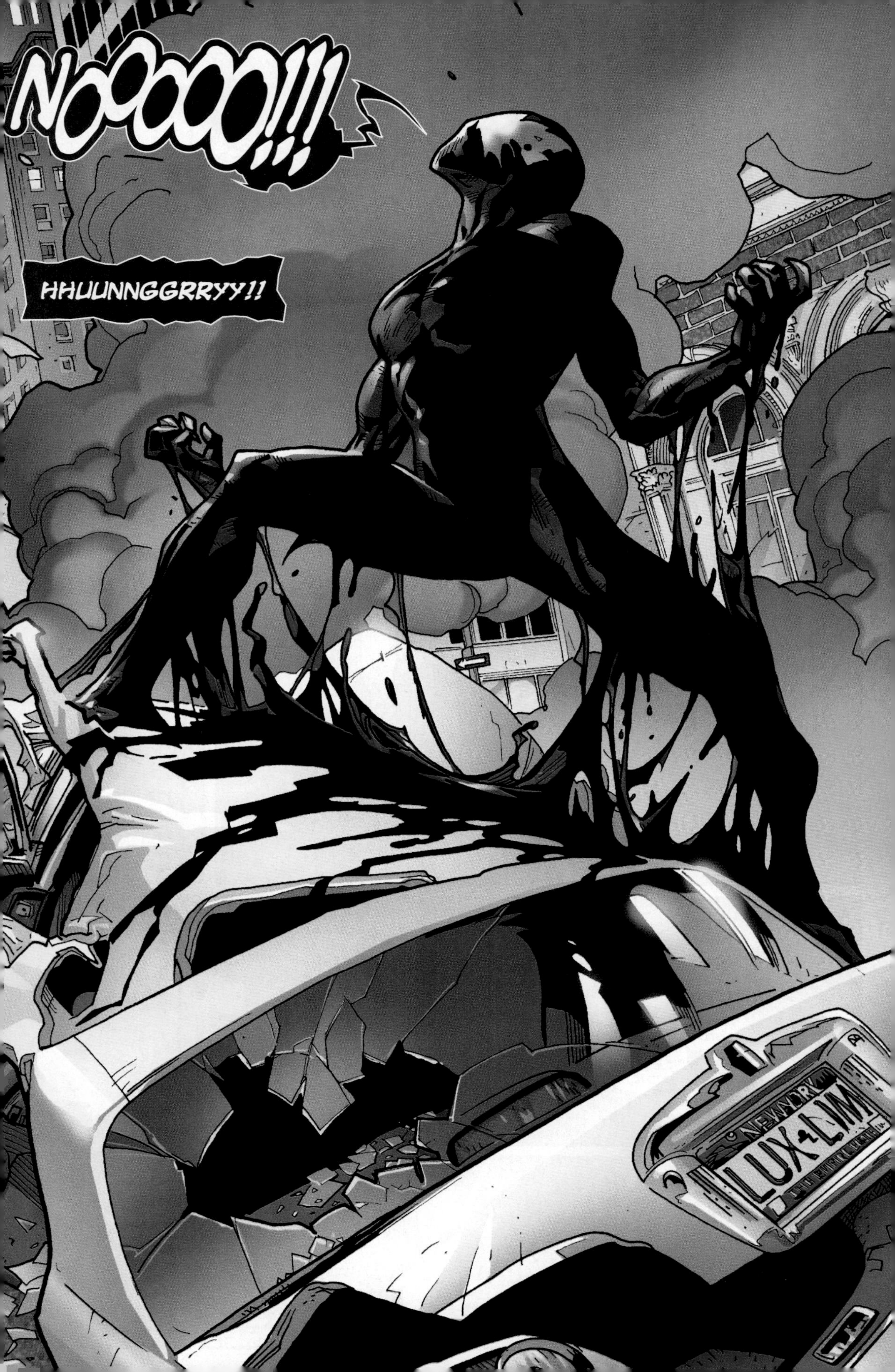
NOOOOO!!!
HHUUNNGGRRYY!!

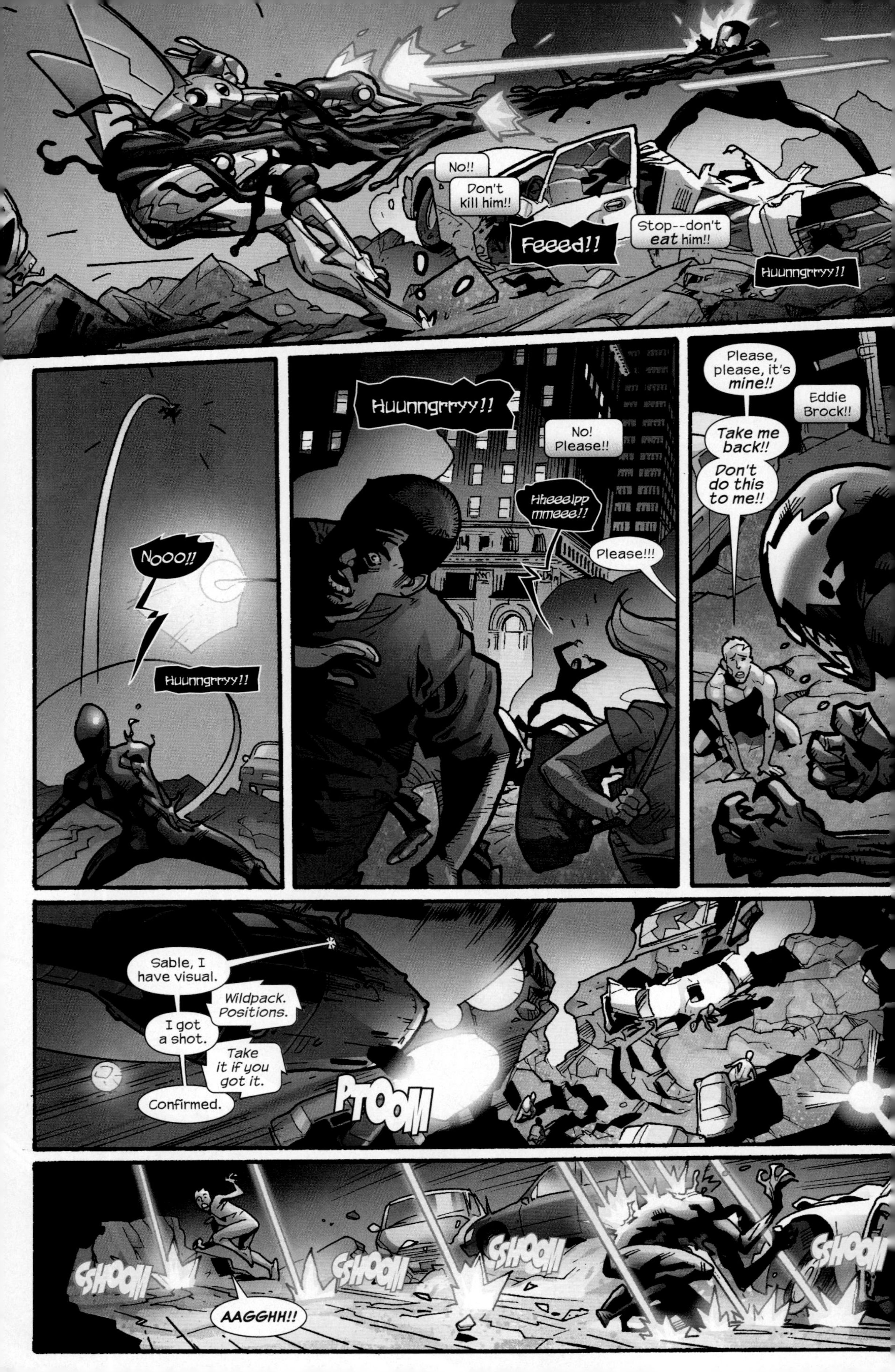
No!!
Don't kill him!!
Feeed!!
Stop--don't eat him!!
Huunngrrryy!!
Nooo!!
Huunngrrryy!!
Huunngrrryy!!
No! Please!!
Hheeelpp mmeee!!
Please!!!
Please, please, it's mine!!
Take me back!!
Don't do this to me!!
Eddie Brock!!
Sable, I have visual.
Wildpack. Positions.
I got a shot.
Take it if you got it.
Confirmed.
PTOOM
CSHOOM
CSHOOM
CSHOOM
CSHOOM
AAGGHH!!

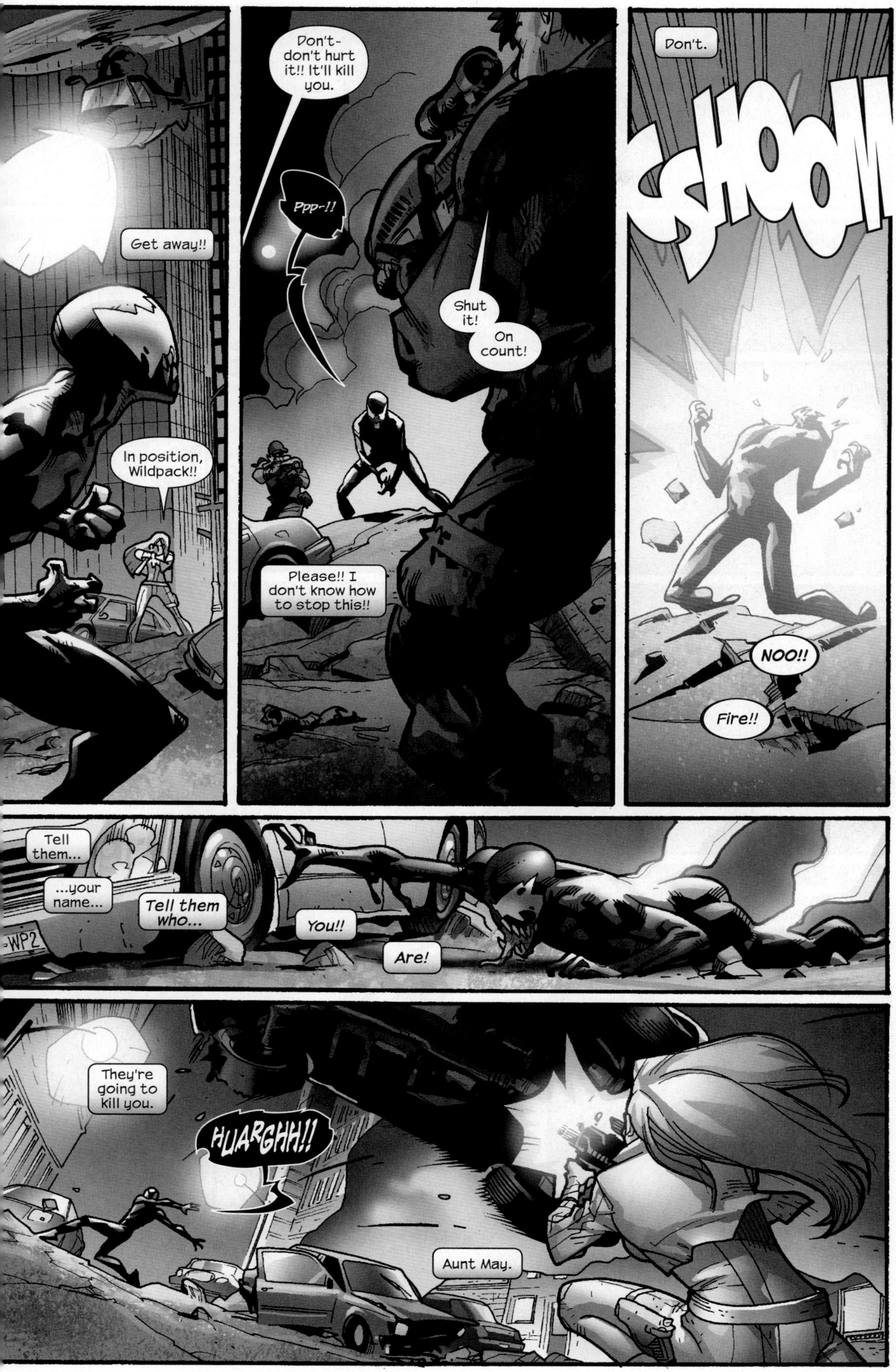
Get away!!
In position, Wildpack!!
Don't- don't hurt it!! It'll kill you.
Ppp-!!
Shut it!
On count!
Please!! I don't know how to stop this!!
Don't.
SHOOM
NOO!!
Fire!!
Tell them...
...your name...
Tell them who...
You!!
Are!
-WP2
They're going to kill you.
HUARGHH!!
Aunt May.

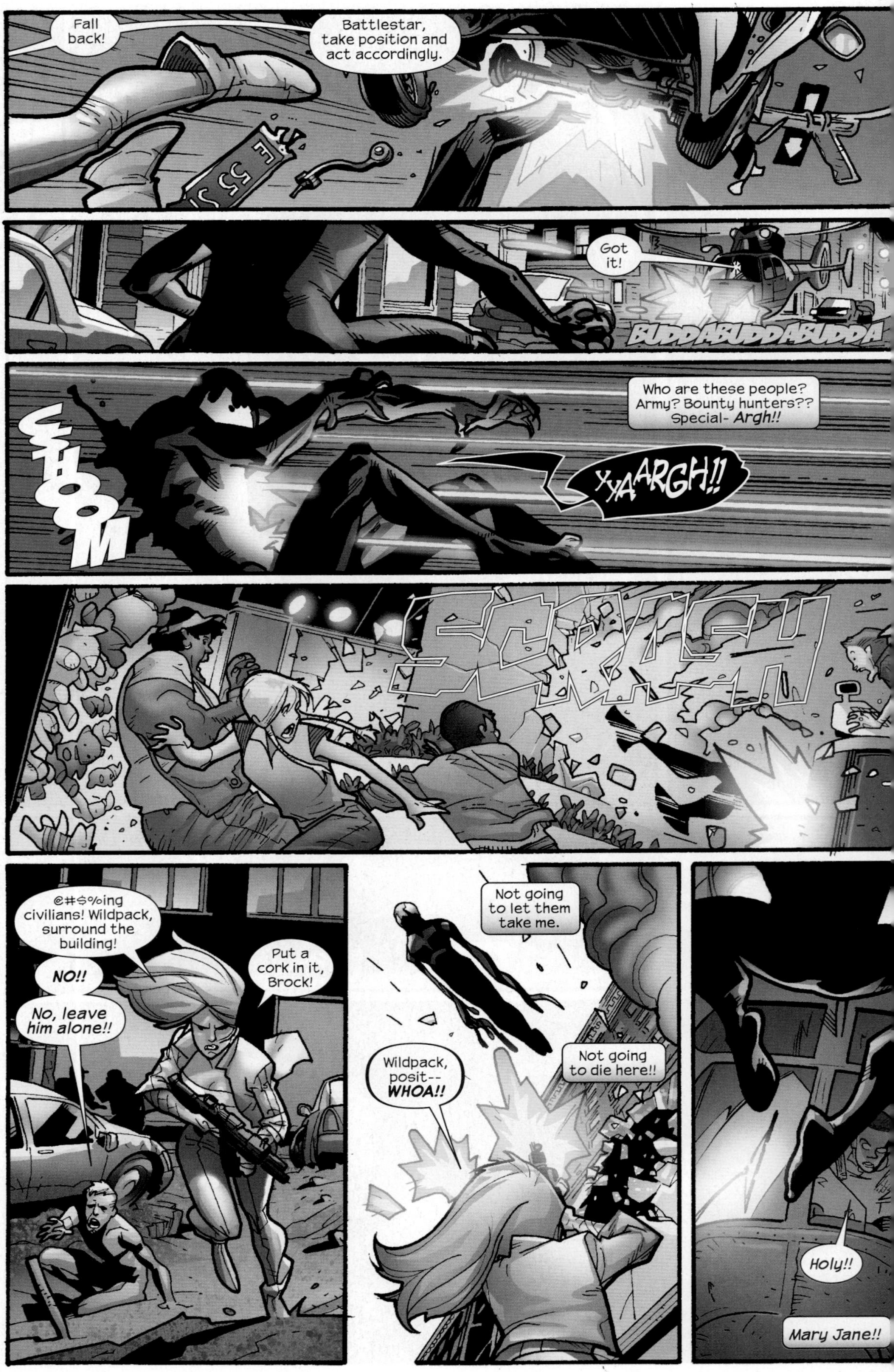
Fall back!
Battlestar, take position and act accordingly.
Got it!
BUDDABUDDABUDDA
Who are these people? Army? Bounty hunters?? Special- Argh!!
WHOOM
YYAARGH!!
SCRAAASH
@#$%ing civilians! Wildpack, surround the building!
NO!!
No, leave him alone!!
Put a cork in it, Brock!
Not going to let them take me.
Not going to die here!!
Wildpack, posit-- WHOA!!
Holy!!
Mary Jane!!

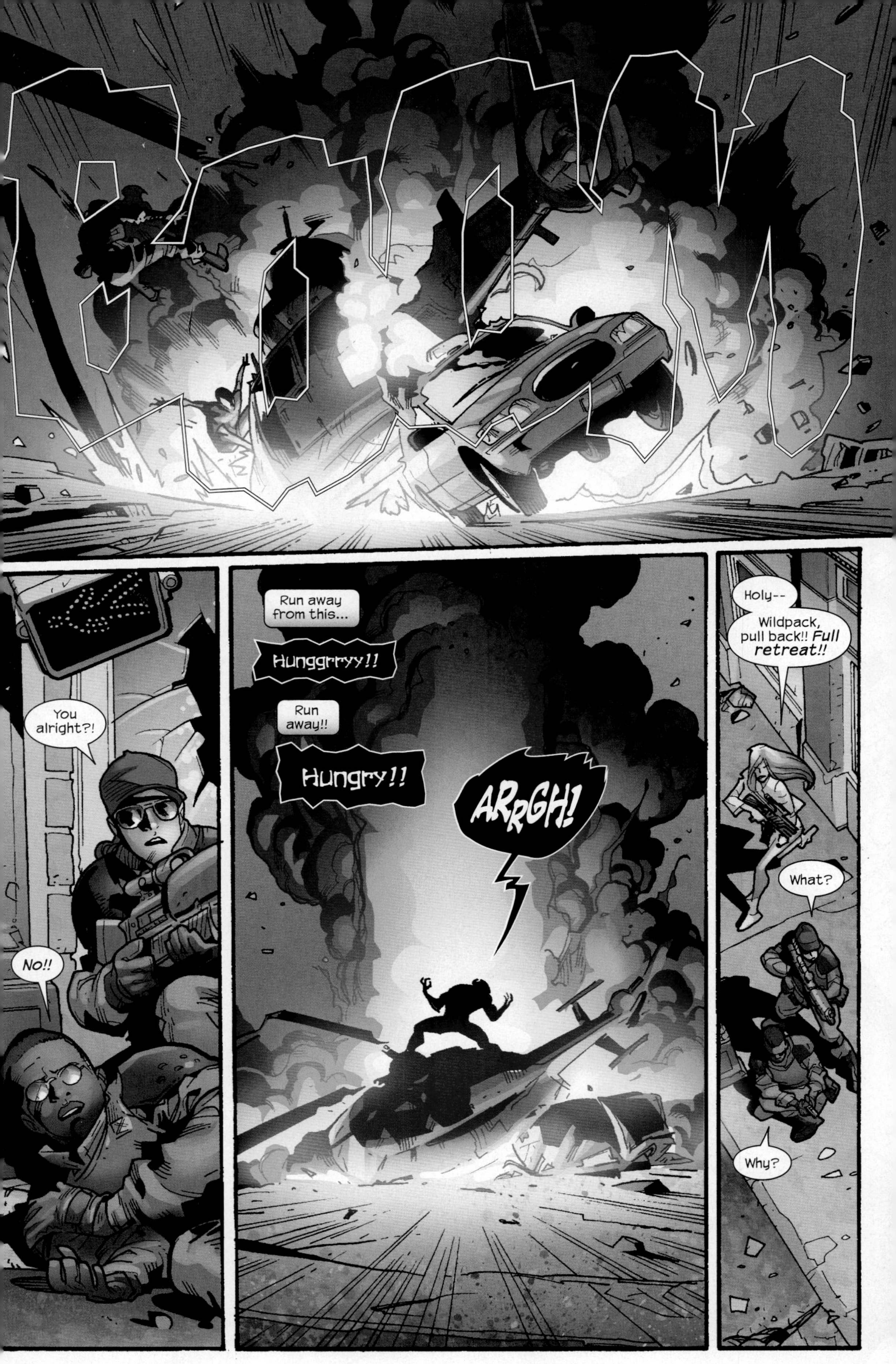
You alright?!
No!!
Run away from this...
Hunggrryy!!
Run away!!
Hungry!!
ARRGH!
Holy--
Wildpack, pull back!! *Full retreat!!*
What?
Why?

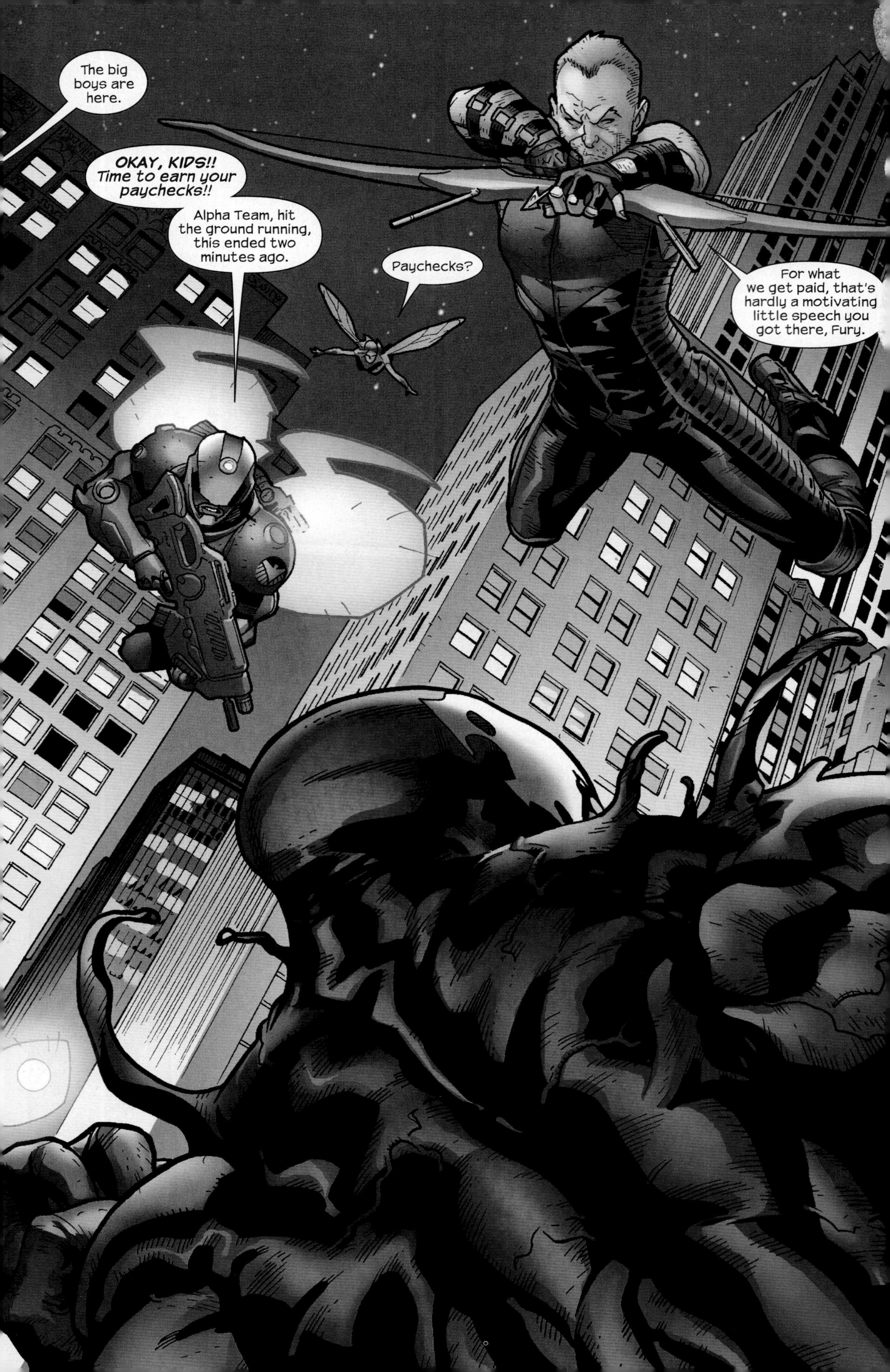

The big boys are here.
OKAY, KIDS!! Time to earn your paychecks!!
Alpha Team, hit the ground running, this ended two minutes ago.
Paychecks?
For what we get paid, that's hardly a motivating little speech you got there, Fury.

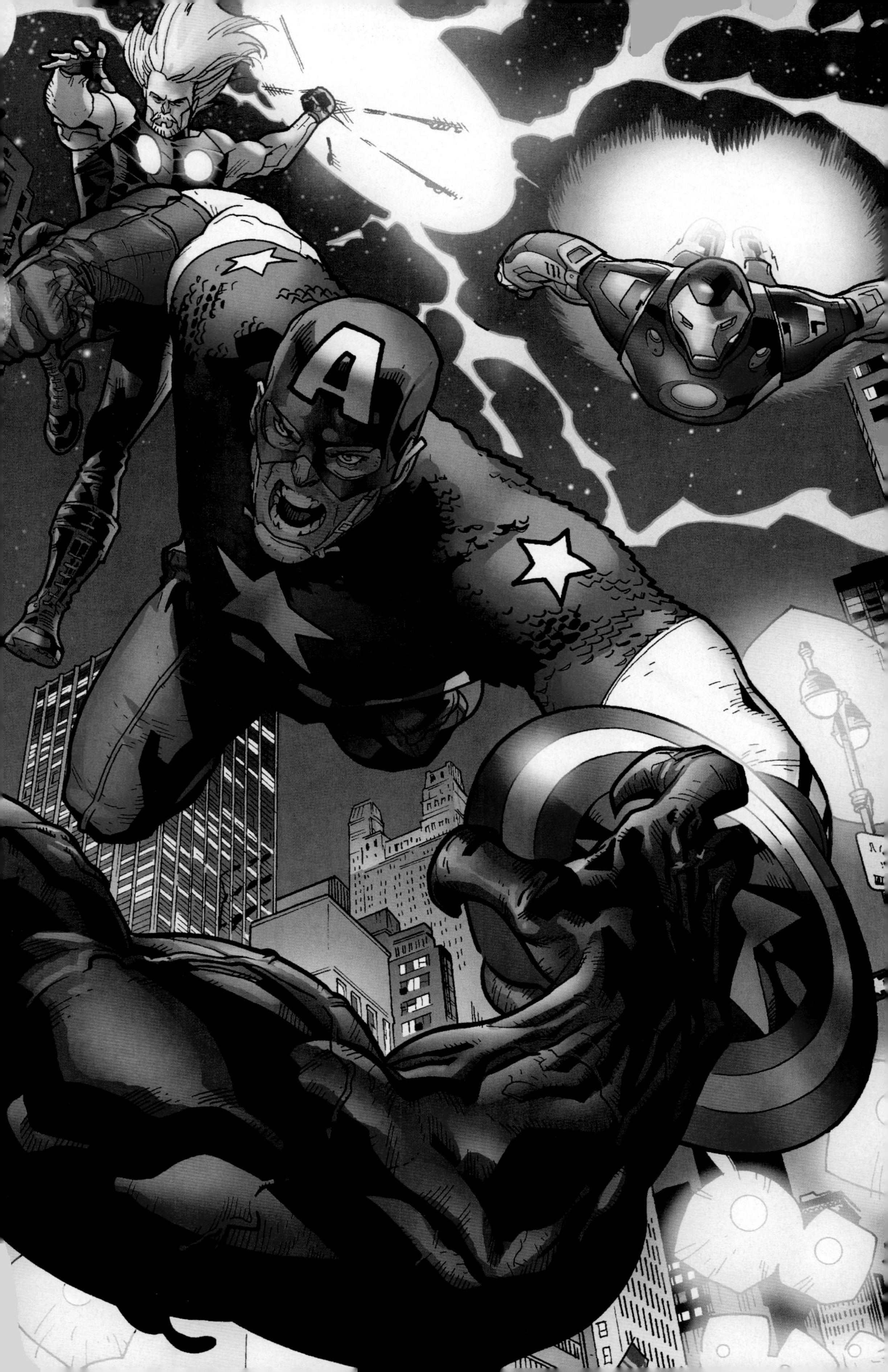

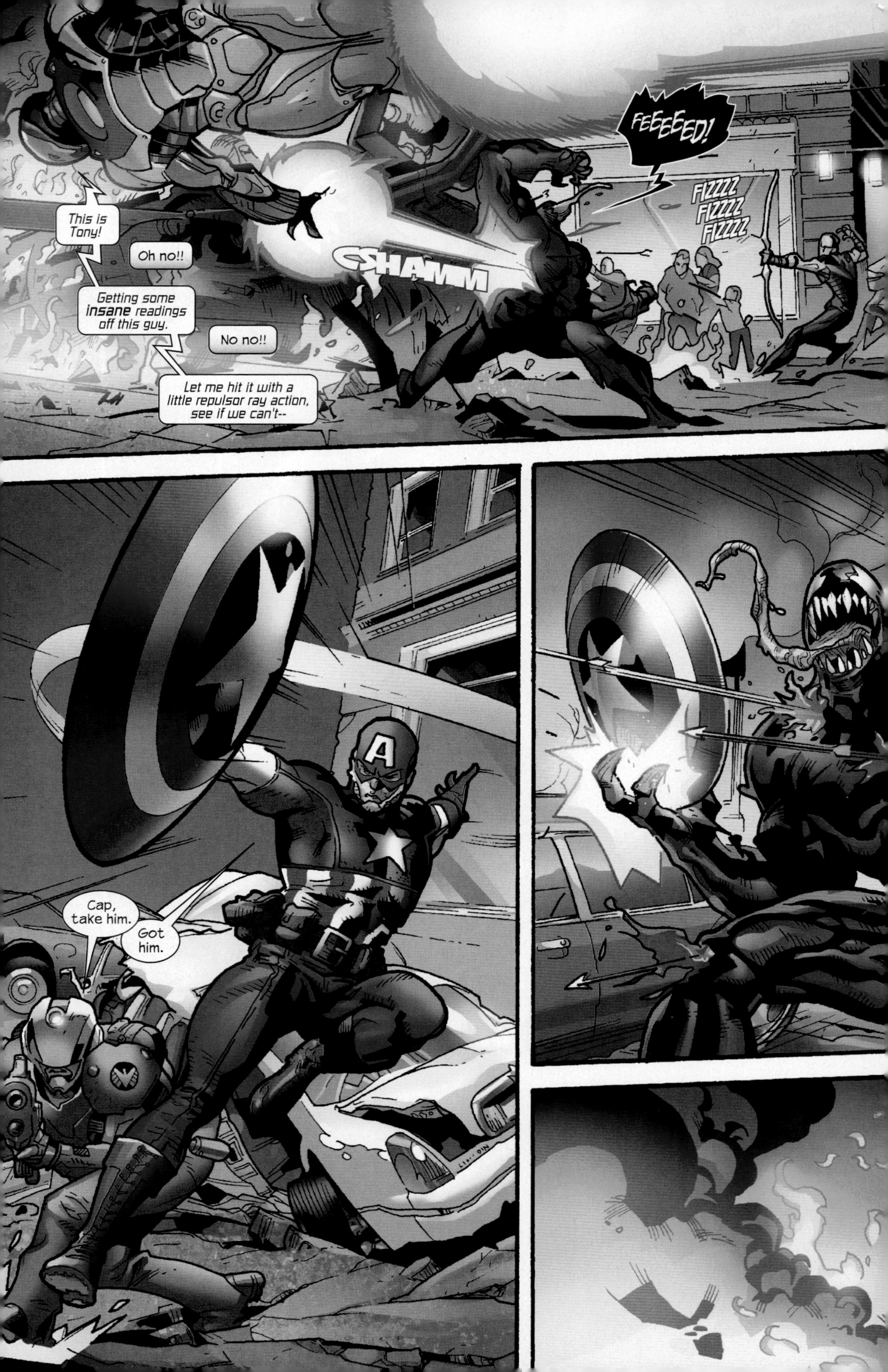
This is Tony!
Oh no!!
Getting some insane readings off this guy.
No no!!
Let me hit it with a little repulsor ray action, see if we can't--
FEEEEEED!
CSHAMM
FIZZZZ FIZZZZ FIZZZZ
Cap, take him.
Got him.

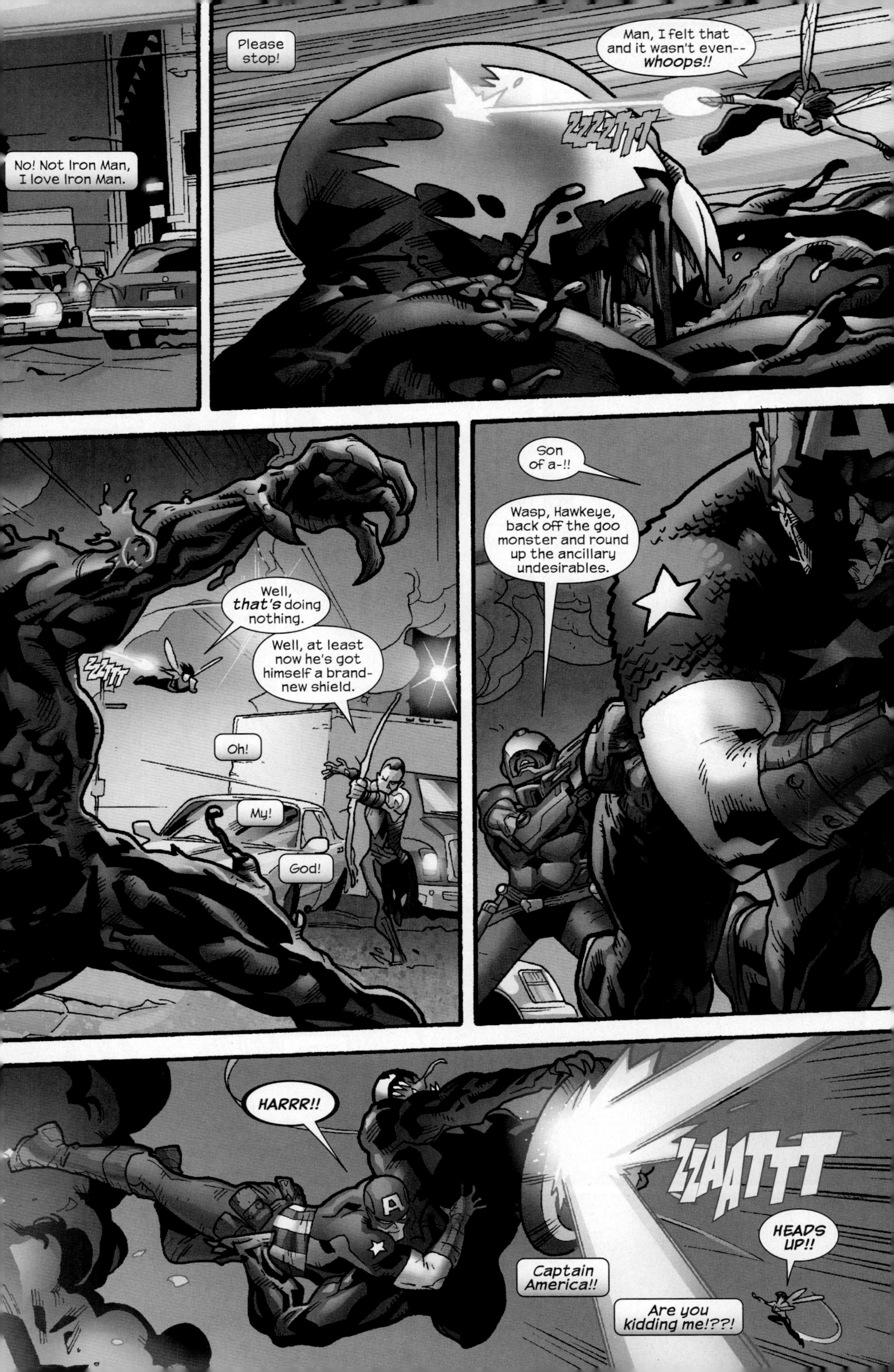
No! Not Iron Man, I love Iron Man.
Please stop!
Man, I felt that and it wasn't even-- *whoops!!*
ZZZTTT
Well, *that's* doing nothing.
ZZZTTT
Well, at least now he's got himself a brand-new shield.
Oh!
My!
God!
Son of a-!!
Wasp, Hawkeye, back off the goo monster and round up the ancillary undesirables.
HARRR!!
ZZAATTT
HEADS UP!!
Captain America!!
Are you kidding me!??!

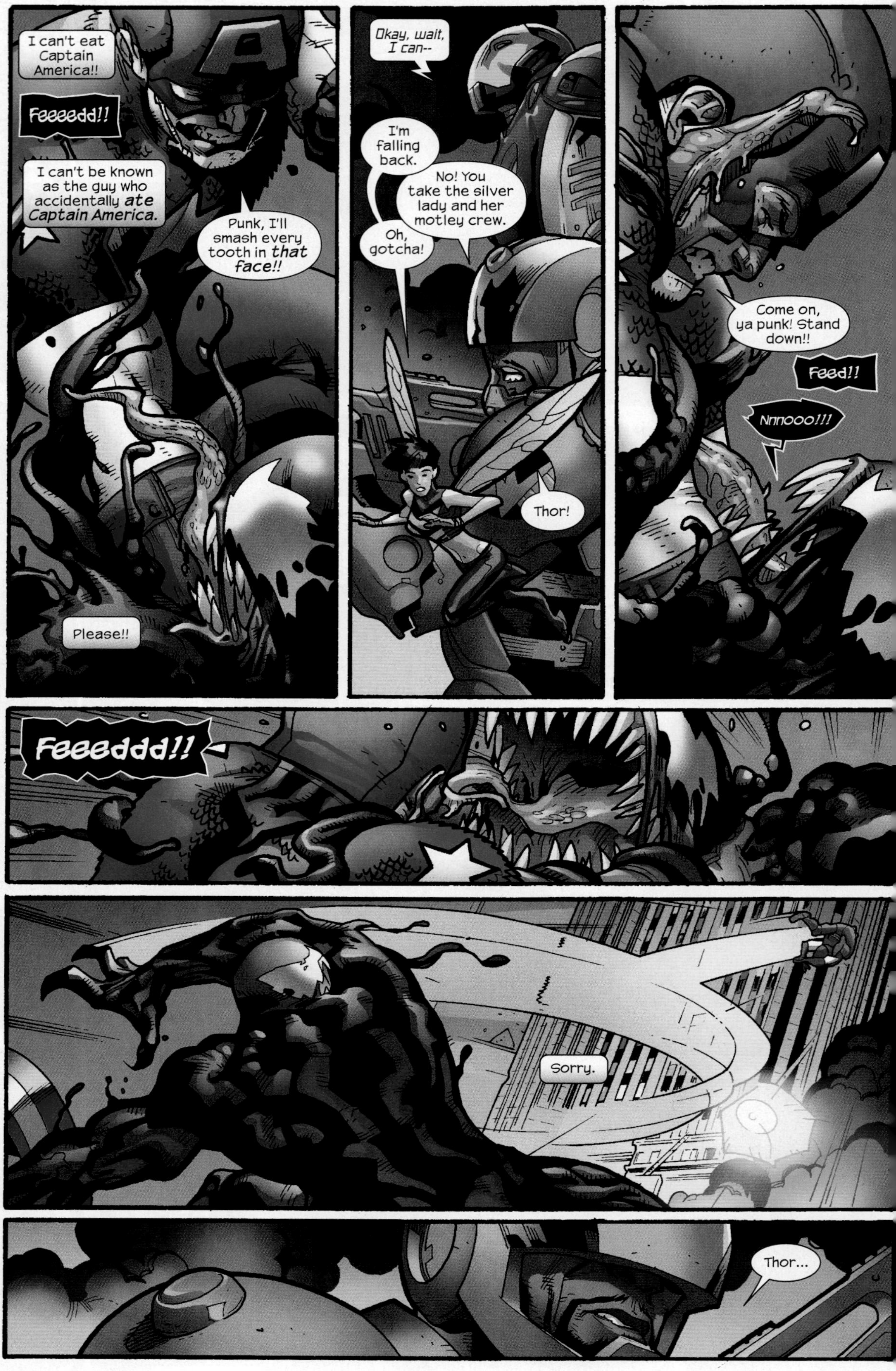
I can't eat Captain America!!
Feeeedd!!
I can't be known as the guy who accidentally *ate* *Captain America*.
Punk, I'll smash every tooth in *that face!!*
Please!!
Okay, wait, I can--
I'm falling back.
No! You take the silver lady and her motley crew.
Oh, gotcha!
Thor!
Come on, ya punk! Stand down!!
Feed!!
Nnnooo!!!
Feeeddd!!
Sorry.
Thor...

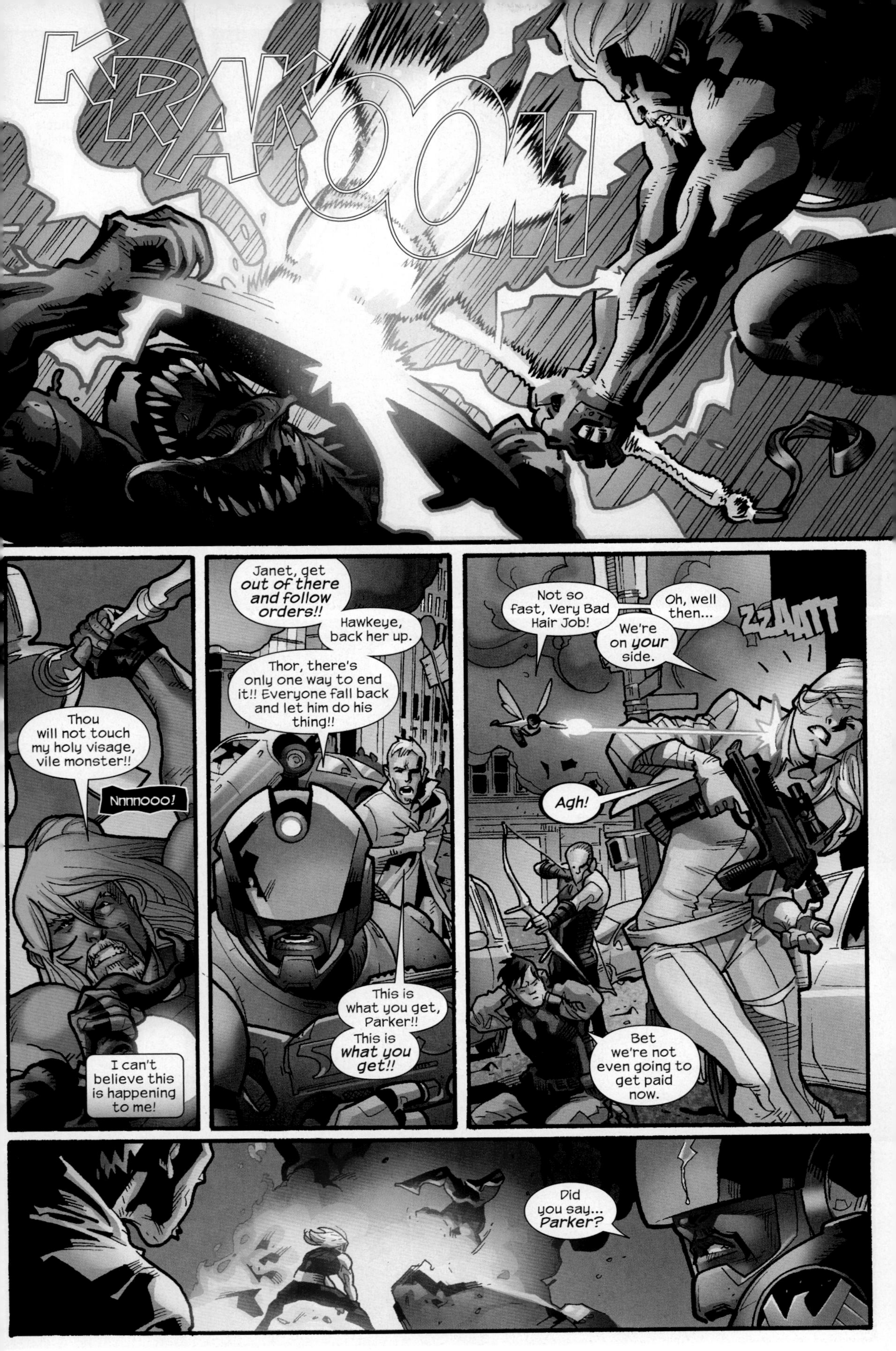

KRAKOOM
Thou will not touch my holy visage, vile monster!!
Nnnnooo!
I can't believe this is happening to me!
Janet, get out of there and follow orders!!
Hawkeye, back her up.
Thor, there's only one way to end it!! Everyone fall back and let him do his thing!!
This is what you get, Parker!!
This is what you get!!
Not so fast, Very Bad Hair Job!
Oh, well then...
We're on your side.
ZZAATT
Agh!
Bet we're not even going to get paid now.
Did you say... Parker?

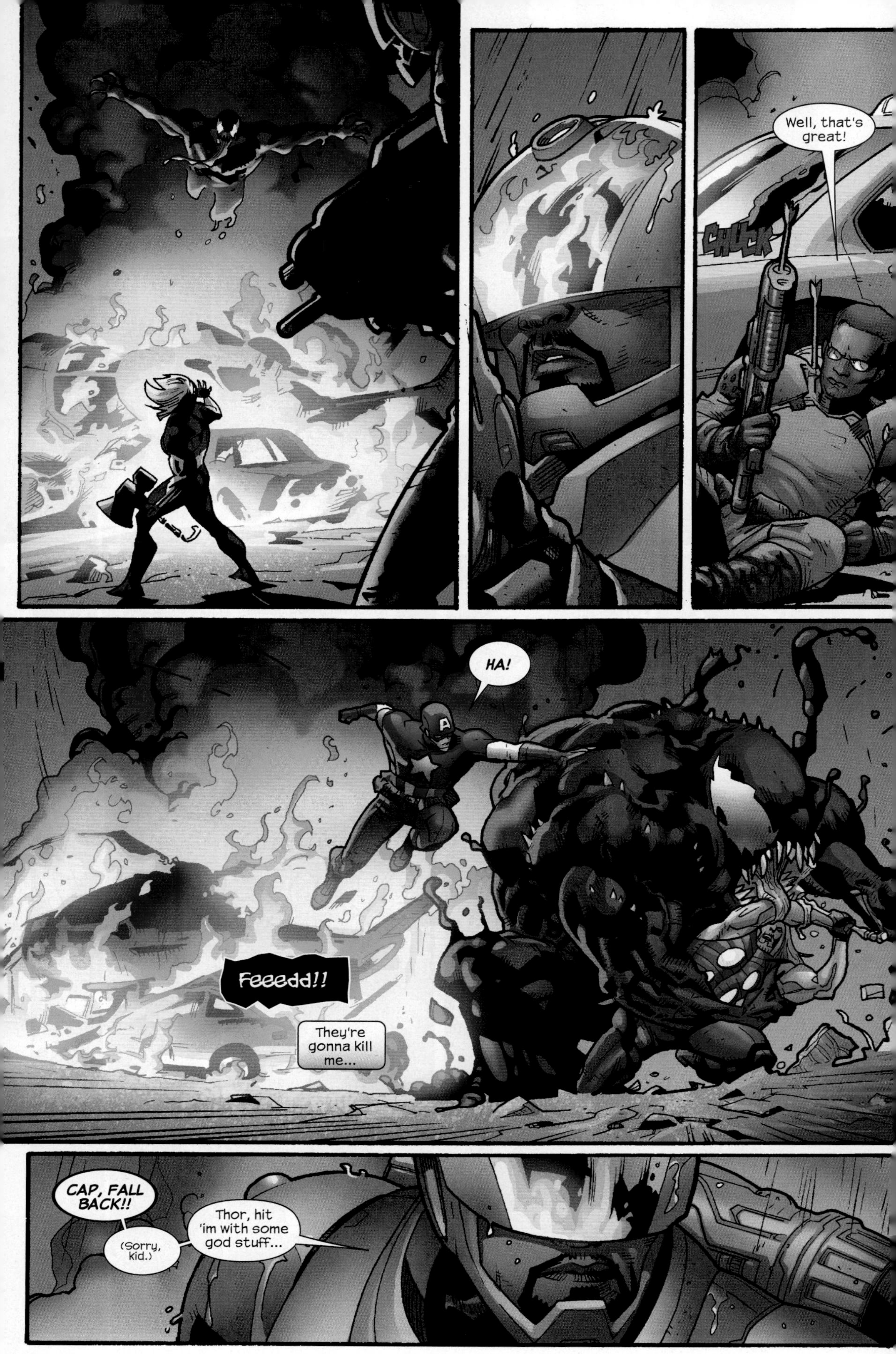
Well, that's great!
CHUCK
HA!
Feeedd!!
They're gonna kill me...
CAP, FALL BACK!!
(Sorry, kid.)
Thor, hit 'im with some god stuff...

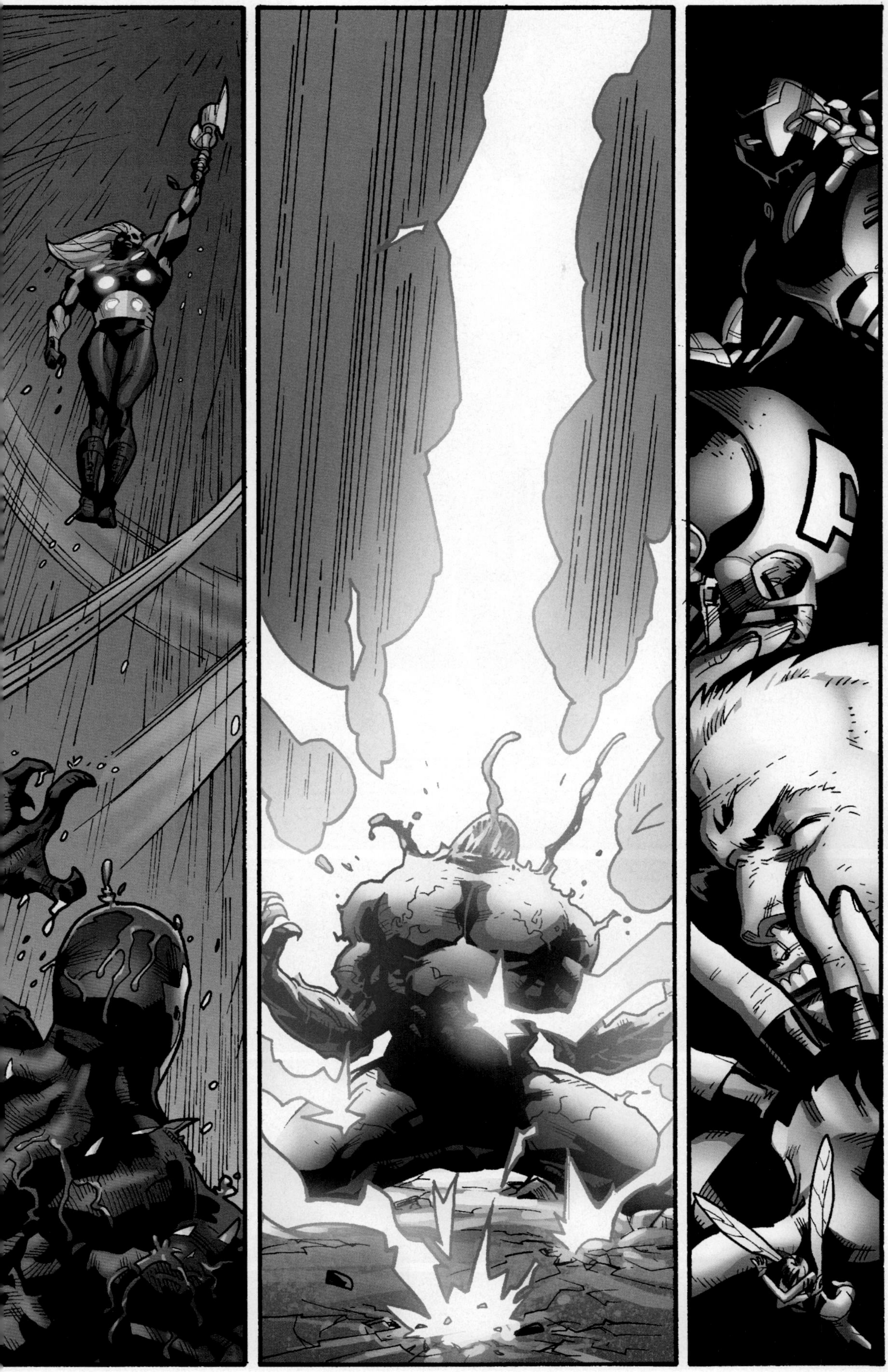

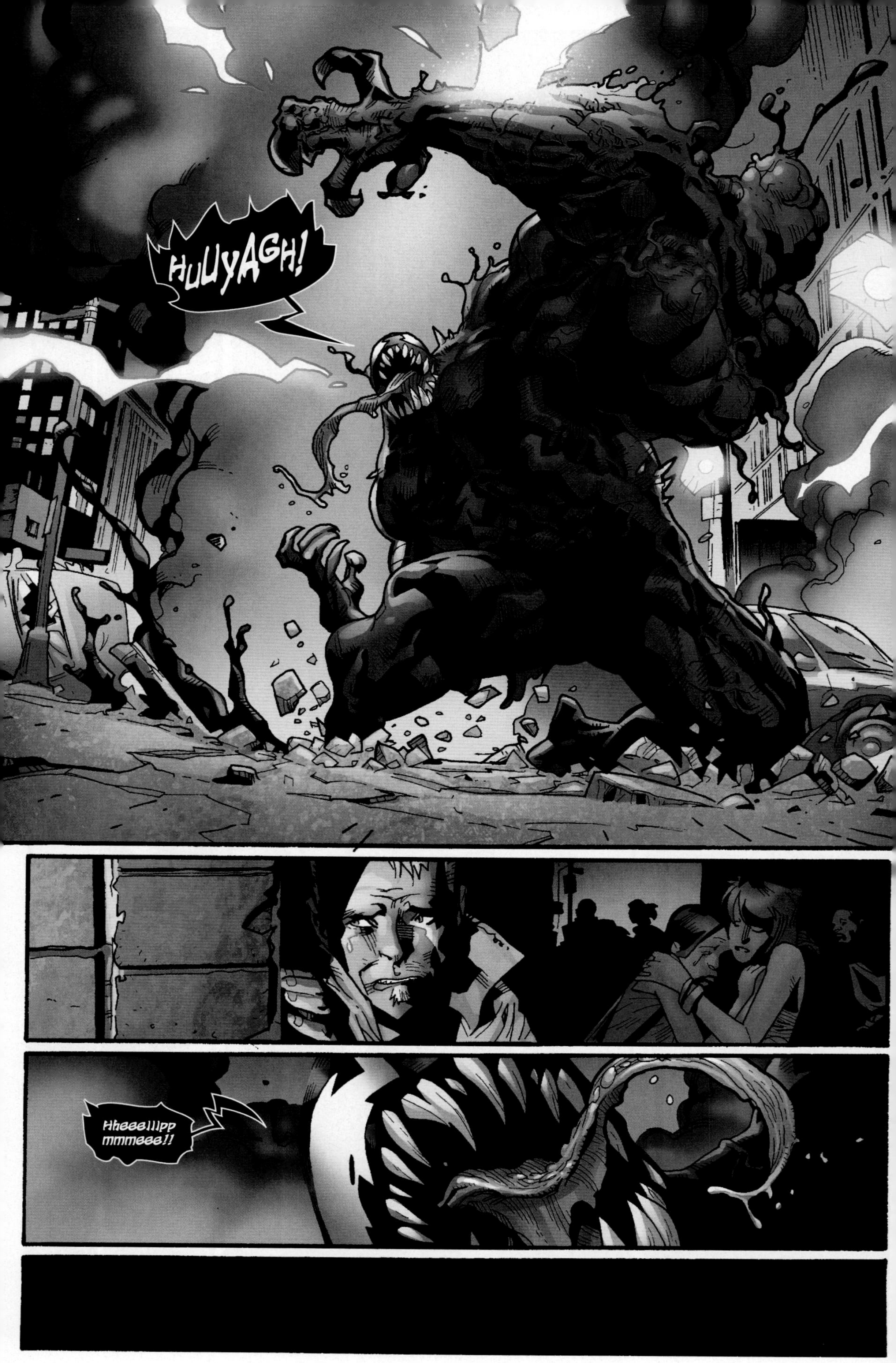
HUUYAGH!
Hheeellllpp mmmeee!!

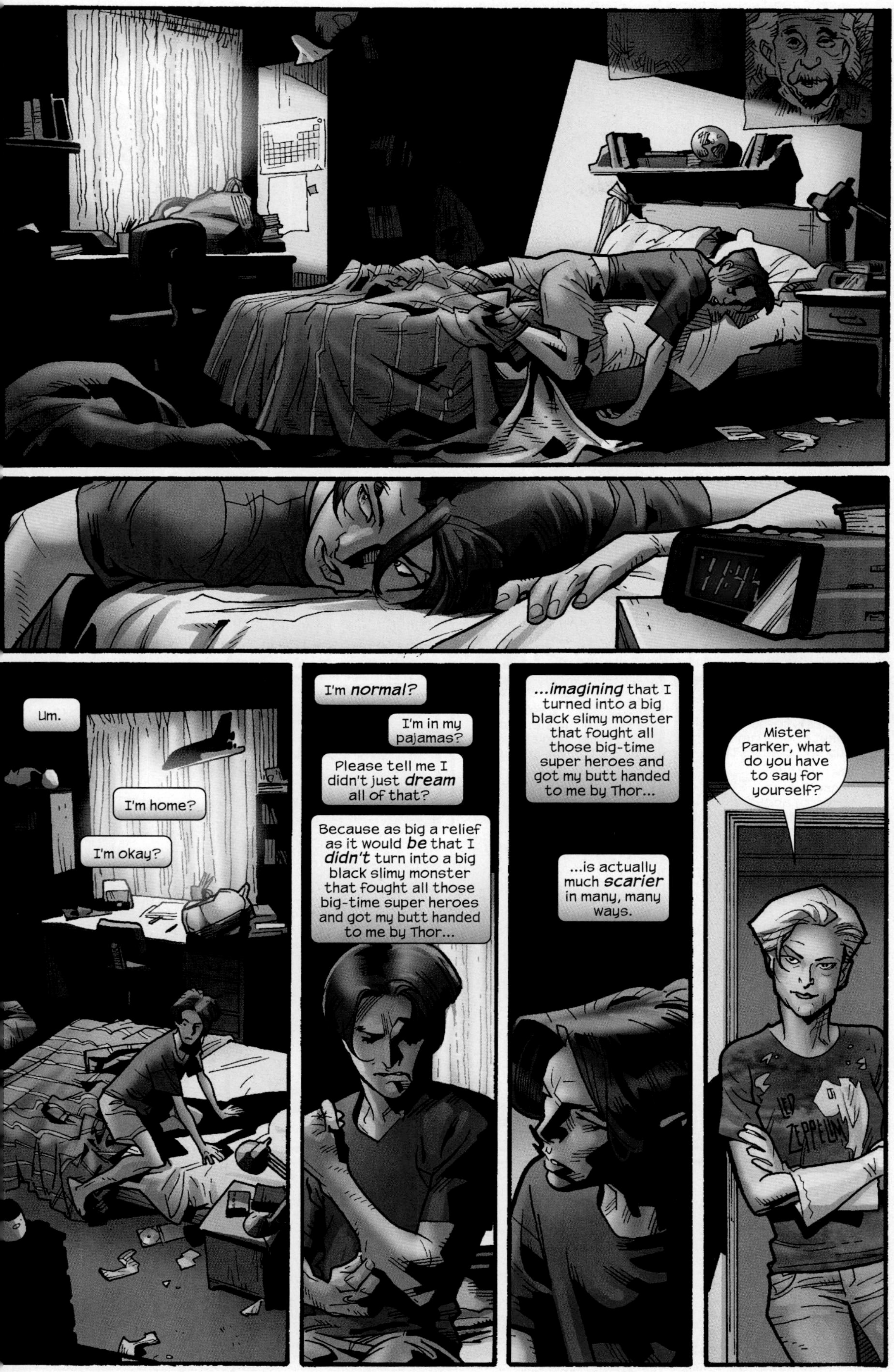
Um.
I'm home?
I'm okay?
I'm normal?
I'm in my pajamas?
Please tell me I didn't just dream all of that?
Because as big a relief as it would be that I didn't turn into a big black slimy monster that fought all those big-time super heroes and got my butt handed to me by Thor...
...imagining that I turned into a big black slimy monster that fought all those big-time super heroes and got my butt handed to me by Thor...
...is actually much scarier in many, many ways.
Mister Parker, what do you have to say for yourself?

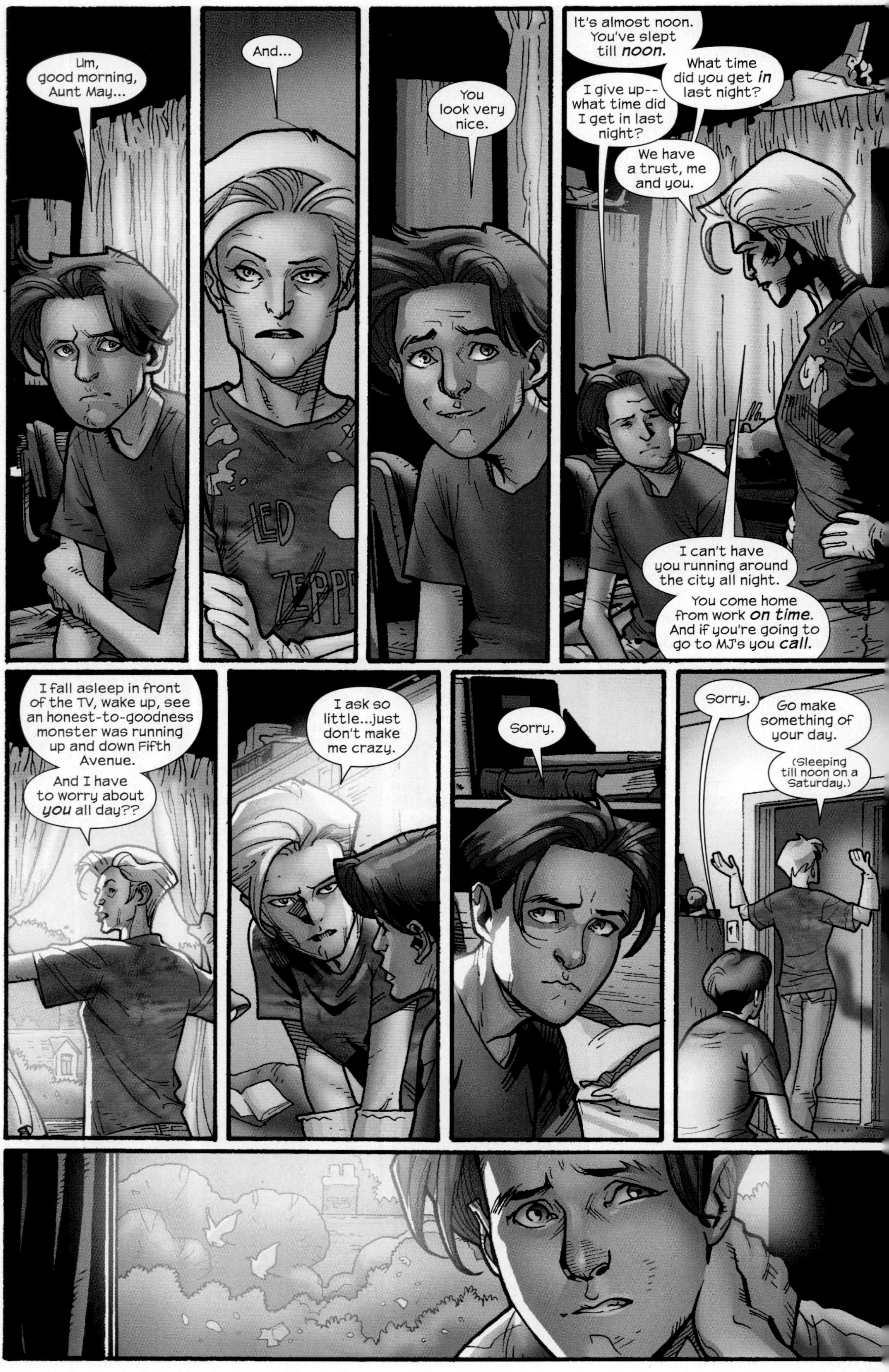
Um, good morning, Aunt May...
And...
You look very nice.
It's almost noon. You've slept till *noon.*
What time did you get *in* last night?
I give up-- what time did I get in last night?
We have a trust, me and you.
I can't have you running around the city all night.
You come home from work *on time.* And if you're going to go to MJ's you *call.*
I fall asleep in front of the TV, wake up, see an honest-to-goodness monster was running up and down Fifth Avenue.
And I have to worry about *you* all day??
I ask so little...just don't make me crazy.
Sorry.
Sorry.
Go make something of your day.
(Sleeping till noon on a Saturday.)

COME OVER WHEN YOU WAKE UP

From	Subject
oneeyedeagle@ultimates.gov	COME OVE

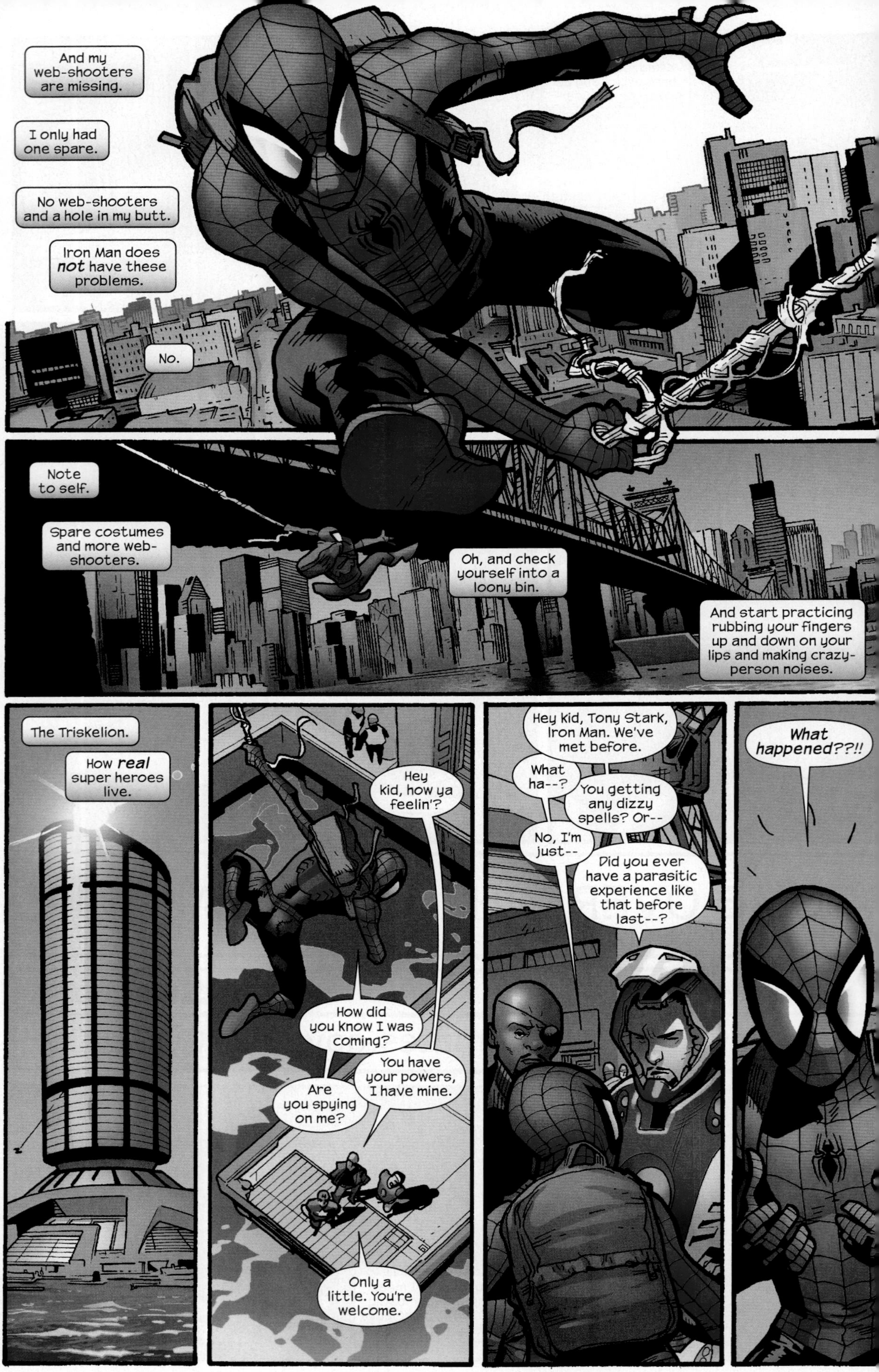

And my web-shooters are missing.
I only had one spare.
No web-shooters and a hole in my butt.
Iron Man does *not* have these problems.
No.
Note to self.
Spare costumes and more web-shooters.
Oh, and check yourself into a loony bin.
And start practicing rubbing your fingers up and down on your lips and making crazy-person noises.
The Triskelion.
How *real* super heroes live.
Hey kid, how ya feelin'?
How did you know I was coming?
Are you spying on me?
You have your powers, I have mine.
Only a little. You're welcome.
Hey kid, Tony Stark, Iron Man. We've met before.
What ha--?
You getting any dizzy spells? Or--
No, I'm just--
Did you ever have a parasitic experience like that before last--?
What happened??!!

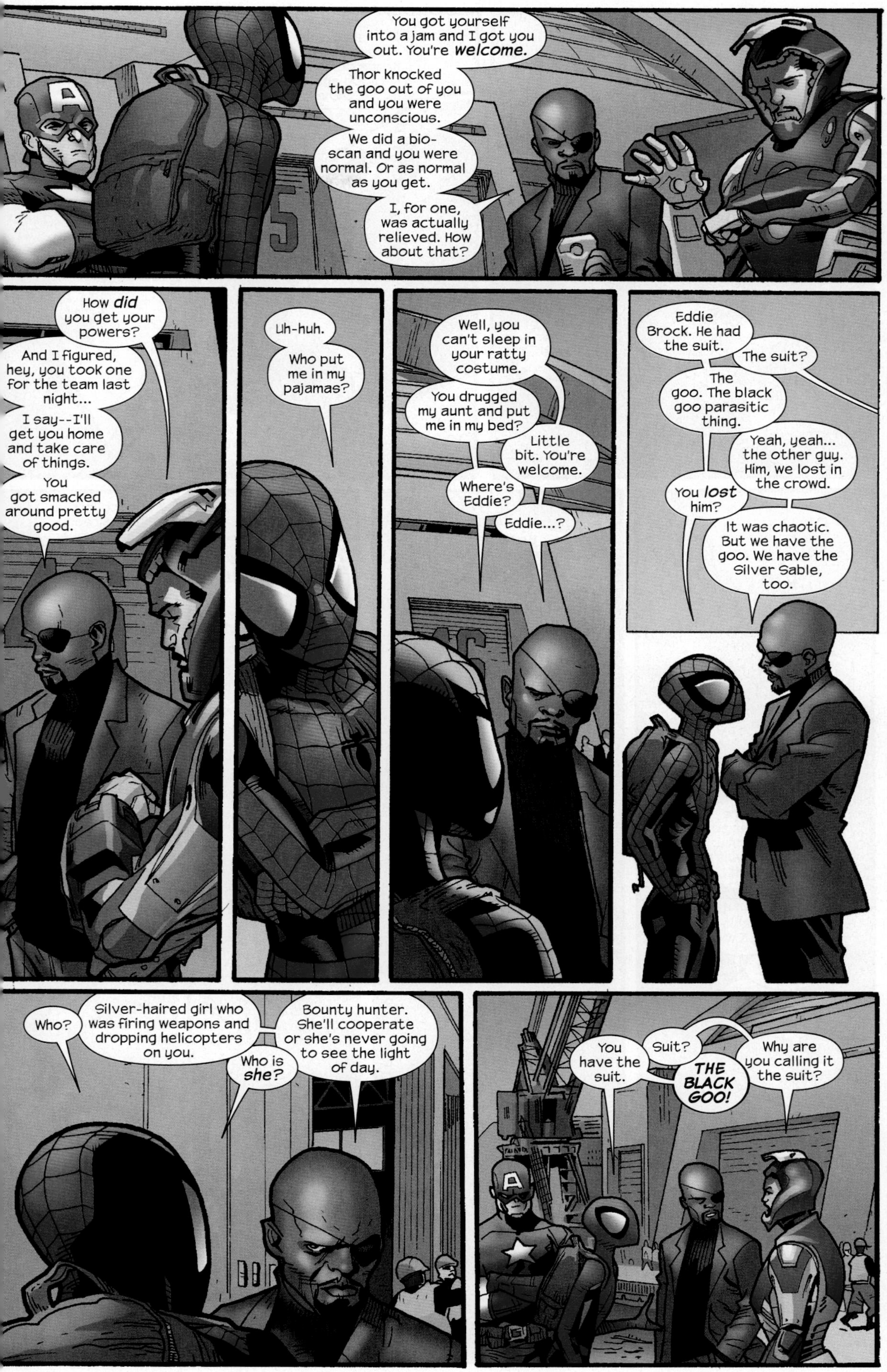
You got yourself into a jam and I got you out. You're *welcome.*
Thor knocked the goo out of you and you were unconscious.
We did a bio-scan and you were normal. Or as normal as you get.
I, for one, was actually relieved. How about that?
How *did* you get your powers?
And I figured, hey, you took one for the team last night...
I say--I'll get you home and take care of things.
You got smacked around pretty good.
Uh-huh.
Who put me in my pajamas?
Well, you can't sleep in your ratty costume.
You drugged my aunt and put me in my bed?
Little bit. You're welcome.
Where's Eddie?
Eddie...?
Eddie Brock. He had the suit.
The suit?
The goo. The black goo parasitic thing.
Yeah, yeah... the other guy. Him, we lost in the crowd.
You *lost* him?
It was chaotic. But we have the goo. We have the Silver Sable, too.
Who?
Silver-haired girl who was firing weapons and dropping helicopters on you.
Who is *she?*
Bounty hunter. She'll cooperate or she's never going to see the light of day.
You have the suit.
Suit?
THE BLACK GOO!
Why are you calling it the suit?

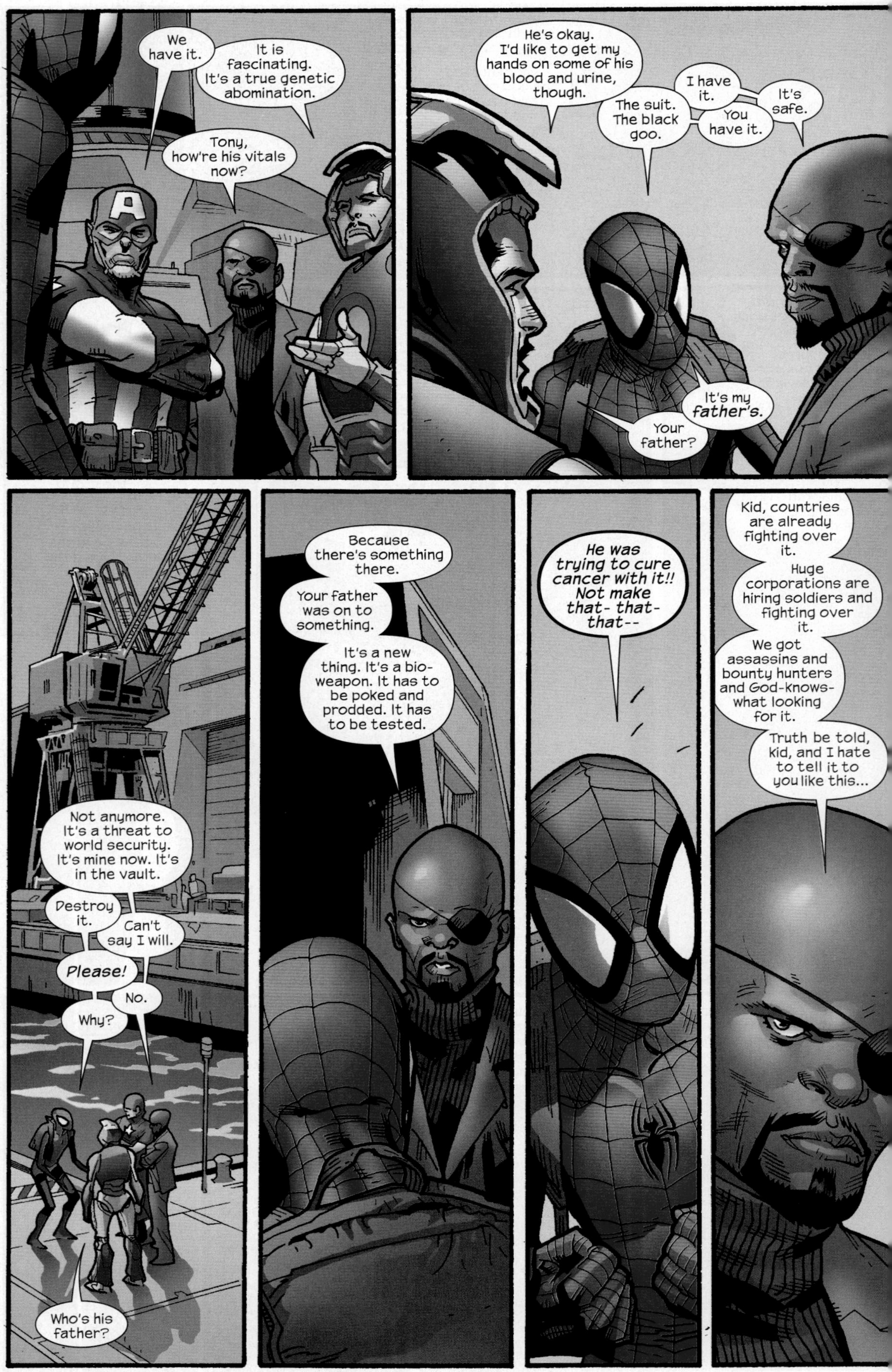
We have it.
It is fascinating. It's a true genetic abomination.
Tony, how're his vitals now?
He's okay. I'd like to get my hands on some of his blood and urine, though.
The suit. The black goo.
I have it.
You have it.
It's safe.
It's my *father's.*
Your father?
Not anymore. It's a threat to world security. It's mine now. It's in the vault.
Destroy it.
Can't say I will.
Please!
No.
Why?
Who's his father?
Because there's something there.
Your father was on to something.
It's a new thing. It's a bio-weapon. It has to be poked and prodded. It has to be tested.
He was trying to cure cancer with it!! Not make that- that- that--
Kid, countries are already fighting over it.
Huge corporations are hiring soldiers and fighting over it.
We got assassins and bounty hunters and God-knows-what looking for it.
Truth be told, kid, and I hate to tell it to you like this...

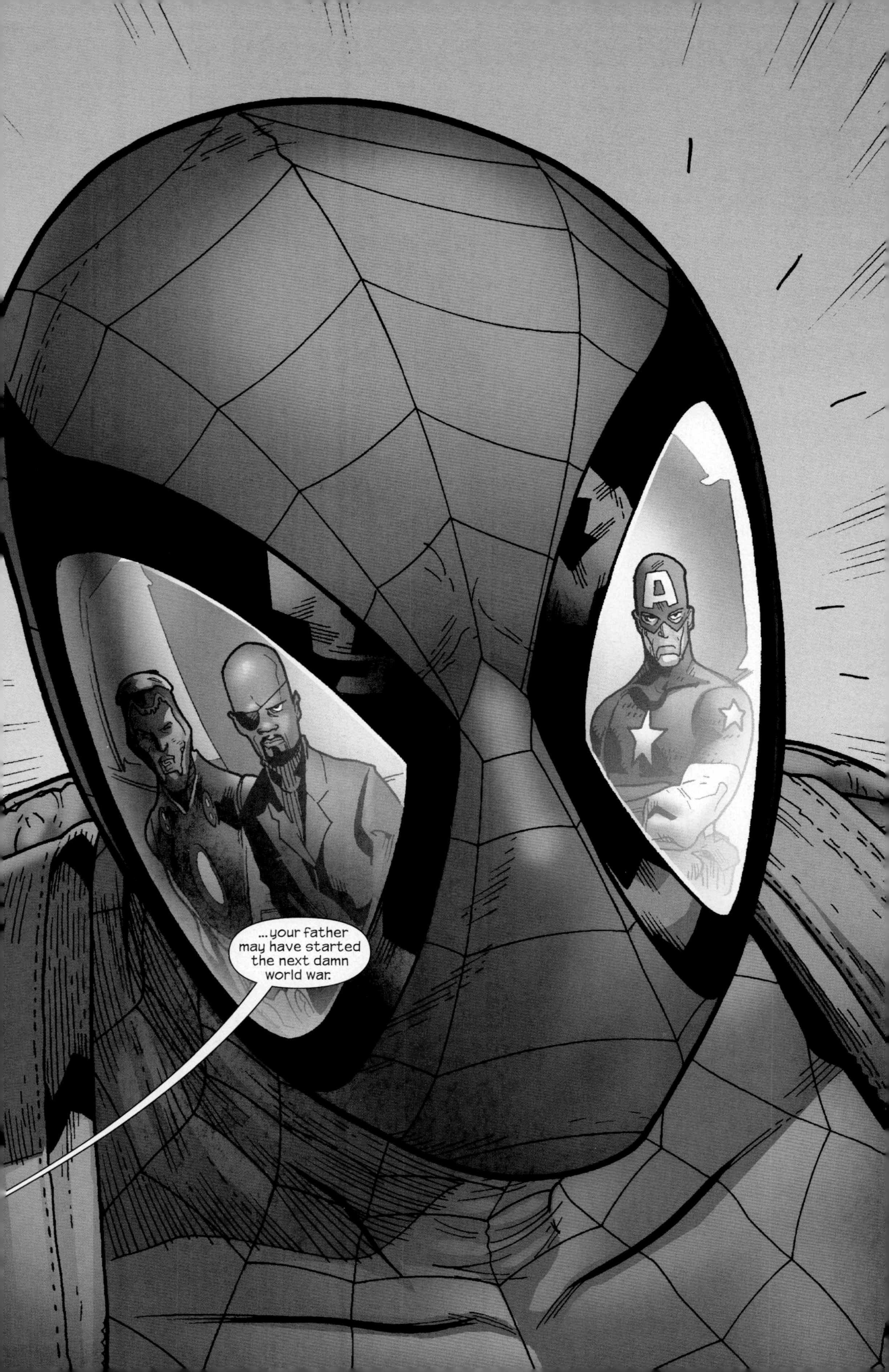
...your father may have started the next damn world war.

127

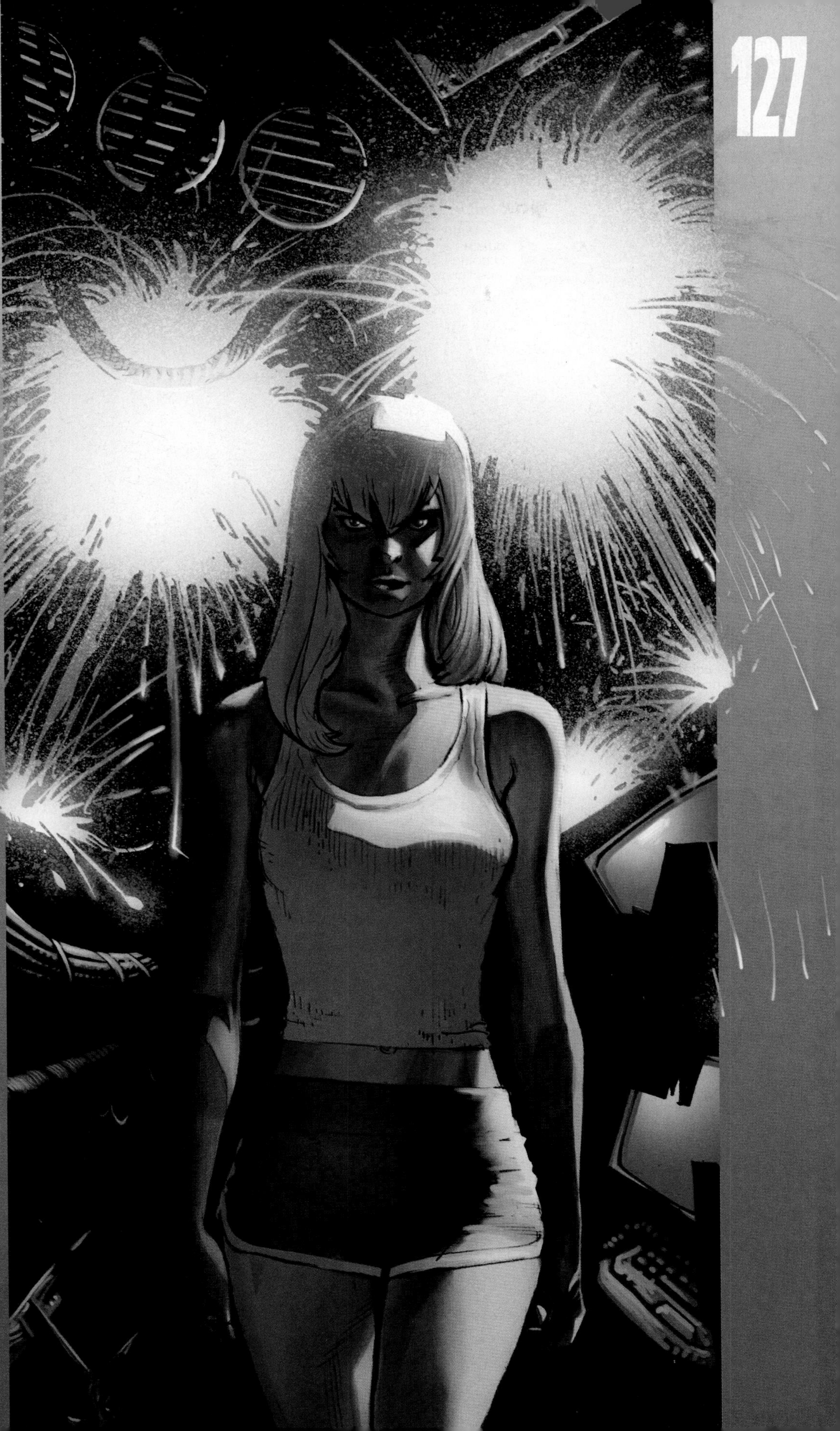

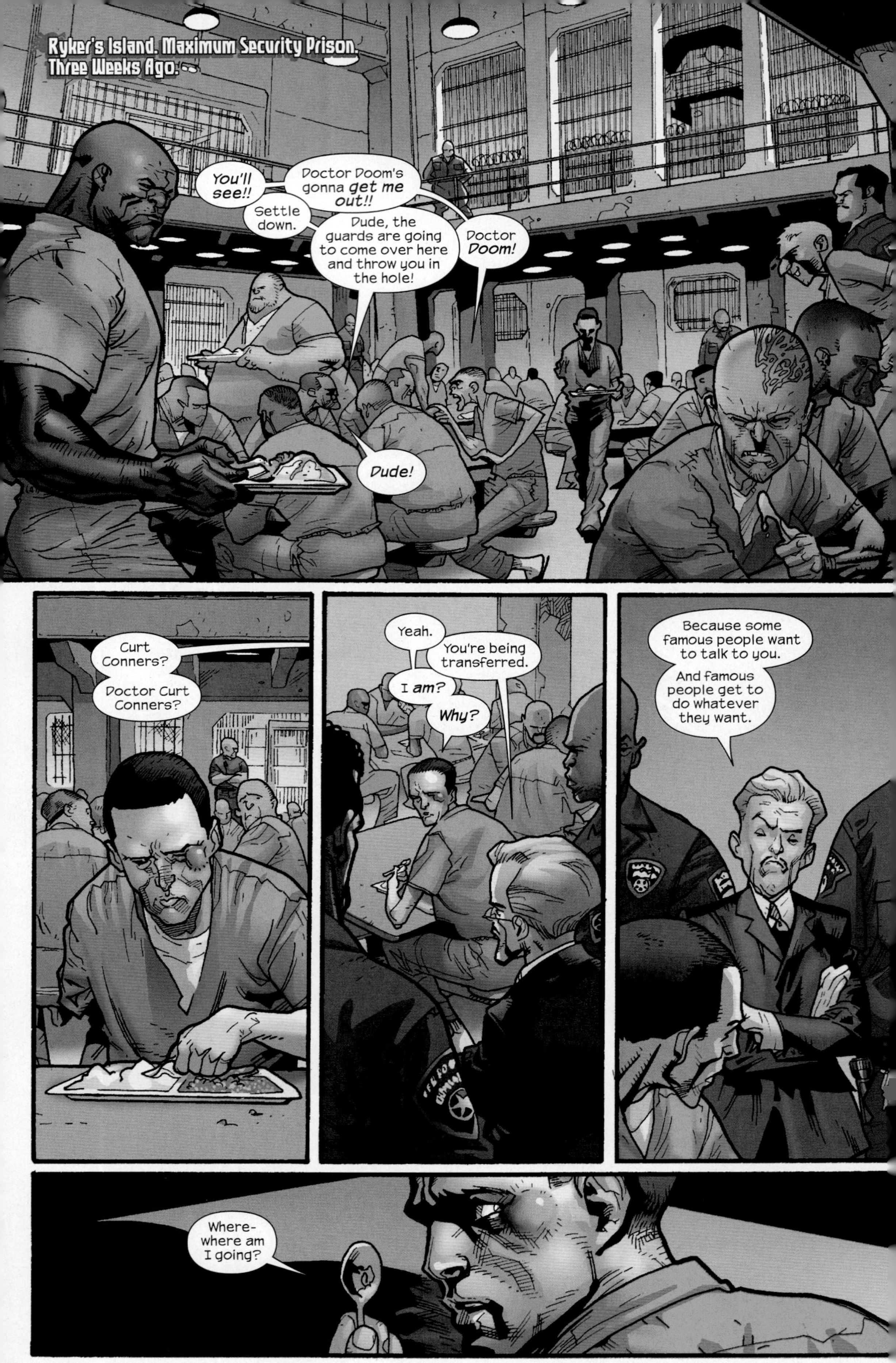
Ryker's Island. Maximum Security Prison.
Three Weeks Ago.
Doctor Doom's gonna get me out!!
You'll see!!
Settle down.
Dude, the guards are going to come over here and throw you in the hole!
Doctor Doom!
Dude!
Curt Conners?
Doctor Curt Conners?
Yeah.
You're being transferred.
I am?
Why?
Because some famous people want to talk to you.
And famous people get to do whatever they want.
Where- where am I going?

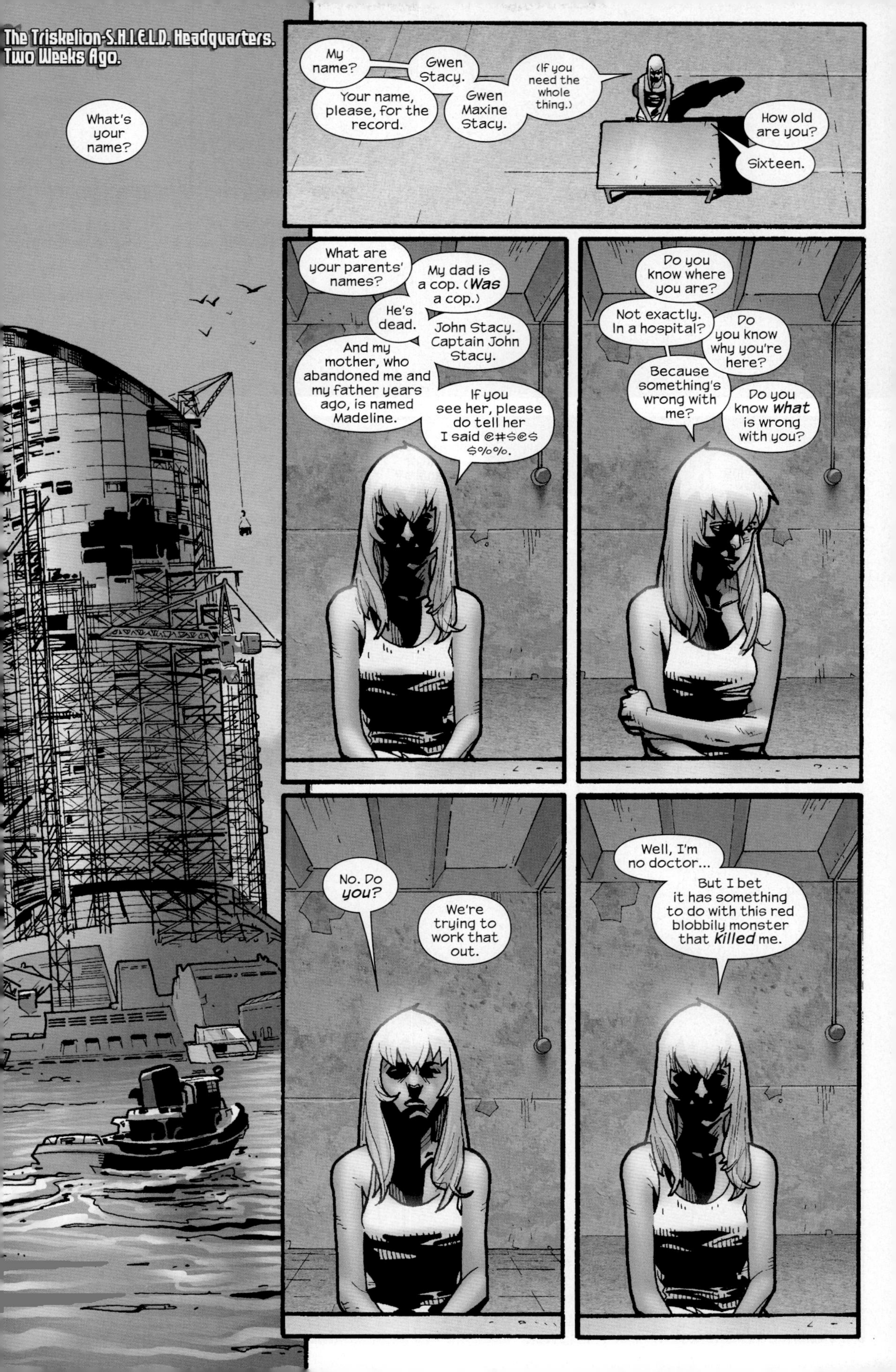

The Triskelion-S.H.I.E.L.D. Headquarters. Two Weeks Ago.
What's your name?
My name?
Your name, please, for the record.
Gwen Stacy.
Gwen Maxine Stacy.
(If you need the whole thing.)
How old are you?
Sixteen.
What are your parents' names?
My dad is a cop. (*Was* a cop.)
He's dead.
John Stacy. Captain John Stacy.
And my mother, who abandoned me and my father years ago, is named Madeline.
If you see her, please do tell her I said @#$@$ $%%.
Do you know where you are?
Not exactly. In a hospital?
Do you know why you're here?
Because something's wrong with me?
Do you know *what* is wrong with you?
No. Do *you*?
We're trying to work that out.
Well, I'm no doctor...
But I bet it has something to do with this red blobbily monster that *killed* me.

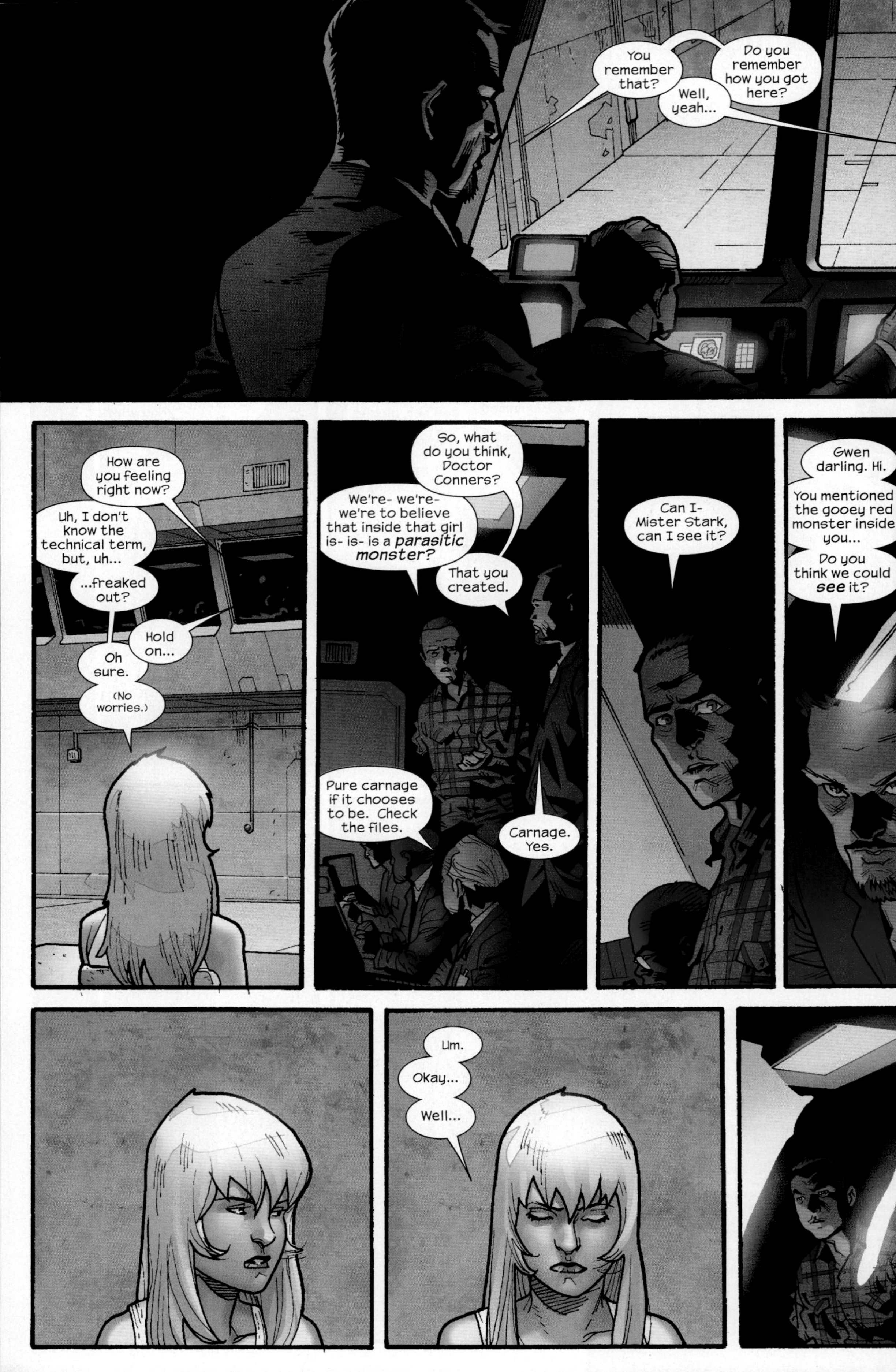
Do you remember how you got here?
Well, yeah...
You remember that?
How are you feeling right now?
Uh, I don't know the technical term, but, uh...
...freaked out?
Hold on...
Oh sure.
(No worries.)
So, what do you think, Doctor Conners?
We're- we're- we're to believe that inside that girl is- is- is a *parasitic monster?*
That you created.
Pure carnage if it chooses to be. Check the files.
Carnage. Yes.
Can I- Mister Stark, can I see it?
Gwen darling. Hi.
You mentioned the gooey red monster inside you...
Do you think we could *see* it?
Um.
Okay...
Well...

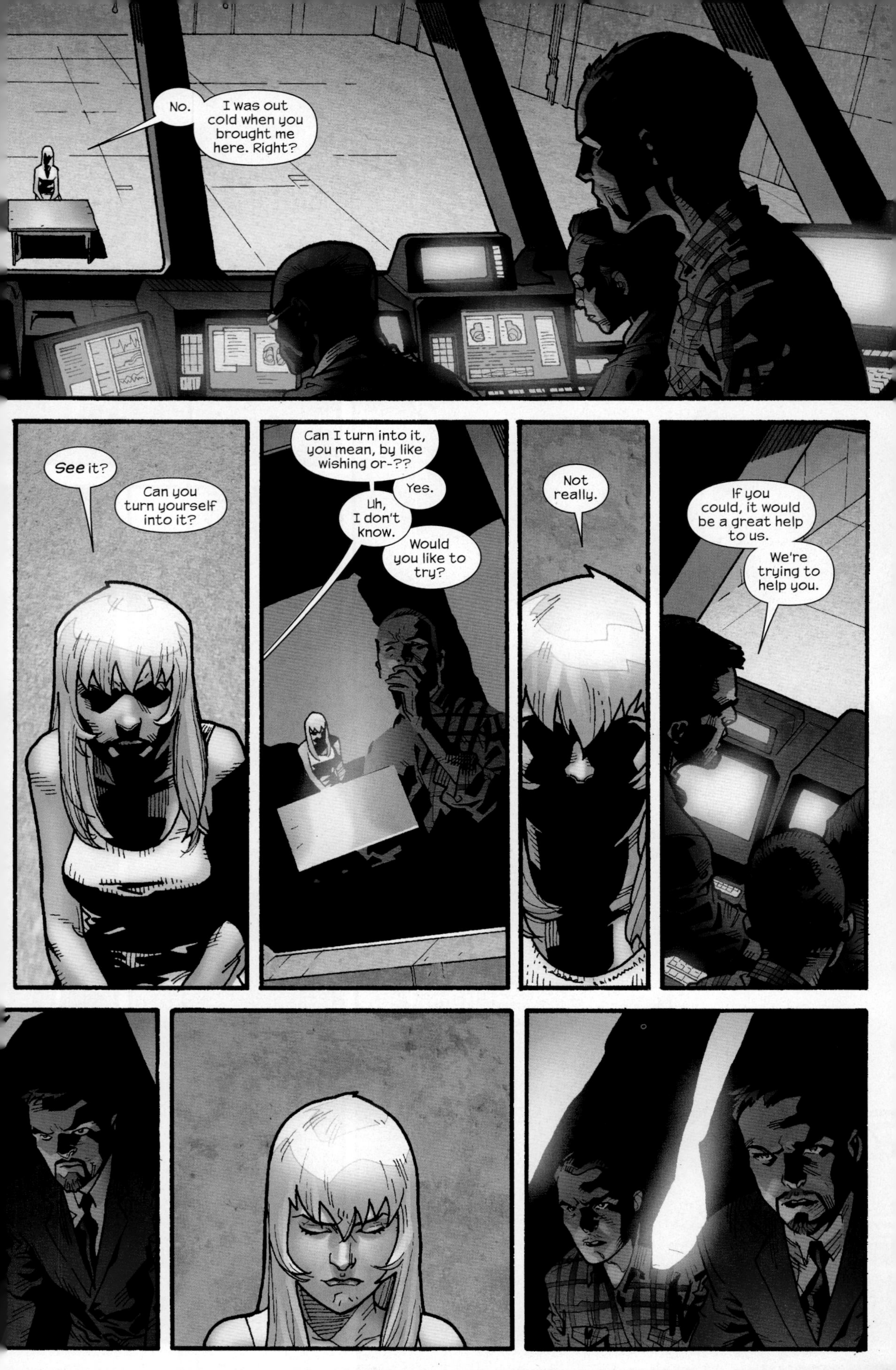
No.
I was out cold when you brought me here. Right?
See it?
Can you turn yourself into it?
Can I turn into it, you mean, by like wishing or-??
Yes.
Uh, I don't know.
Would you like to try?
Not really.
If you could, it would be a great help to us.
We're trying to help you.

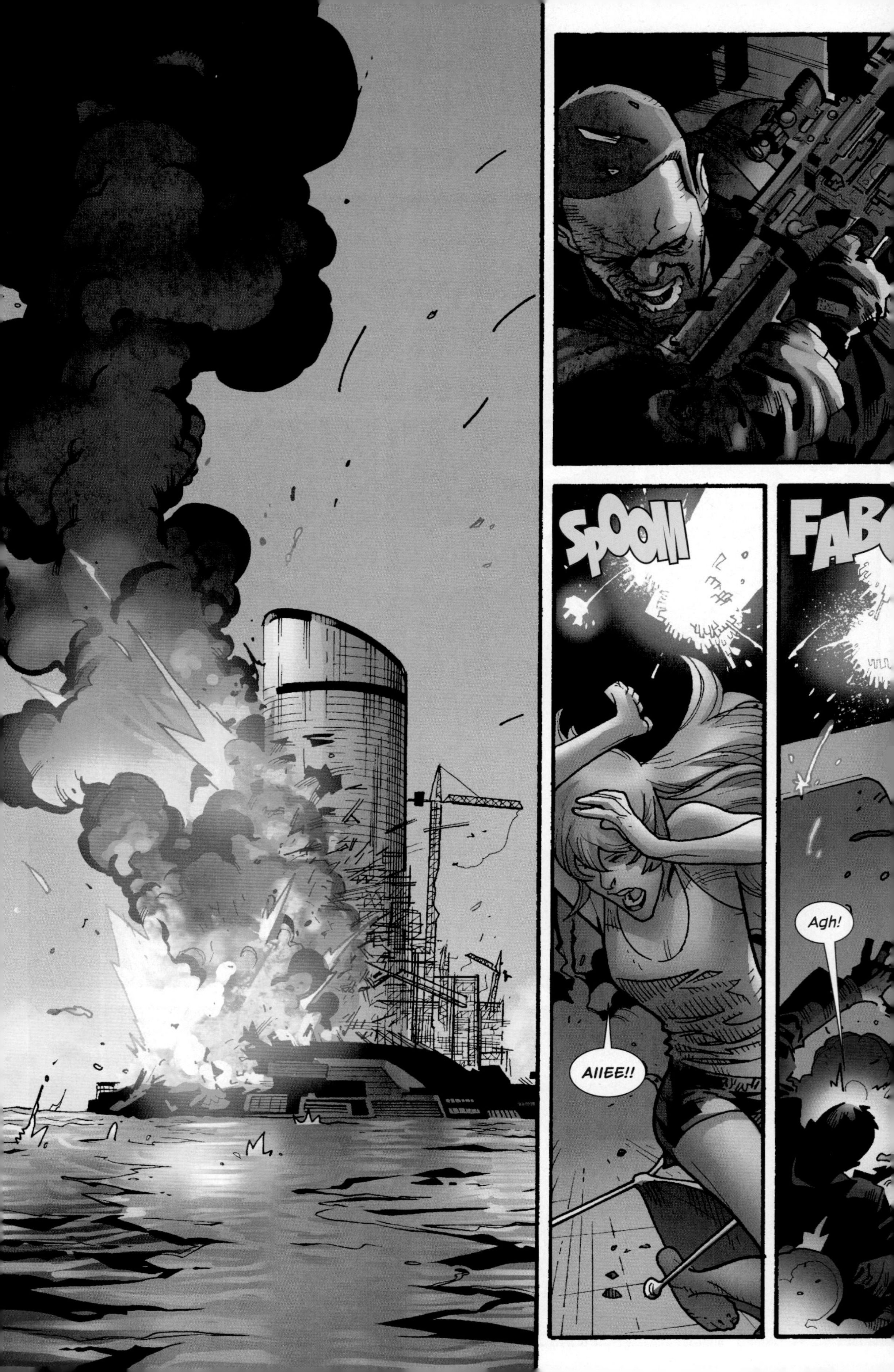
SPOOM
AIIEE!!
FAB
Agh!

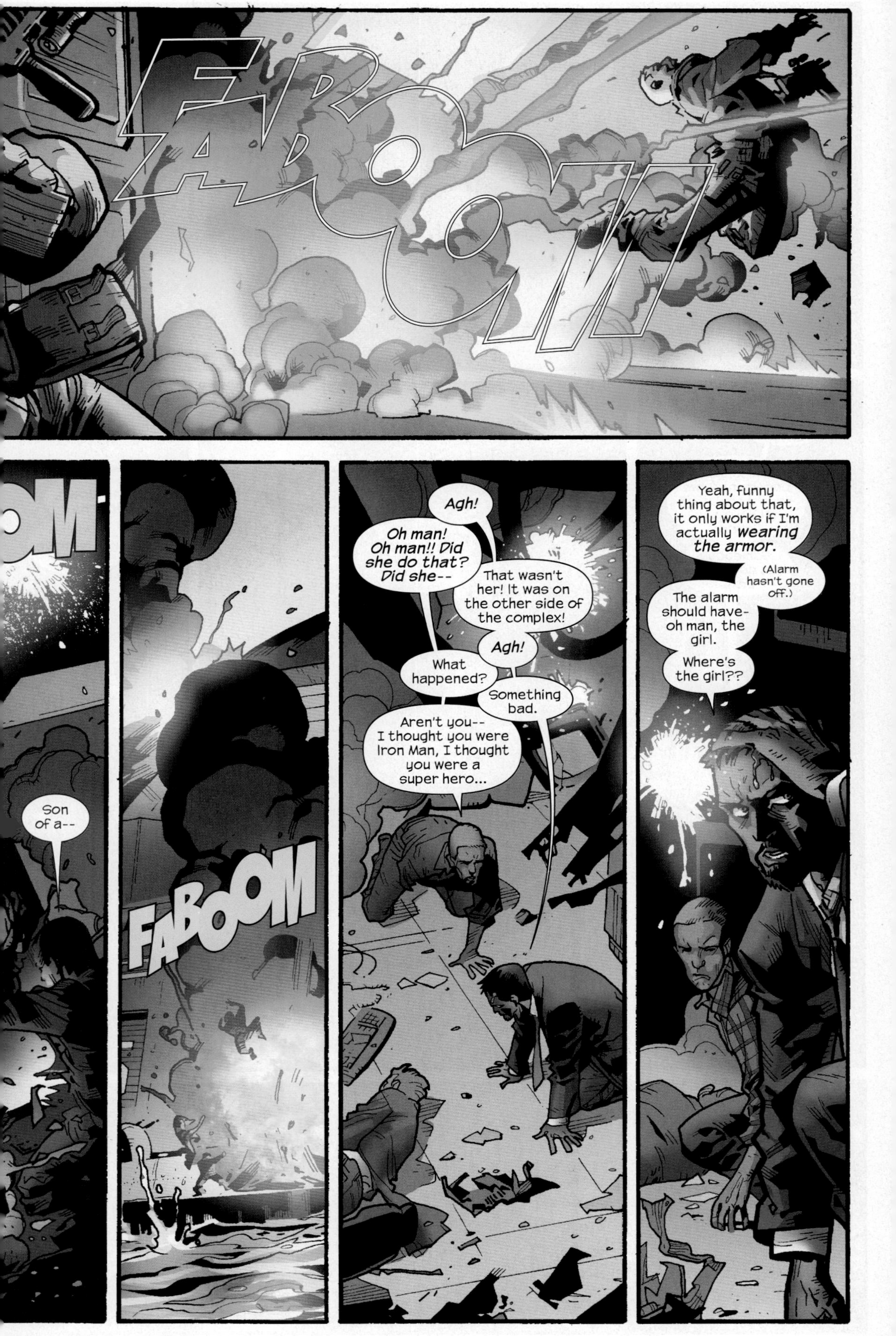
FABOOM!!
OOM
Son of a--
FABOOM
Agh!
Oh man! Oh man!! Did she do that? Did she--
That wasn't her! It was on the other side of the complex!
Agh!
What happened?
Something bad.
Aren't you-- I thought you were Iron Man, I thought you were a super hero...
Yeah, funny thing about that, it only works if I'm actually *wearing the armor.*
(Alarm hasn't gone off.)
The alarm should have-oh man, the girl.
Where's the girl??

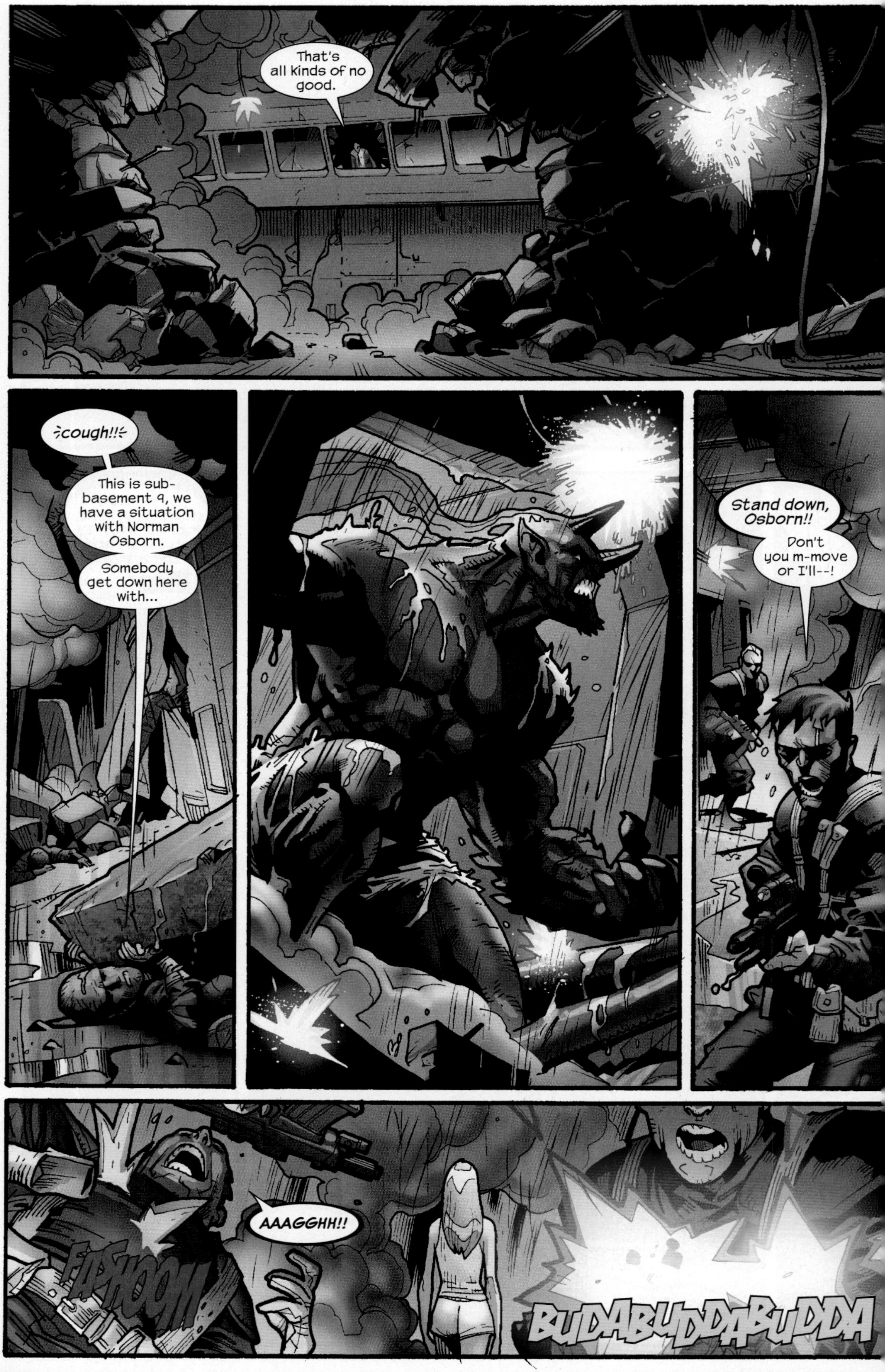
That's all kinds of no good.
cough!!
This is sub-basement 9, we have a situation with Norman Osborn.
Somebody get down here with...
Stand down, Osborn!!
Don't you m-move or I'll--!
FASHOOM
AAAGGHH!!
BUDABUDDABUDDA

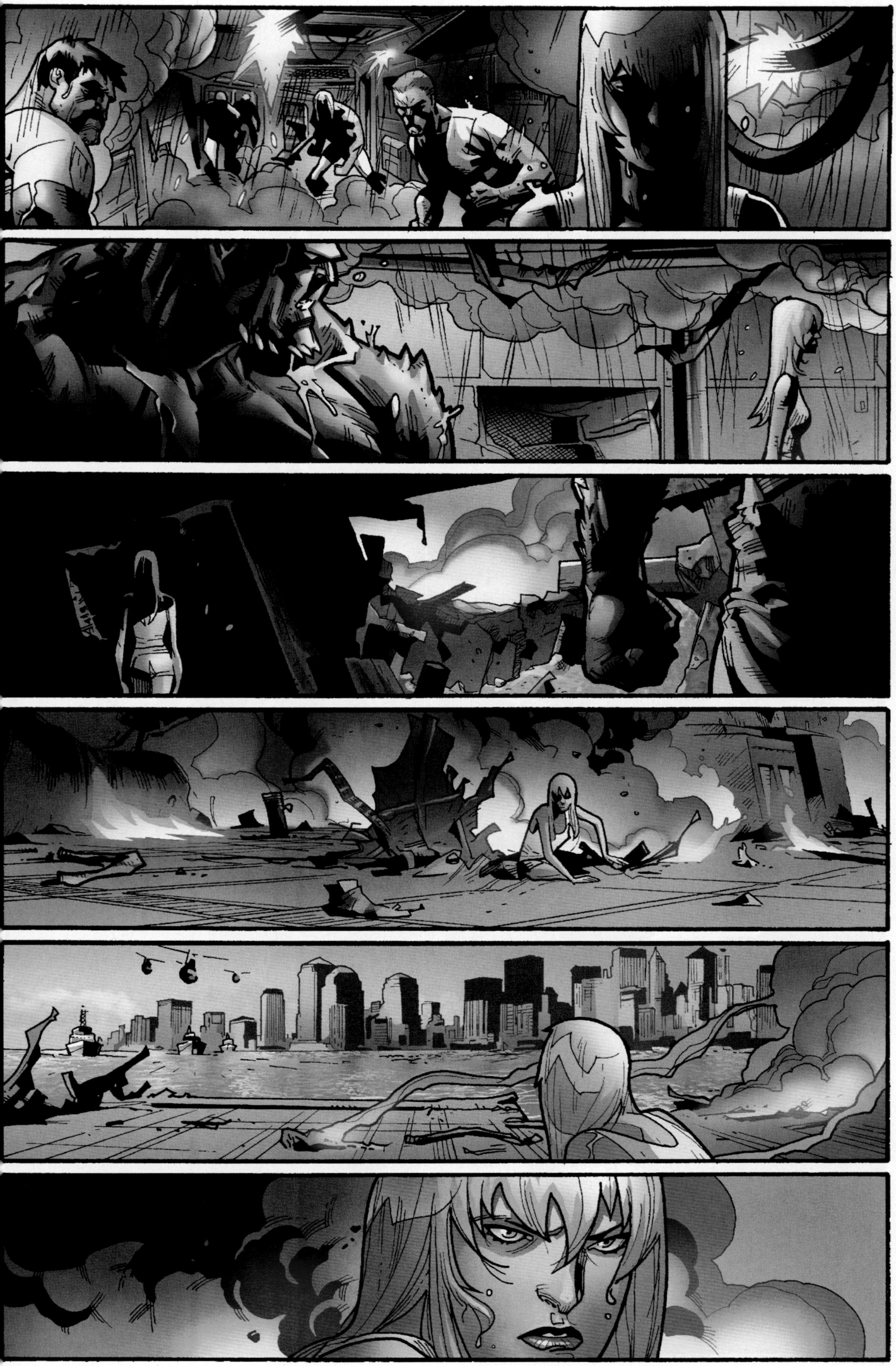

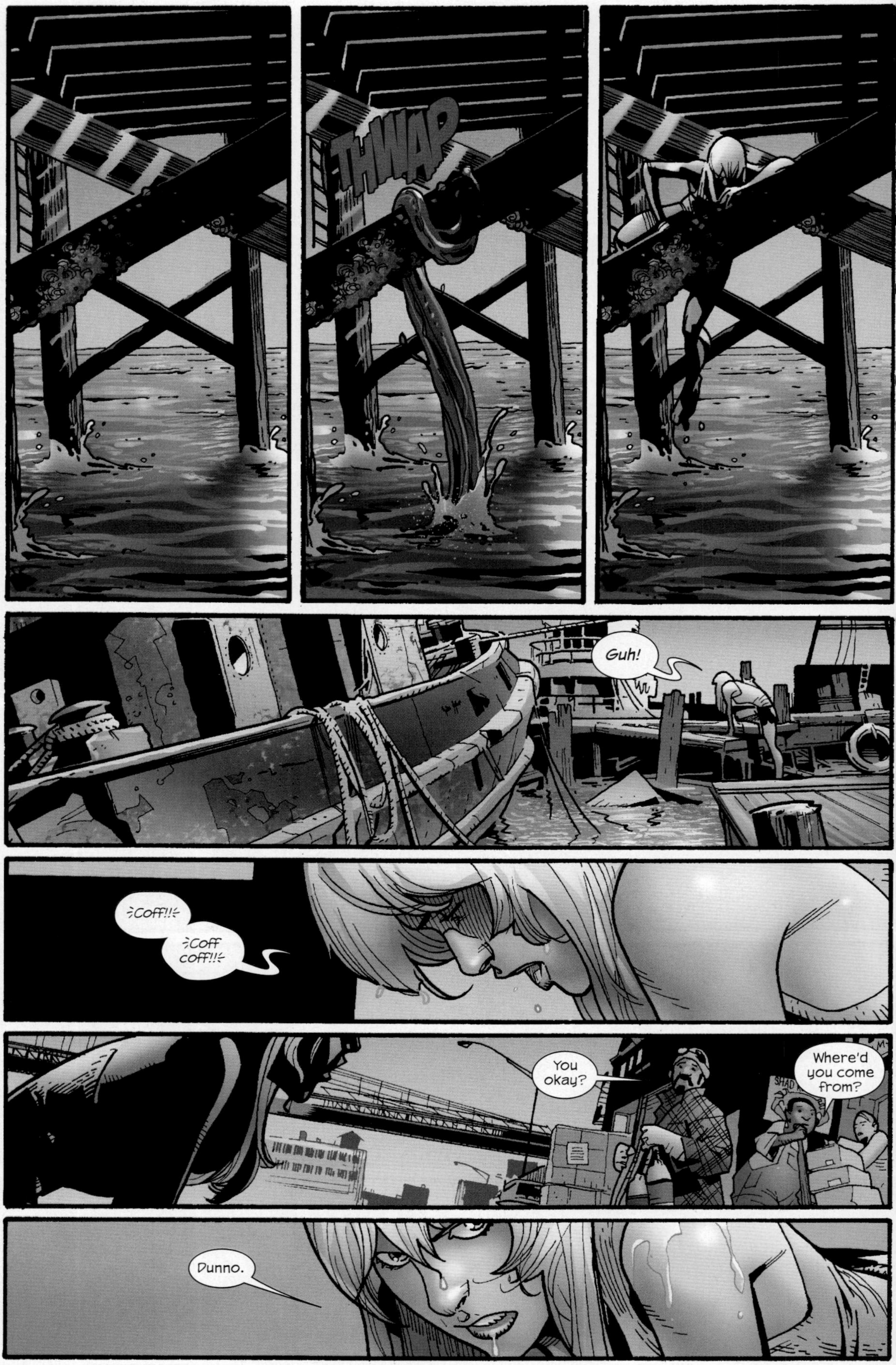
THWAP
Guh!
Coff!!
Coff coff!!
You okay?
Where'd you come from?
Dunno.

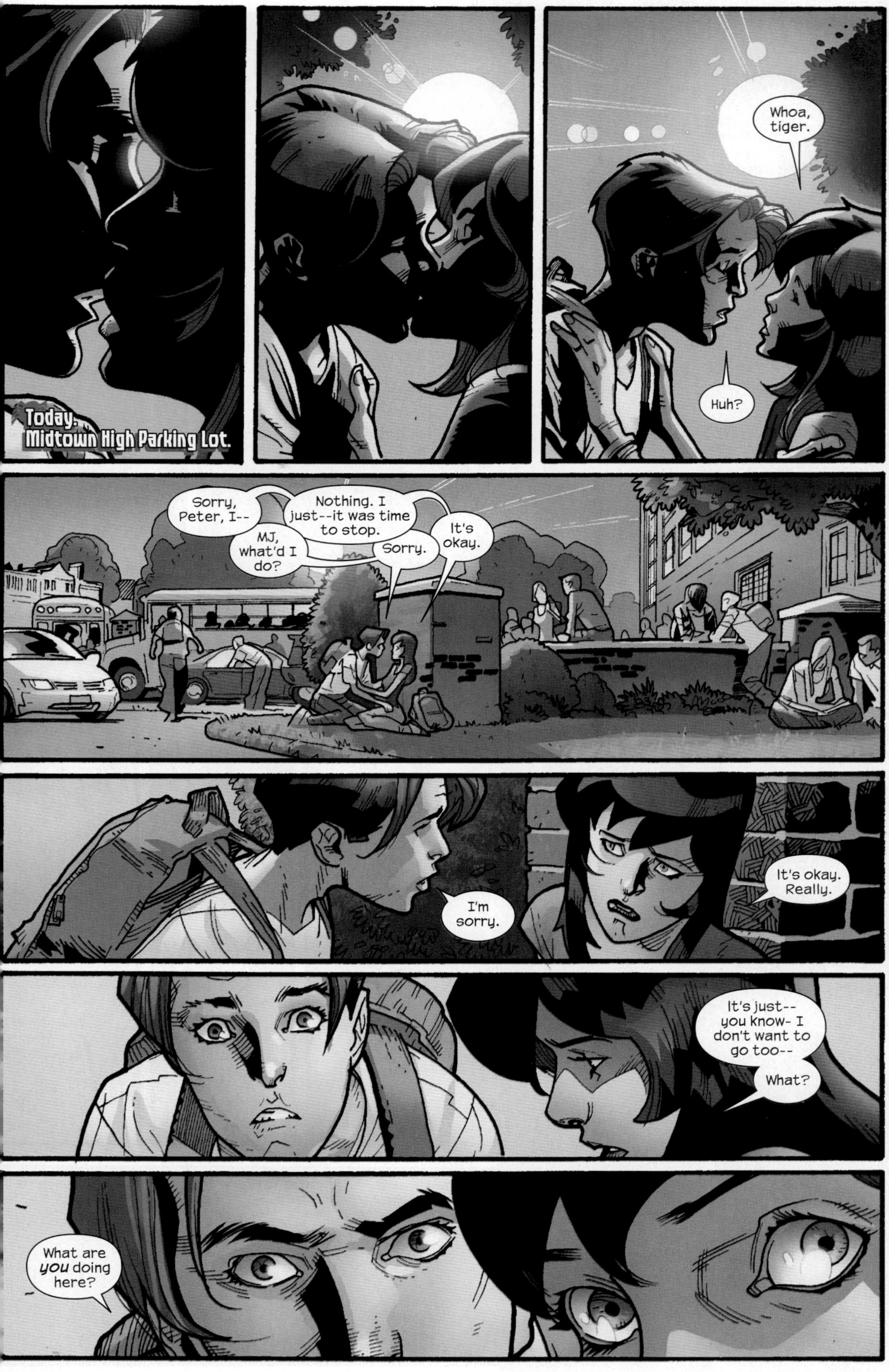
Today.
Midtown High Parking Lot.
Whoa, tiger.
Huh?
Sorry, Peter, I--
MJ, what'd I do?
Nothing. I just--it was time to stop.
Sorry.
It's okay.
I'm sorry.
It's okay. Really.
It's just-- you know- I don't want to go too--
What?
What are *you* doing here?

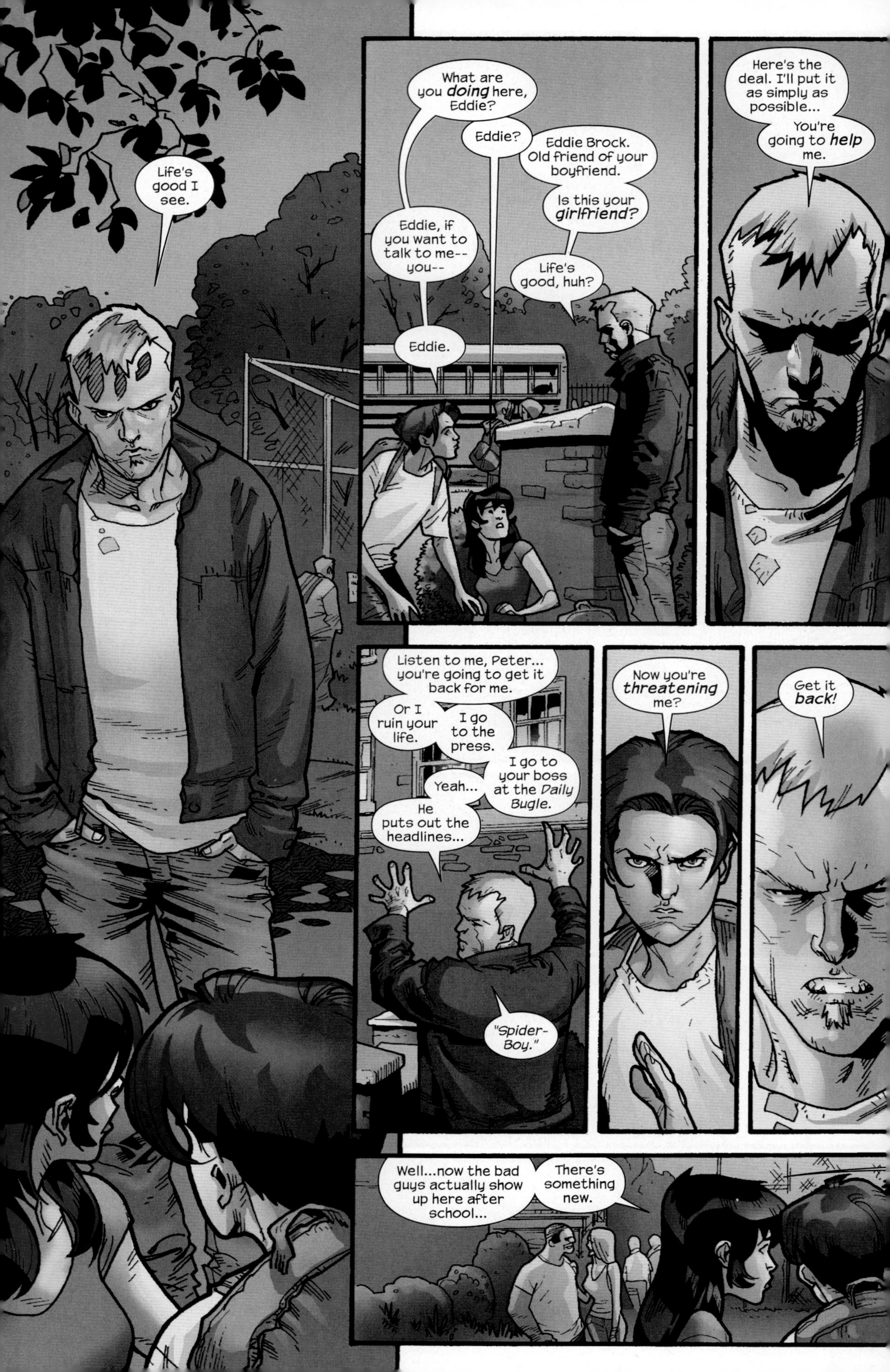
Life's good I see.
What are you *doing* here, Eddie?
Eddie?
Eddie Brock. Old friend of your boyfriend.
Is this your *girlfriend?*
Eddie, if you want to talk to me-- you--
Life's good, huh?
Eddie.
Here's the deal. I'll put it as simply as possible...
You're going to *help* me.
Listen to me, Peter... you're going to get it back for me.
Or I ruin your life.
I go to the press.
I go to your boss at the *Daily Bugle.*
Yeah...
He puts out the headlines...
"Spider-Boy."
Now you're *threatening* me?
Get it *back!*
Well...now the bad guys actually show up here after school...
There's something new.

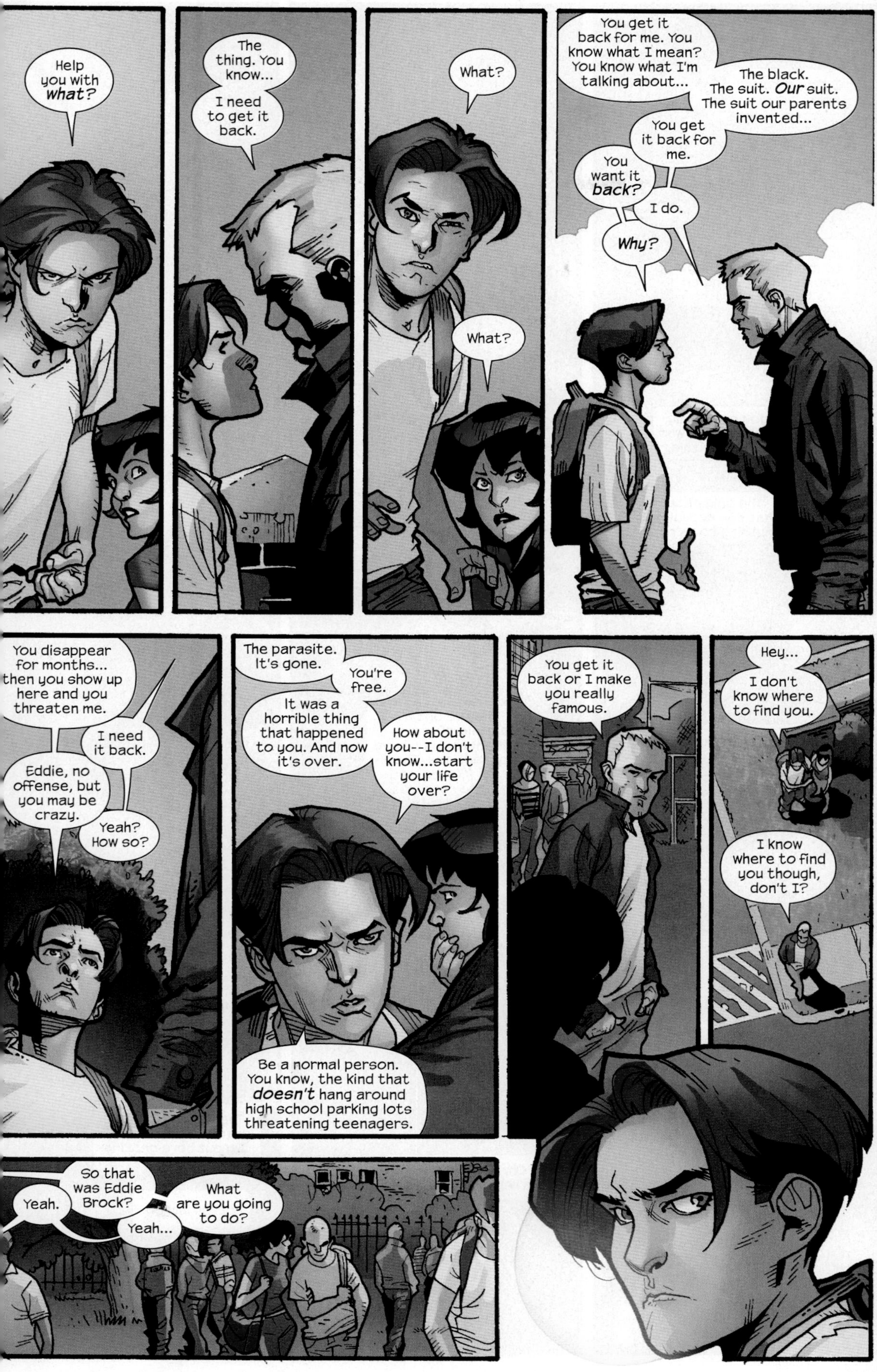
Help you with *what?*
The thing. You know...
I need to get it back.
What?
What?
You get it back for me. You know what I mean? You know what I'm talking about...
The black. The suit. *Our* suit. The suit our parents invented...
You get it back for me.
You want it *back?*
I do.
Why?
You disappear for months... then you show up here and you threaten me.
I need it back.
Eddie, no offense, but you may be crazy.
Yeah? How so?
The parasite. It's gone.
You're free.
It was a horrible thing that happened to you. And now it's over.
How about you--I don't know...start your life over?
Be a normal person. You know, the kind that *doesn't* hang around high school parking lots threatening teenagers.
You get it back or I make you really famous.
Hey...
I don't know where to find you.
I know where to find you though, don't I?
So that was Eddie Brock?
Yeah.
What are you going to do?
Yeah...

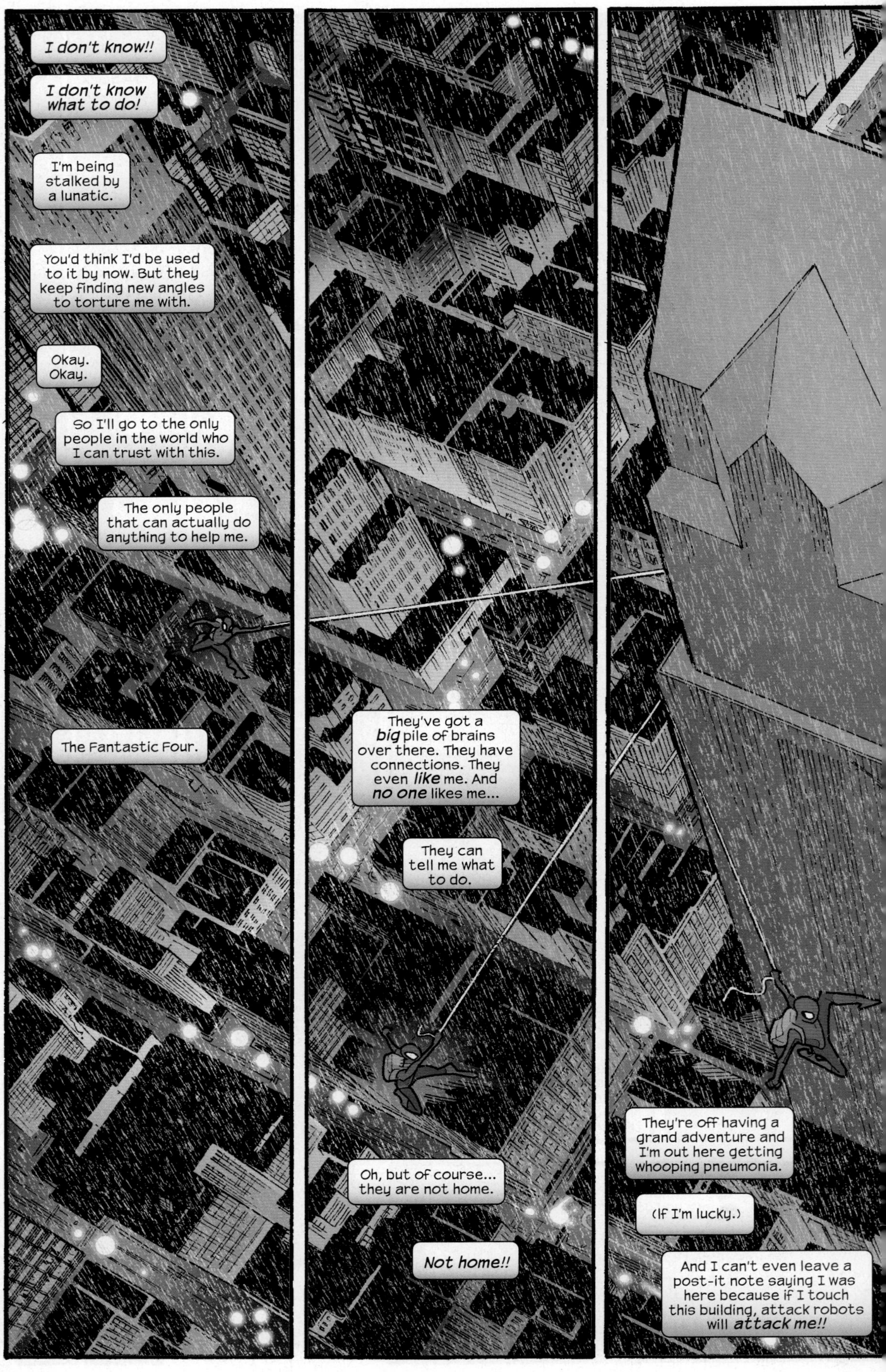
I don't know!!
I don't know what to do!
I'm being stalked by a lunatic.
You'd think I'd be used to it by now. But they keep finding new angles to torture me with.
Okay. Okay.
So I'll go to the only people in the world who I can trust with this.
The only people that can actually do anything to help me.
The Fantastic Four.
They've got a *big* pile of brains over there. They have connections. They even *like* me. And *no one* likes me...
They can tell me what to do.
Oh, but of course... they are not home.
Not home!!
They're off having a grand adventure and I'm out here getting whooping pneumonia.
(If I'm lucky.)
And I can't even leave a post-it note saying I was here because if I touch this building, attack robots will *attack me!!*

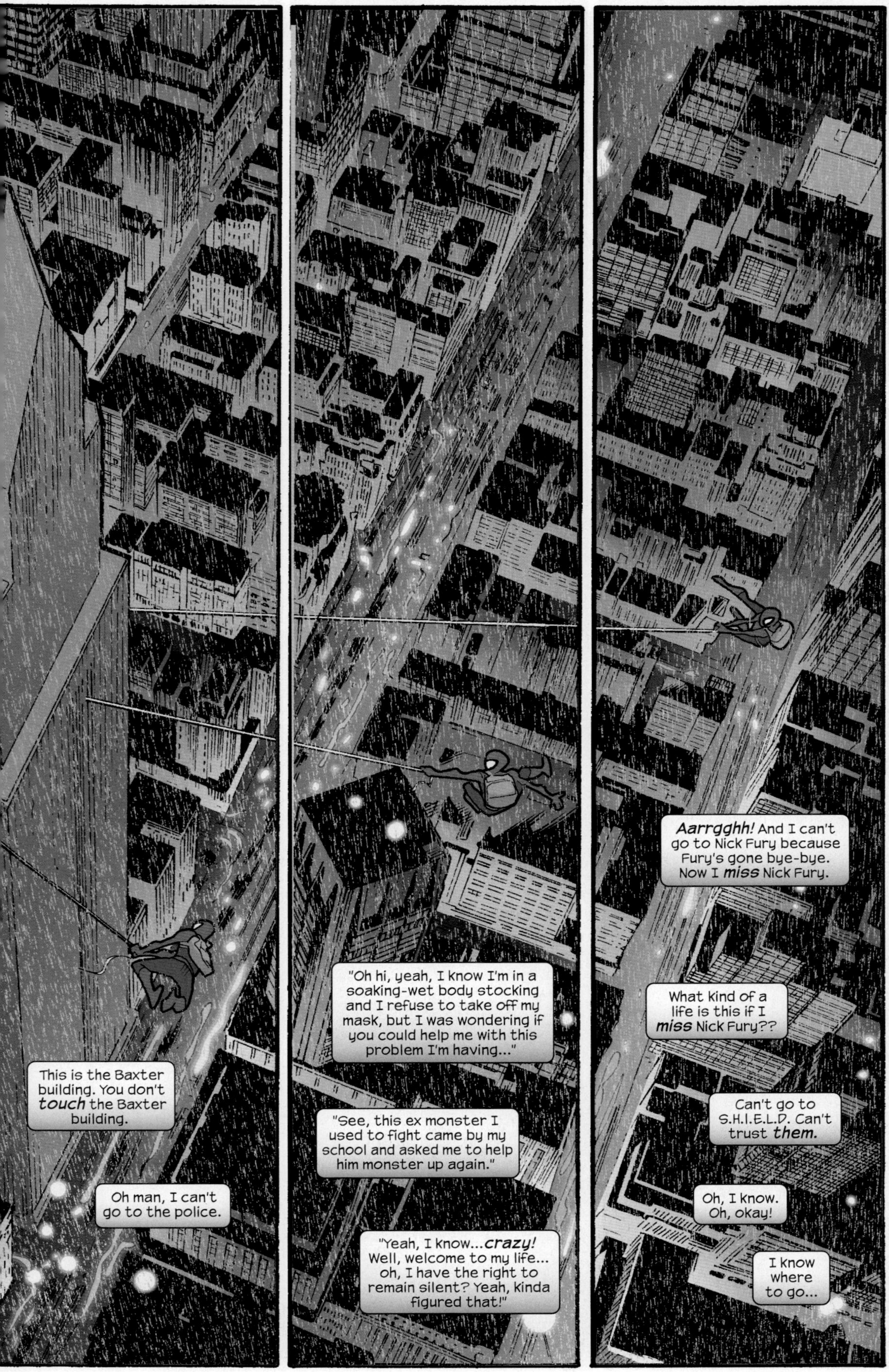
This is the Baxter building. You don't *touch* the Baxter building.
Oh man, I can't go to the police.
"Oh hi, yeah, I know I'm in a soaking-wet body stocking and I refuse to take off my mask, but I was wondering if you could help me with this problem I'm having..."
"See, this ex monster I used to fight came by my school and asked me to help him monster up again."
"Yeah, I know...*crazy!* Well, welcome to my life... oh, I have the right to remain silent? Yeah, kinda figured that!"
Aarrgghh! And I can't go to Nick Fury because Fury's gone bye-bye. Now I *miss* Nick Fury.
What kind of a life is this if I *miss* Nick Fury??
Can't go to S.H.I.E.L.D. Can't trust *them.*
Oh, I know. Oh, okay!
I know where to go...

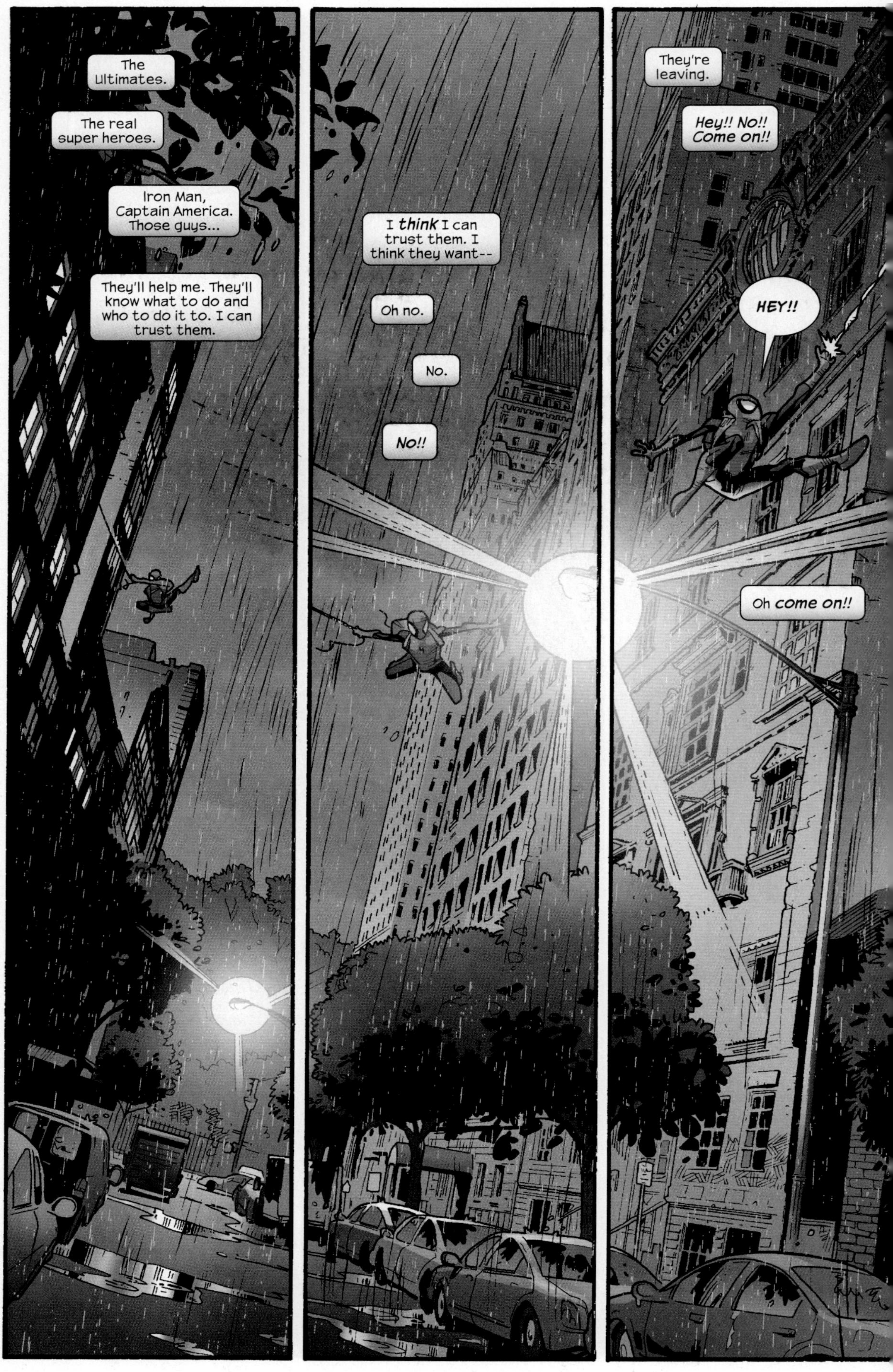

The Ultimates.
The real super heroes.
Iron Man, Captain America. Those guys...
They'll help me. They'll know what to do and who to do it to. I can trust them.
I *think* I can trust them. I think they want--
Oh no.
No.
No!!
They're leaving.
Hey!! No!! Come on!!
HEY!!
Oh *come on!!*

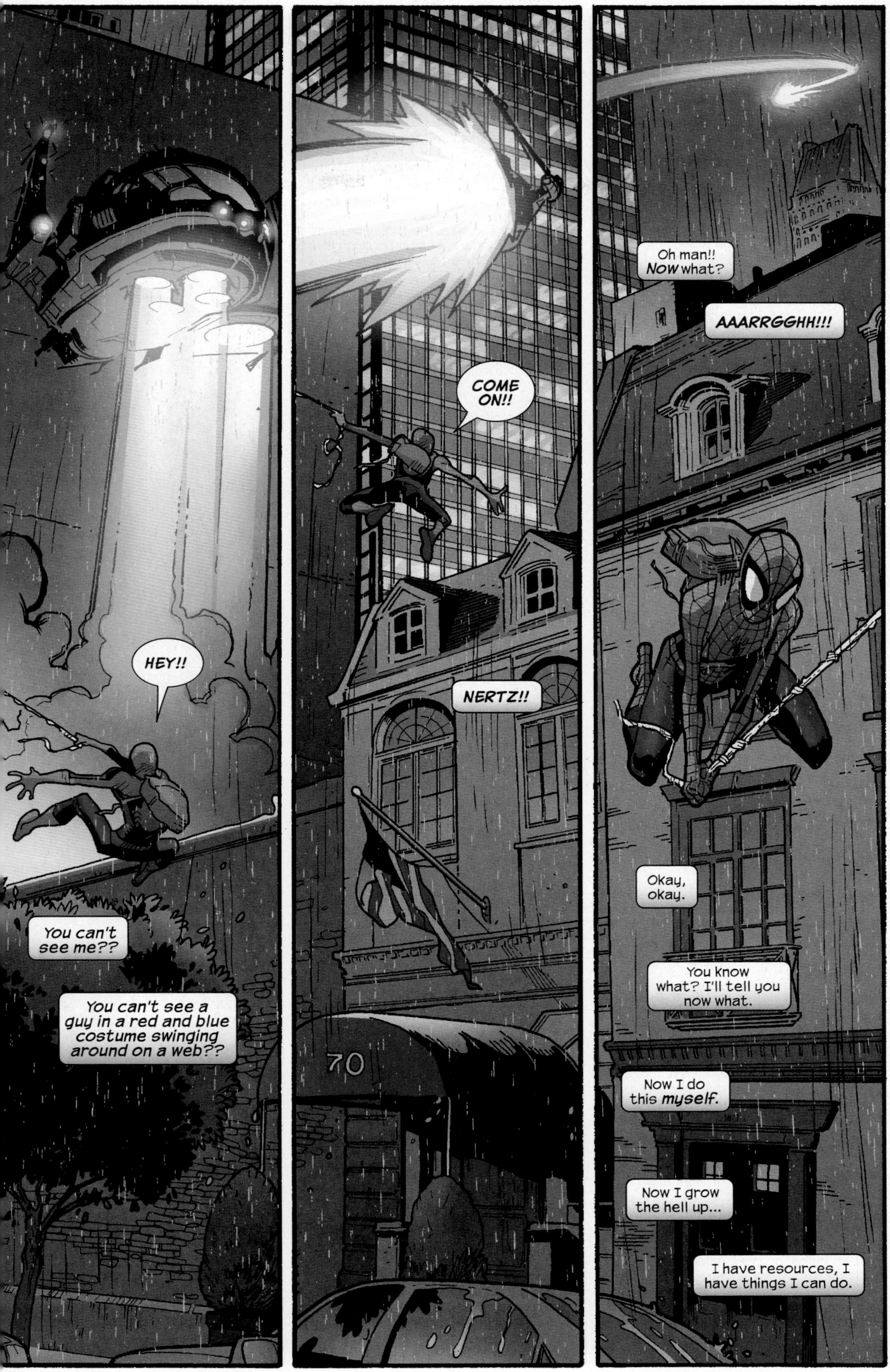
HEY!!
You can't see me??
You can't see a guy in a red and blue costume swinging around on a web??
COME ON!!
NERTZ!!
70
Oh man!! NOW what?
AAARRGGHH!!!
Okay, okay.
You know what? I'll tell you now what.
Now I do this myself.
Now I grow the hell up...
I have resources, I have things I can do.

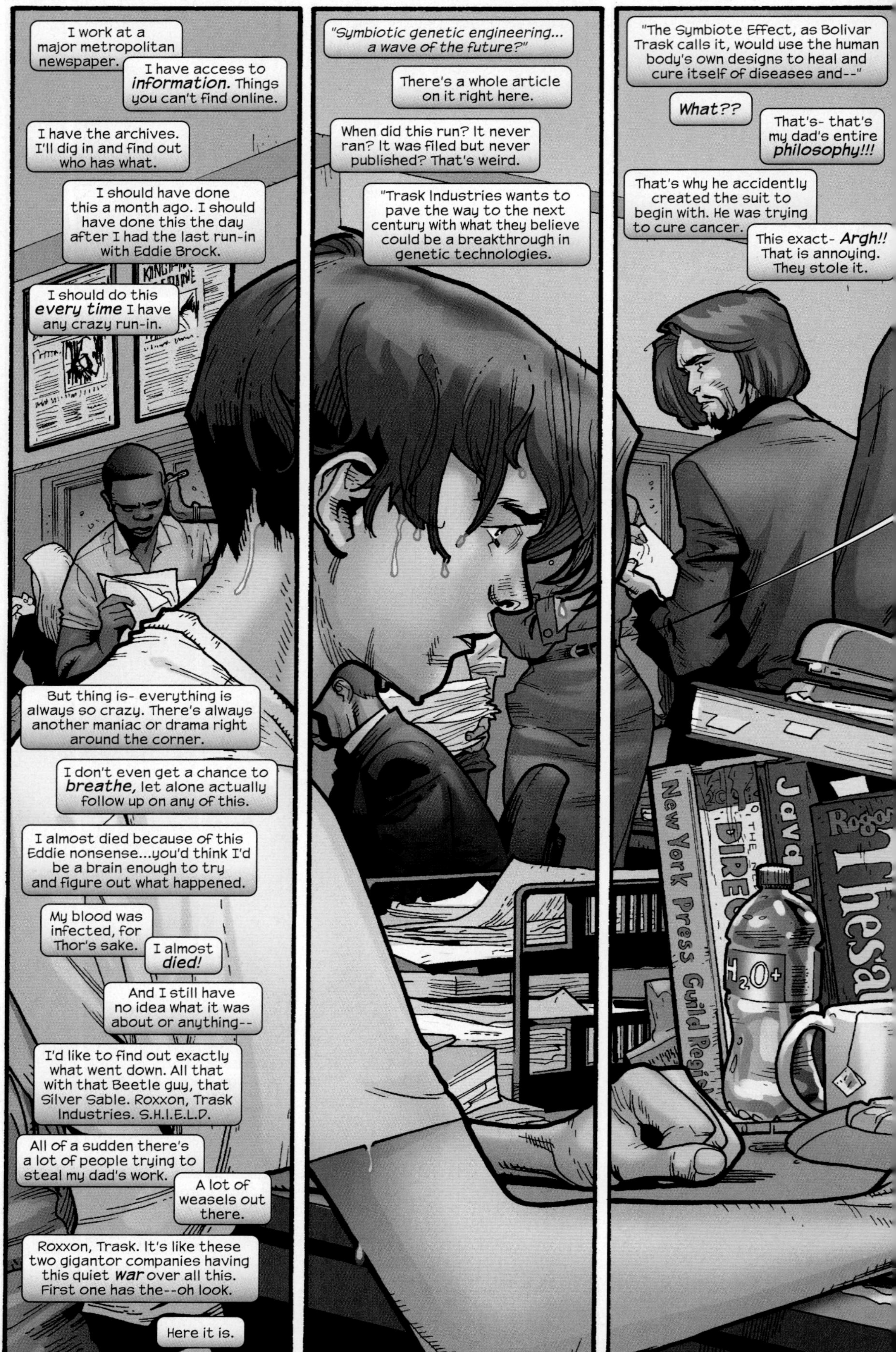
I work at a major metropolitan newspaper.
I have access to *information.* Things you can't find online.
I have the archives. I'll dig in and find out who has what.
I should have done this a month ago. I should have done this the day after I had the last run-in with Eddie Brock.
I should do this *every time* I have any crazy run-in.
But thing is- everything is always so crazy. There's always another maniac or drama right around the corner.
I don't even get a chance to *breathe,* let alone actually follow up on any of this.
I almost died because of this Eddie nonsense...you'd think I'd be a brain enough to try and figure out what happened.
My blood was infected, for Thor's sake.
I almost *died!*
And I still have no idea what it was about or anything--
I'd like to find out exactly what went down. All that with that Beetle guy, that Silver Sable. Roxxon, Trask Industries. S.H.I.E.L.D.
All of a sudden there's a lot of people trying to steal my dad's work.
A lot of weasels out there.
Roxxon, Trask. It's like these two gigantor companies having this quiet *war* over all this. First one has the--oh look.
Here it is.
"Symbiotic genetic engineering... a wave of the future?"
There's a whole article on it right here.
When did this run? It never ran? It was filed but never published? That's weird.
"Trask Industries wants to pave the way to the next century with what they believe could be a breakthrough in genetic technologies.
"The Symbiote Effect, as Bolivar Trask calls it, would use the human body's own designs to heal and cure itself of diseases and--"
What??
That's- that's my dad's entire *philosophy!!!*
That's why he accidently created the suit to begin with. He was trying to cure cancer.
This exact- *Argh!!* That is annoying. They stole it.

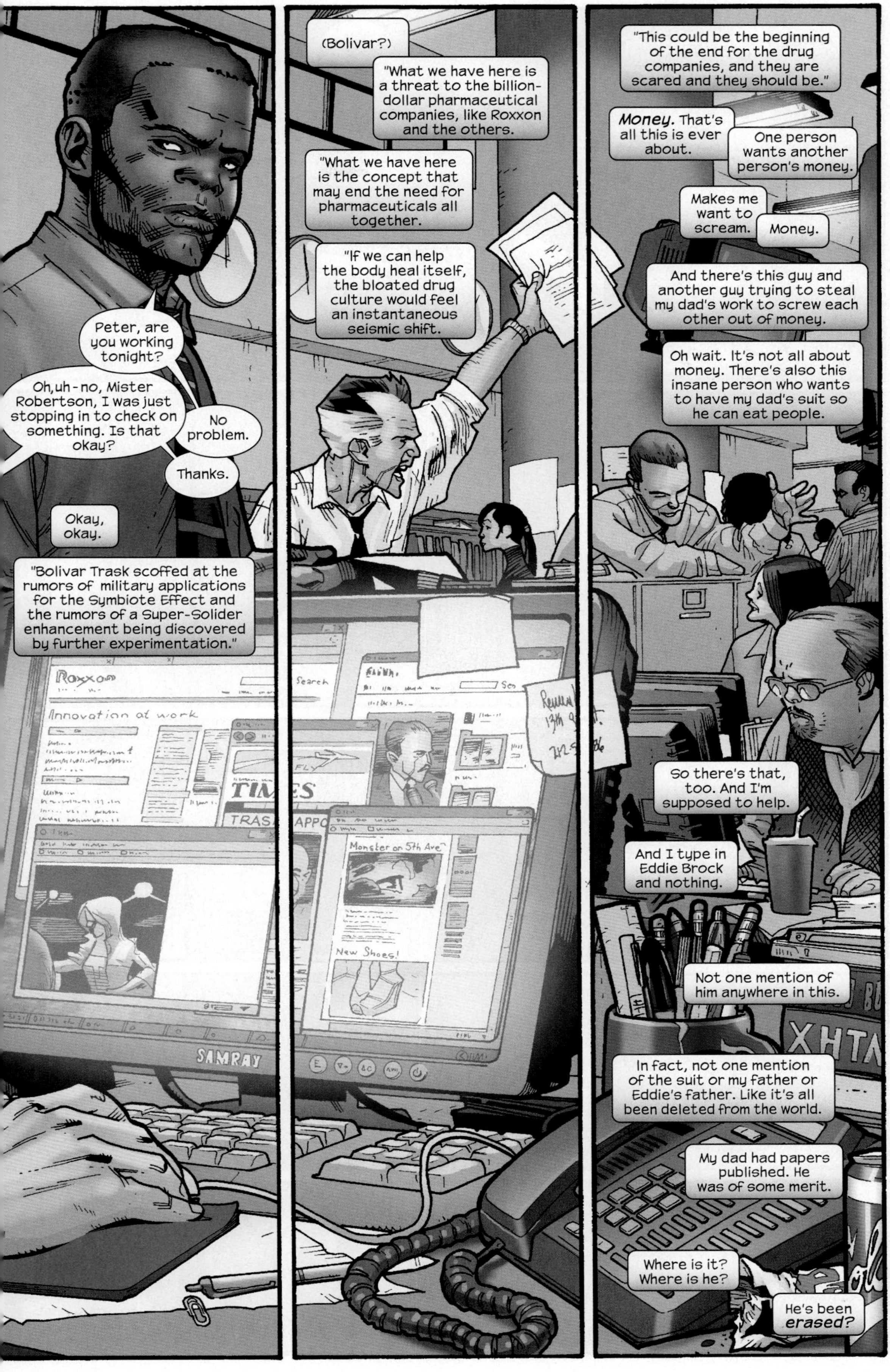
Peter, are you working tonight?
Oh, uh - no, Mister Robertson, I was just stopping in to check on something. Is that okay?
No problem.
Thanks.
Okay, okay.
"Bolivar Trask scoffed at the rumors of military applications for the Symbiote Effect and the rumors of a Super-Solider enhancement being discovered by further experimentation."
Roxxon
Innovation at work
Search
TIMES
Monster on 5th Ave
New Shoes!
SAMRAY
(Bolivar?)
"What we have here is a threat to the billion-dollar pharmaceutical companies, like Roxxon and the others.
"What we have here is the concept that may end the need for pharmaceuticals all together.
"If we can help the body heal itself, the bloated drug culture would feel an instantaneous seismic shift.
"This could be the beginning of the end for the drug companies, and they are scared and they should be."
Money. That's all this is ever about.
One person wants another person's money.
Makes me want to scream.
Money.
And there's this guy and another guy trying to steal my dad's work to screw each other out of money.
Oh wait. It's not all about money. There's also this insane person who wants to have my dad's suit so he can eat people.
So there's that, too. And I'm supposed to help.
And I type in Eddie Brock and nothing.
Not one mention of him anywhere in this.
In fact, not one mention of the suit or my father or Eddie's father. Like it's all been deleted from the world.
My dad had papers published. He was of some merit.
Where is it? Where is he?
He's been *erased?*

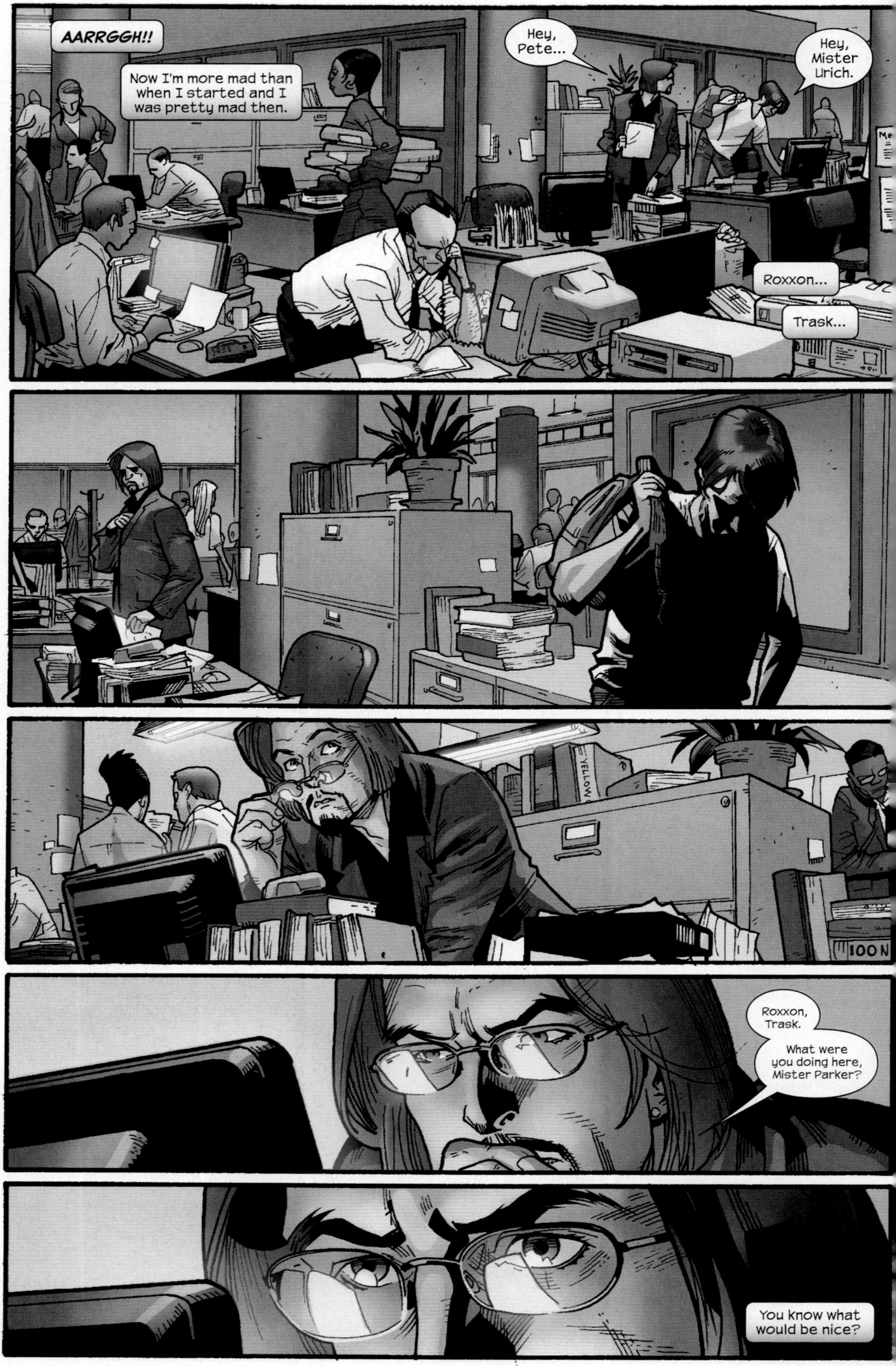
AARRGGH!!
Now I'm more mad than when I started and I was pretty mad then.
Hey, Pete...
Hey, Mister Urich.
Roxxon...
Trask...
Roxxon, Trask.
What were you doing here, Mister Parker?
You know what would be nice?

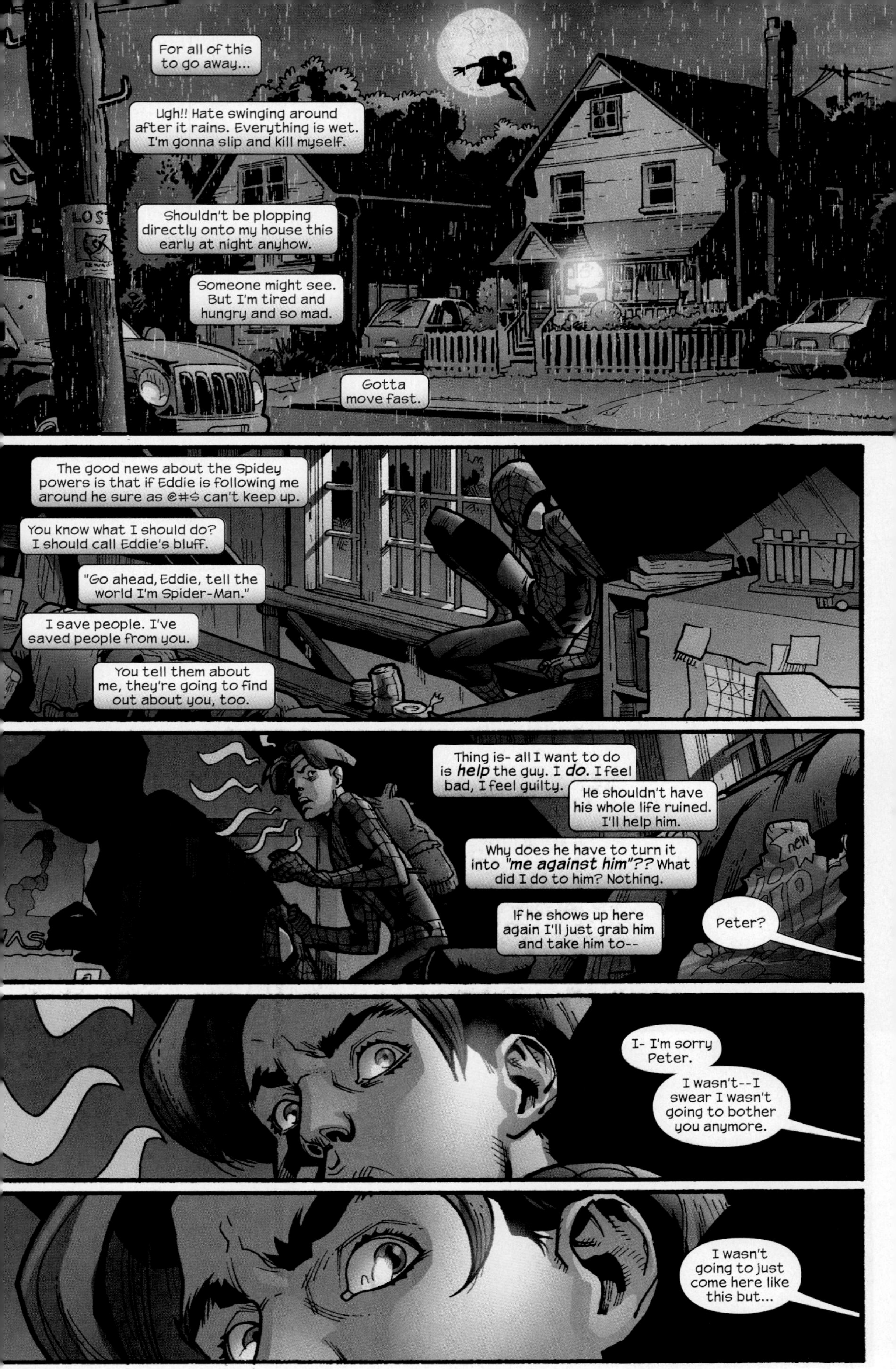
For all of this to go away...
Ugh!! Hate swinging around after it rains. Everything is wet. I'm gonna slip and kill myself.
Shouldn't be plopping directly onto my house this early at night anyhow.
Someone might see. But I'm tired and hungry and so mad.
Gotta move fast.
The good news about the Spidey powers is that if Eddie is following me around he sure as @#$ can't keep up.
You know what I should do? I should call Eddie's bluff.
"Go ahead, Eddie, tell the world I'm Spider-Man."
I save people. I've saved people from you.
You tell them about me, they're going to find out about you, too.
Thing is- all I want to do is *help* the guy. I *do.* I feel bad, I feel guilty.
He shouldn't have his whole life ruined. I'll help him.
Why does he have to turn it into *"me against him"*?? What did I do to him? Nothing.
If he shows up here again I'll just grab him and take him to--
Peter?
I- I'm sorry Peter.
I wasn't--I swear I wasn't going to bother you anymore.
I wasn't going to just come here like this but...

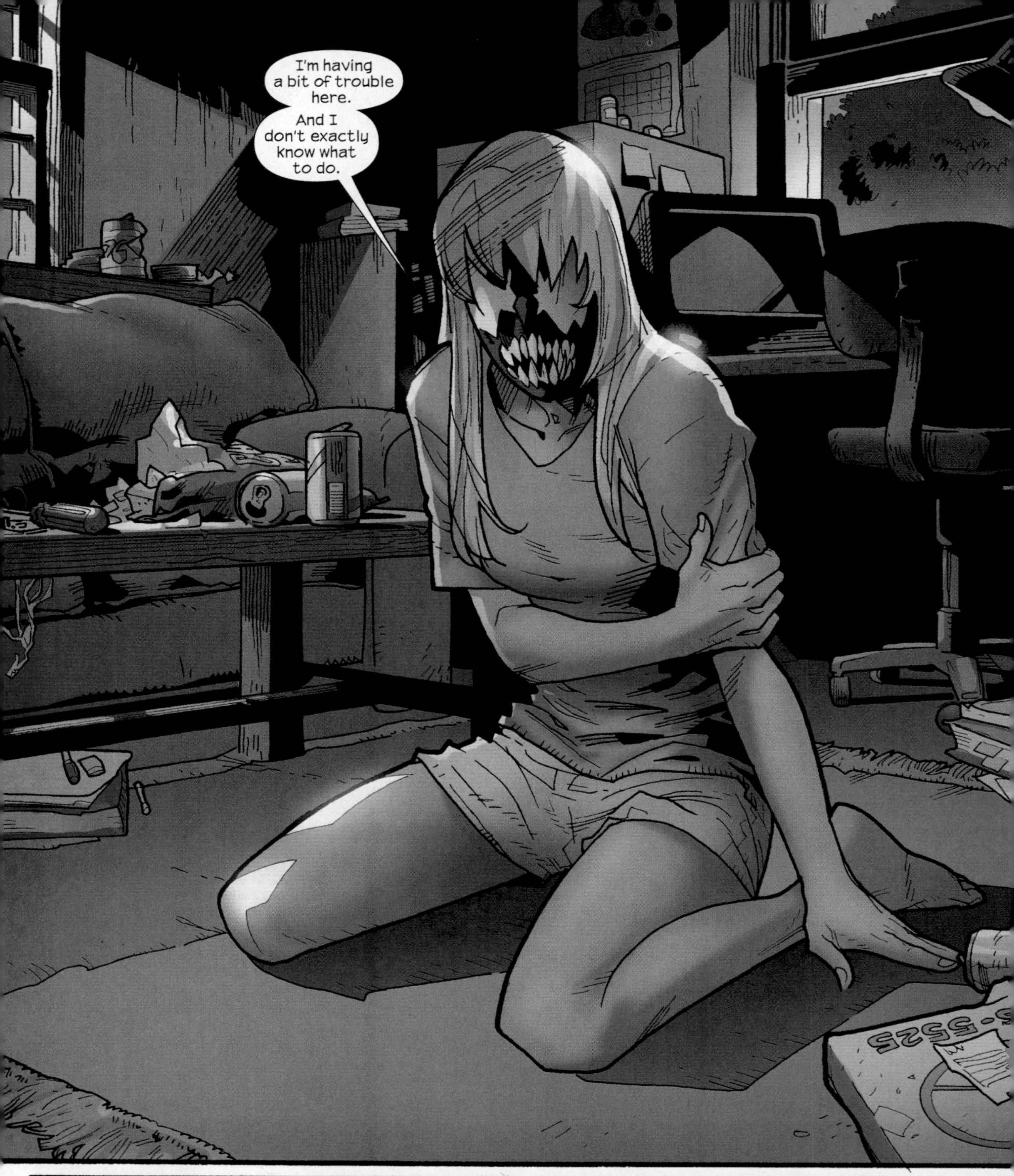
I'm having a bit of trouble here.
And I don't exactly know what to do.

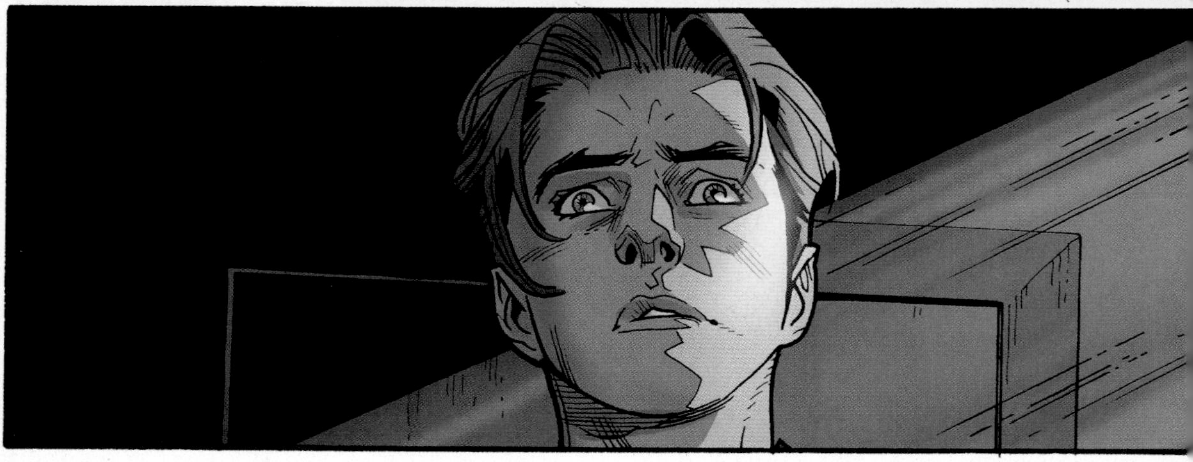

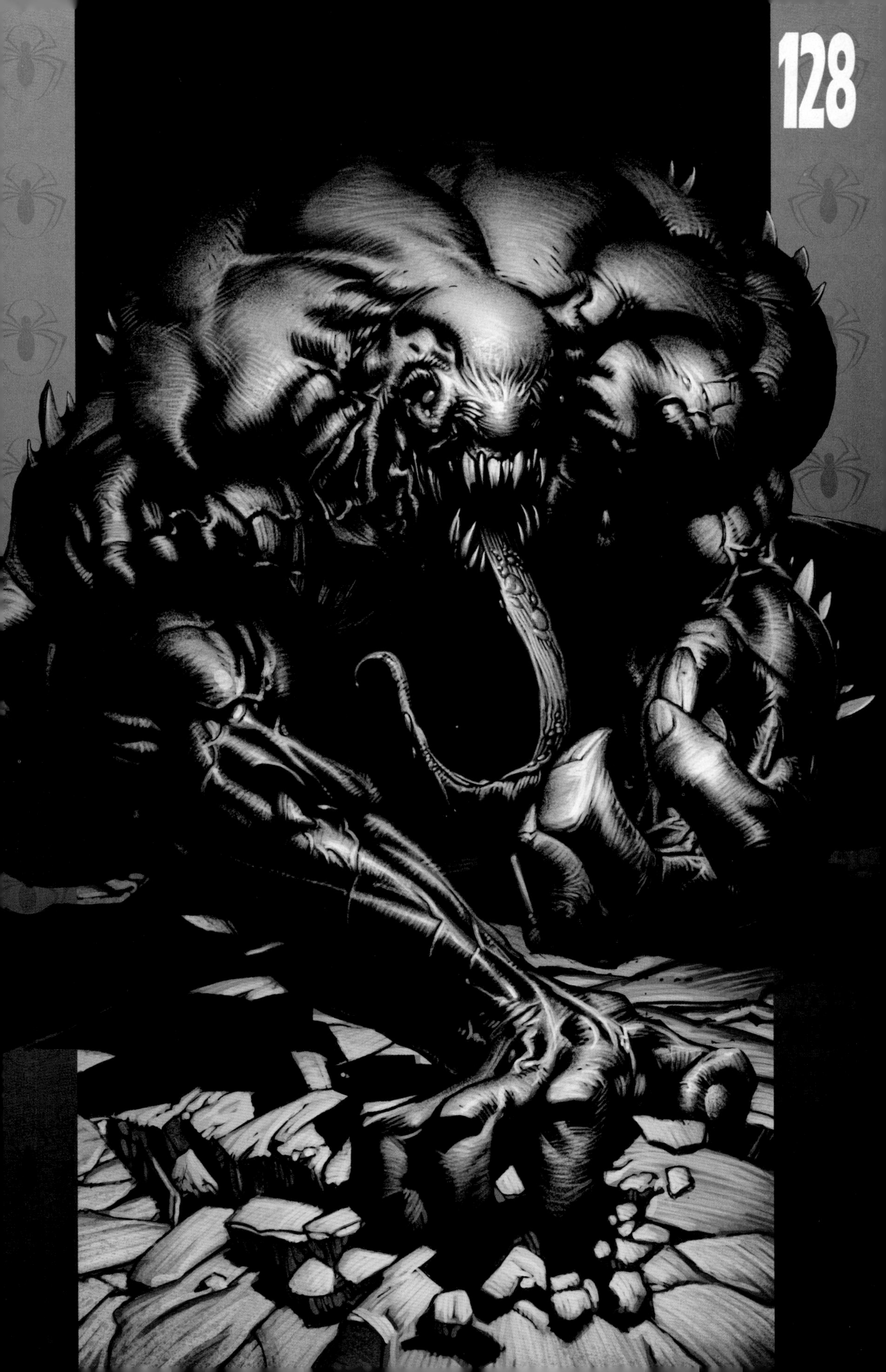
128

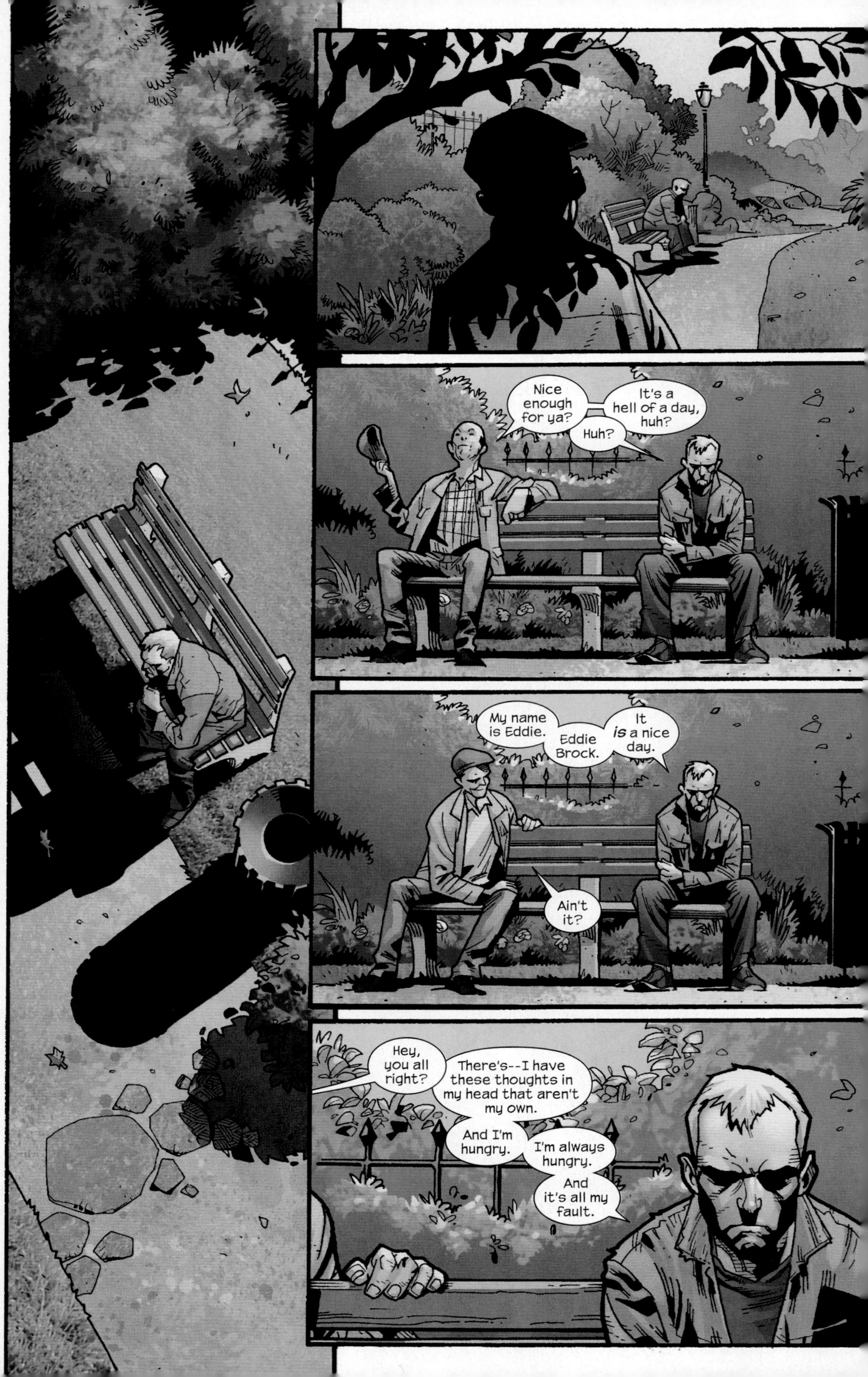
Nice enough for ya?
It's a hell of a day, huh?
Huh?
My name is Eddie.
Eddie Brock.
It *is* a nice day.
Ain't it?
Hey, you all right?
There's--I have these thoughts in my head that aren't my own.
And I'm hungry.
I'm always hungry.
And it's all my fault.

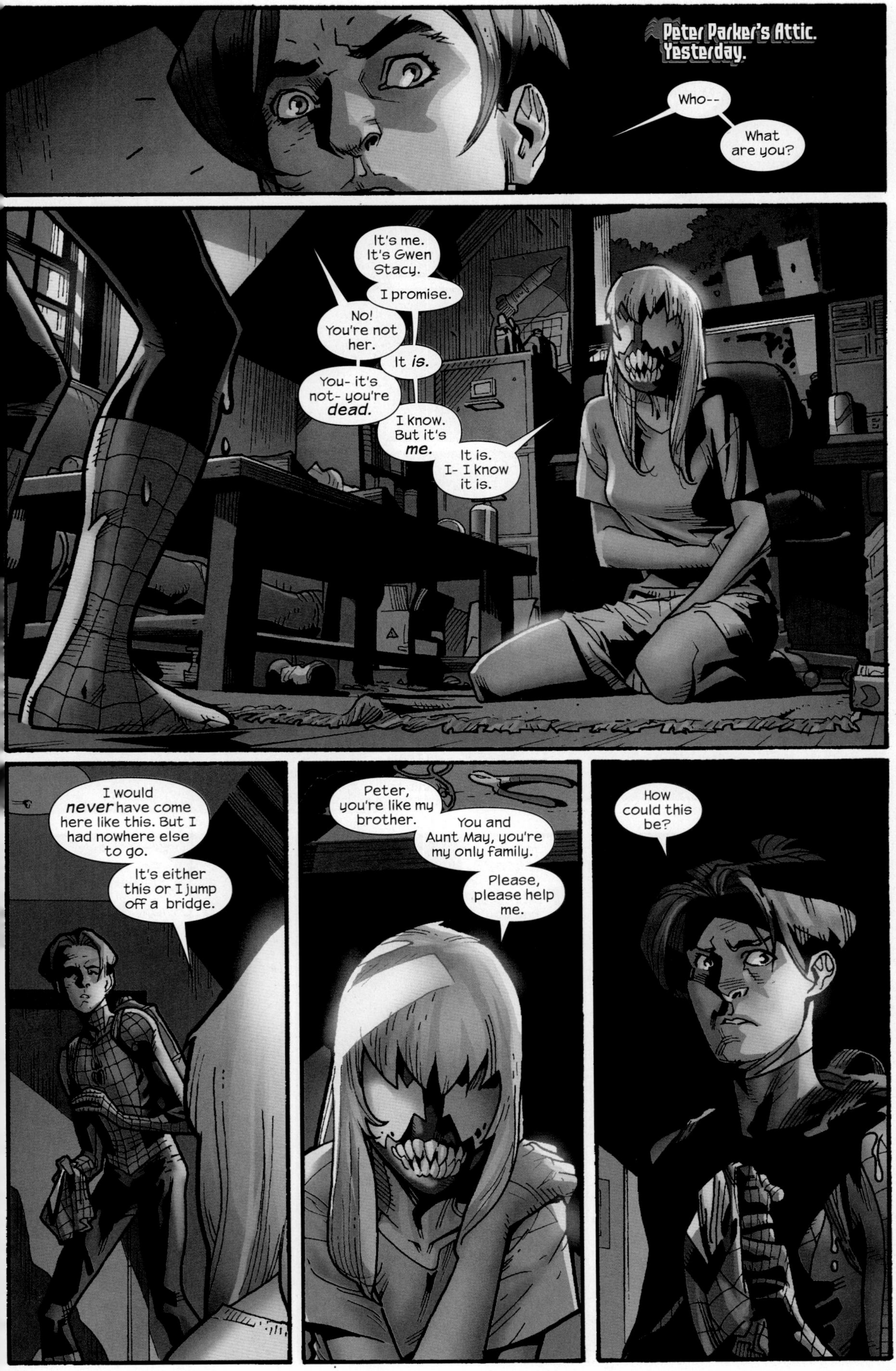
Peter Parker's Attic. Yesterday.
Who--
What are you?
It's me. It's Gwen Stacy.
I promise.
No! You're not her.
It *is.*
You- it's not- you're ***dead.***
I know. But it's ***me.***
It is. I- I know it is.
I would ***never*** have come here like this. But I had nowhere else to go.
It's either this or I jump off a bridge.
Peter, you're like my brother.
You and Aunt May, you're my only family.
Please, please help me.
How could this be?

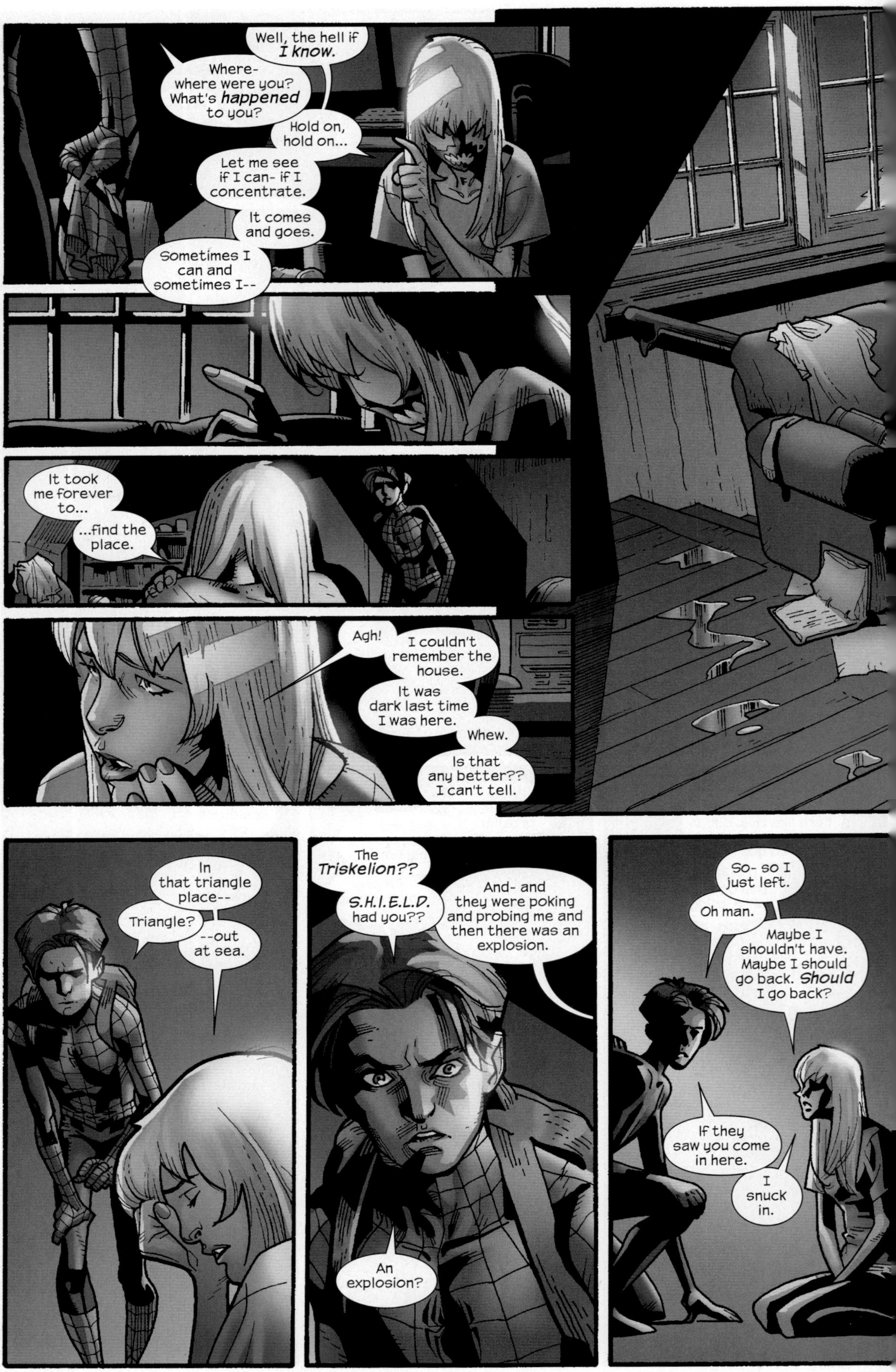
Well, the hell if I know.
Where- where were you? What's happened to you?
Hold on, hold on...
Let me see if I can- if I concentrate.
It comes and goes.
Sometimes I can and sometimes I--
It took me forever to...
...find the place.
Agh!
I couldn't remember the house.
It was dark last time I was here.
Whew.
Is that any better?? I can't tell.
In that triangle place--
Triangle?
--out at sea.
The Triskelion??
S.H.I.E.L.D. had you??
And- and they were poking and probing me and then there was an explosion.
An explosion?
So- so I just left.
Oh man.
Maybe I shouldn't have. Maybe I should go back. Should I go back?
If they saw you come in here.
I snuck in.

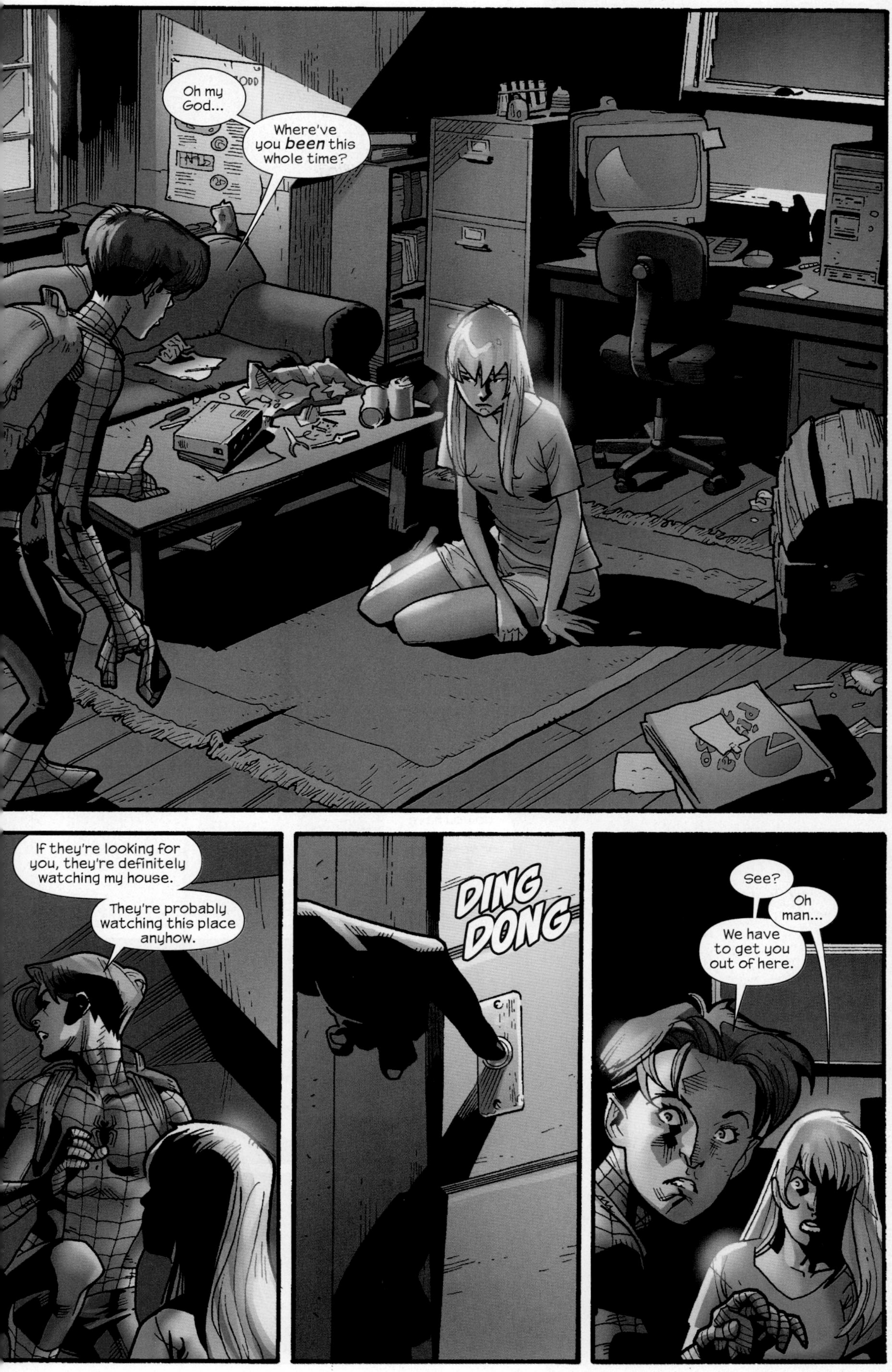
Oh my God...
Where've you *been* this whole time?
If they're looking for you, they're definitely watching my house.
They're probably watching this place anyhow.
DING DONG
See?
Oh man...
We have to get you out of here.

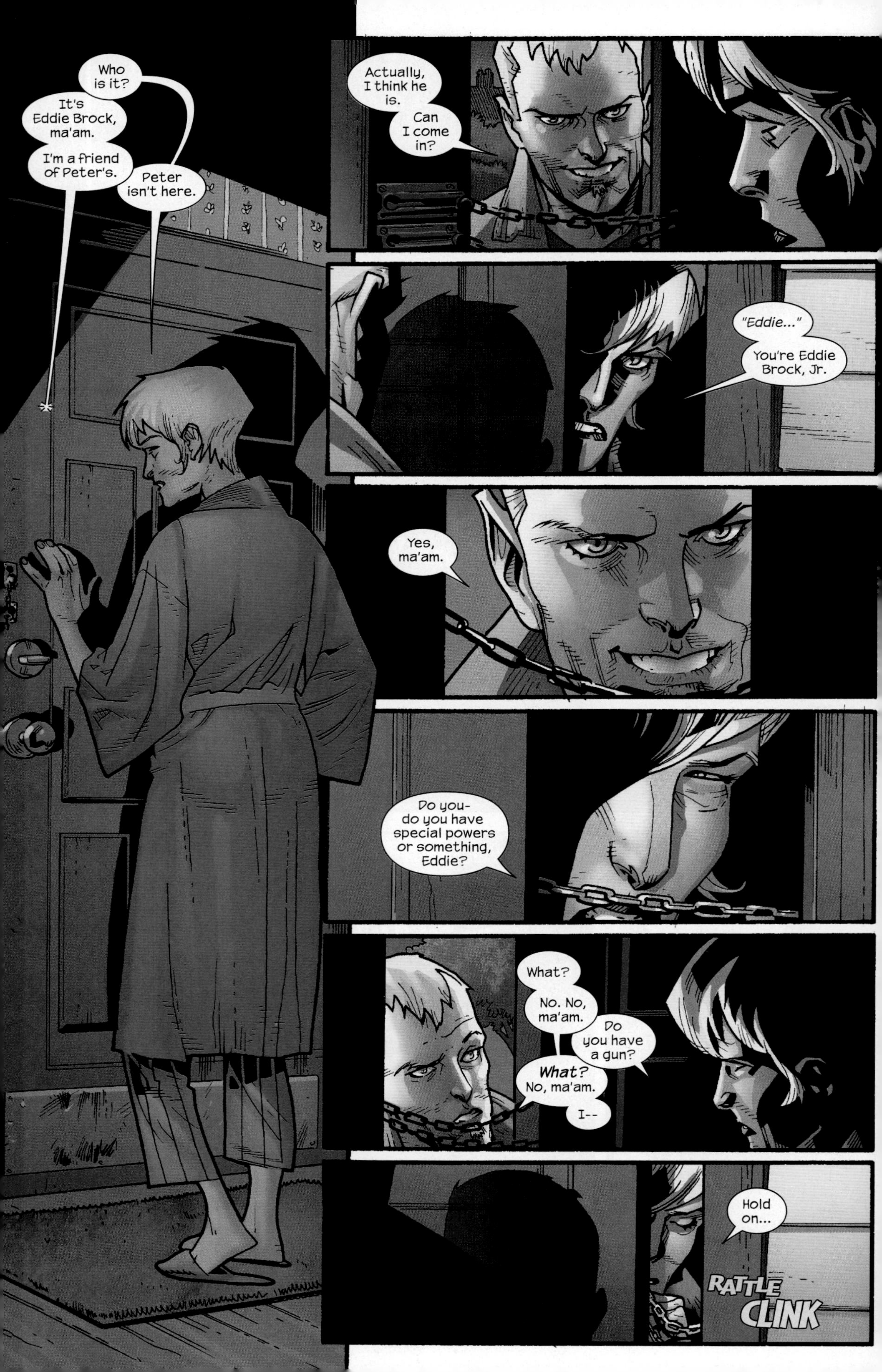

Who is it?
It's Eddie Brock, ma'am.
I'm a friend of Peter's.
Peter isn't here.
Actually, I think he is.
Can I come in?
"Eddie..."
You're Eddie Brock, Jr.
Yes, ma'am.
Do you- do you have special powers or something, Eddie?
What?
No. No, ma'am.
Do you have a gun?
What? No, ma'am.
I--
Hold on...
RATTLE
CLINK

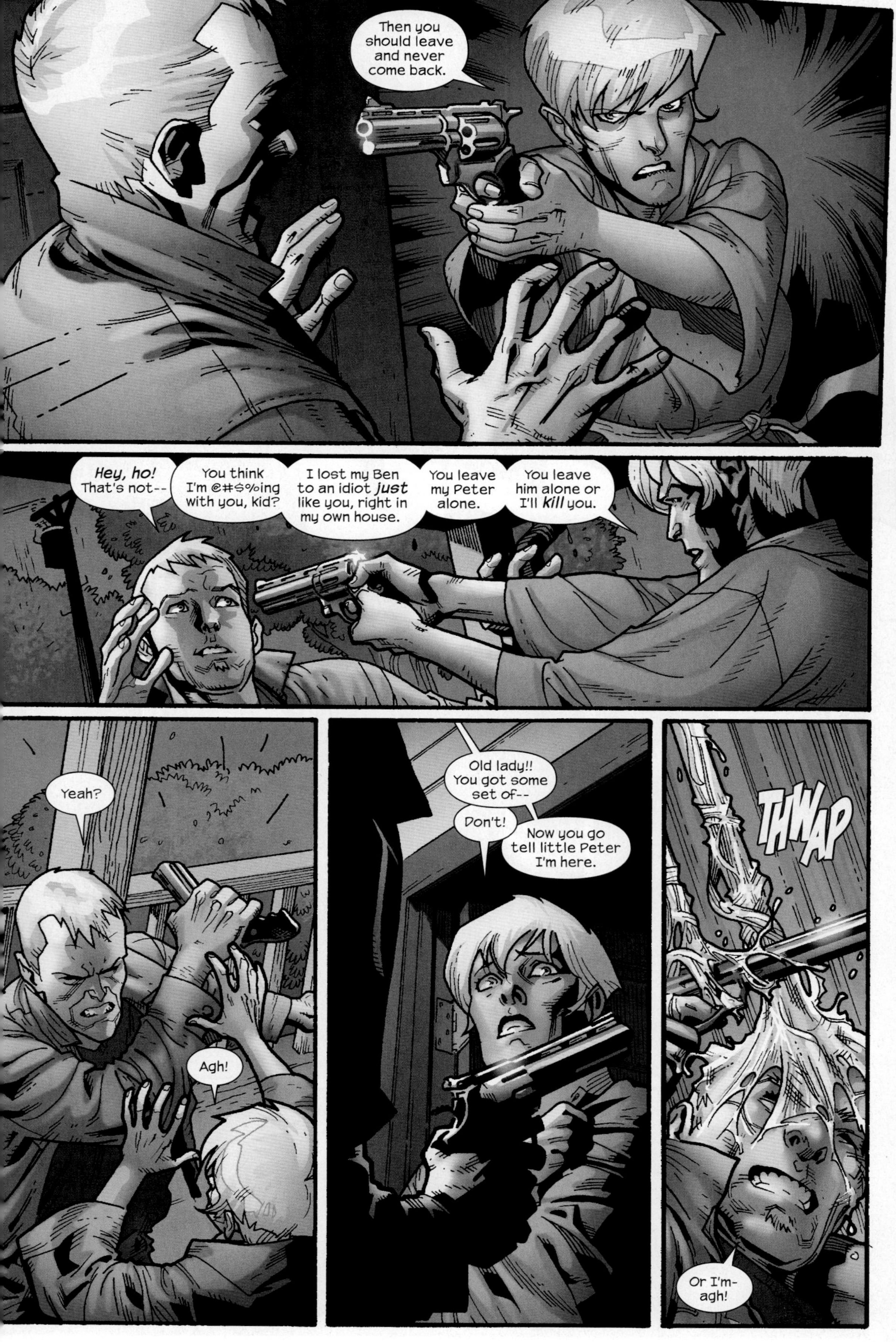
Then you should leave and never come back.
Hey, ho! That's not--
You think I'm @#$%ing with you, kid?
I lost my Ben to an idiot just like you, right in my own house.
You leave my Peter alone.
You leave him alone or I'll kill you.
Yeah?
Agh!
Old lady!! You got some set of--
Don't!
Now you go tell little Peter I'm here.
THWAP
Or I'm-agh!

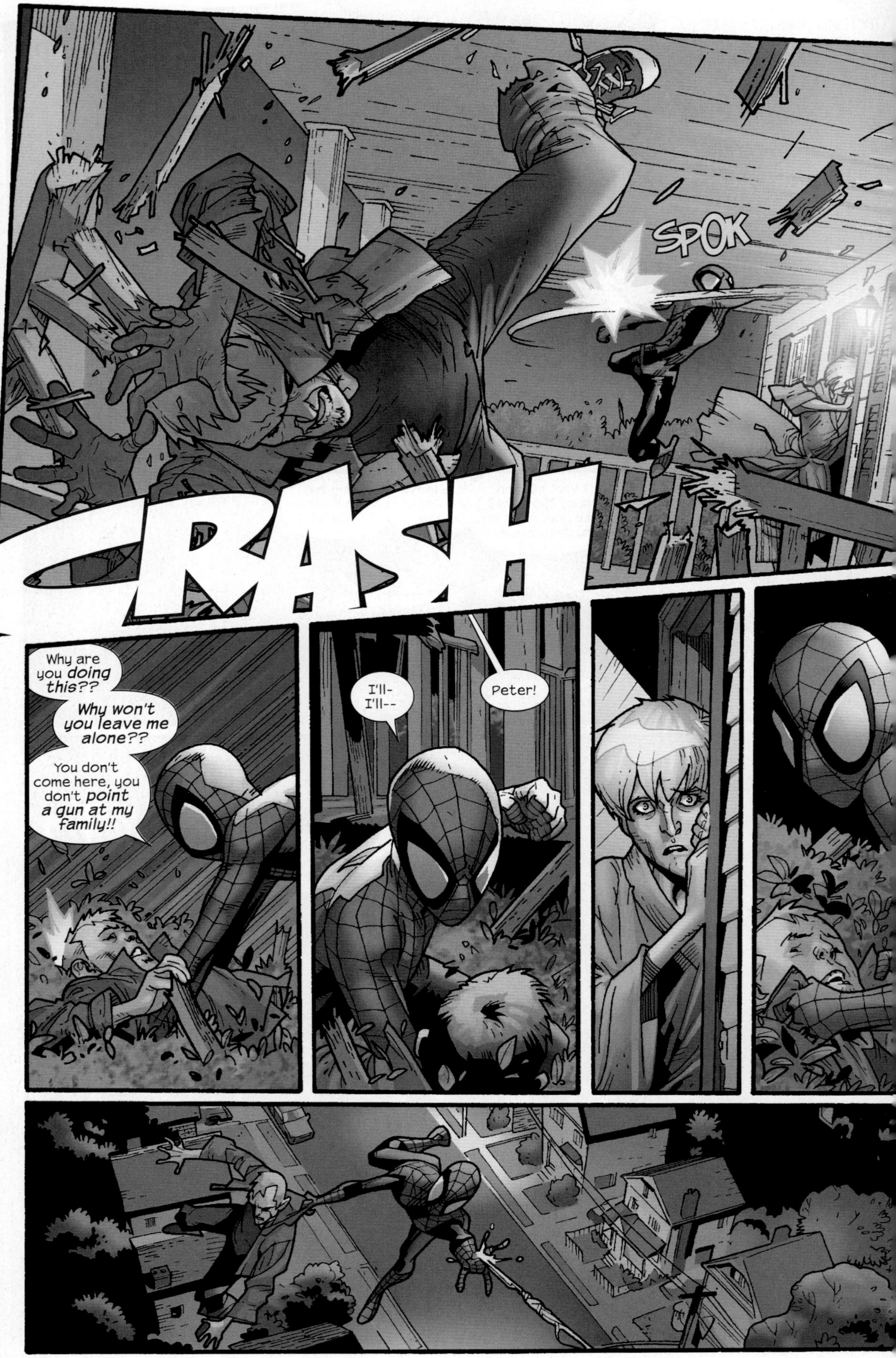
SPOK
CRASH
Why are you doing this??
Why won't you leave me alone??
You don't come here, you don't point a gun at my family!!
I'll-- I'll--
Peter!

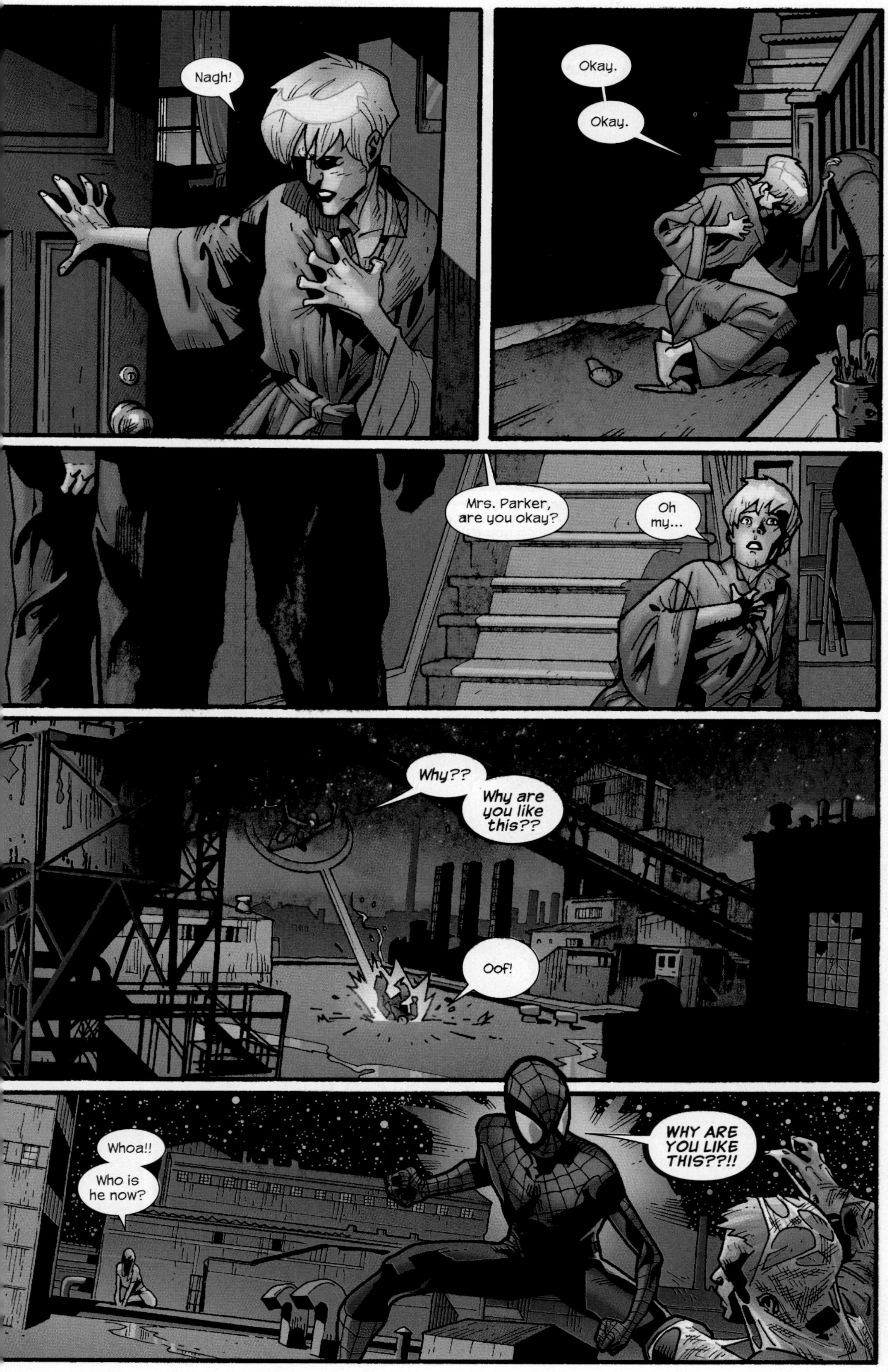

Nagh!
Okay.
Okay.
Mrs. Parker, are you okay?
Oh my...
Why??
Why are you like this??
Oof!
Whoa!!
Who is he now?
WHY ARE YOU LIKE THIS??!!

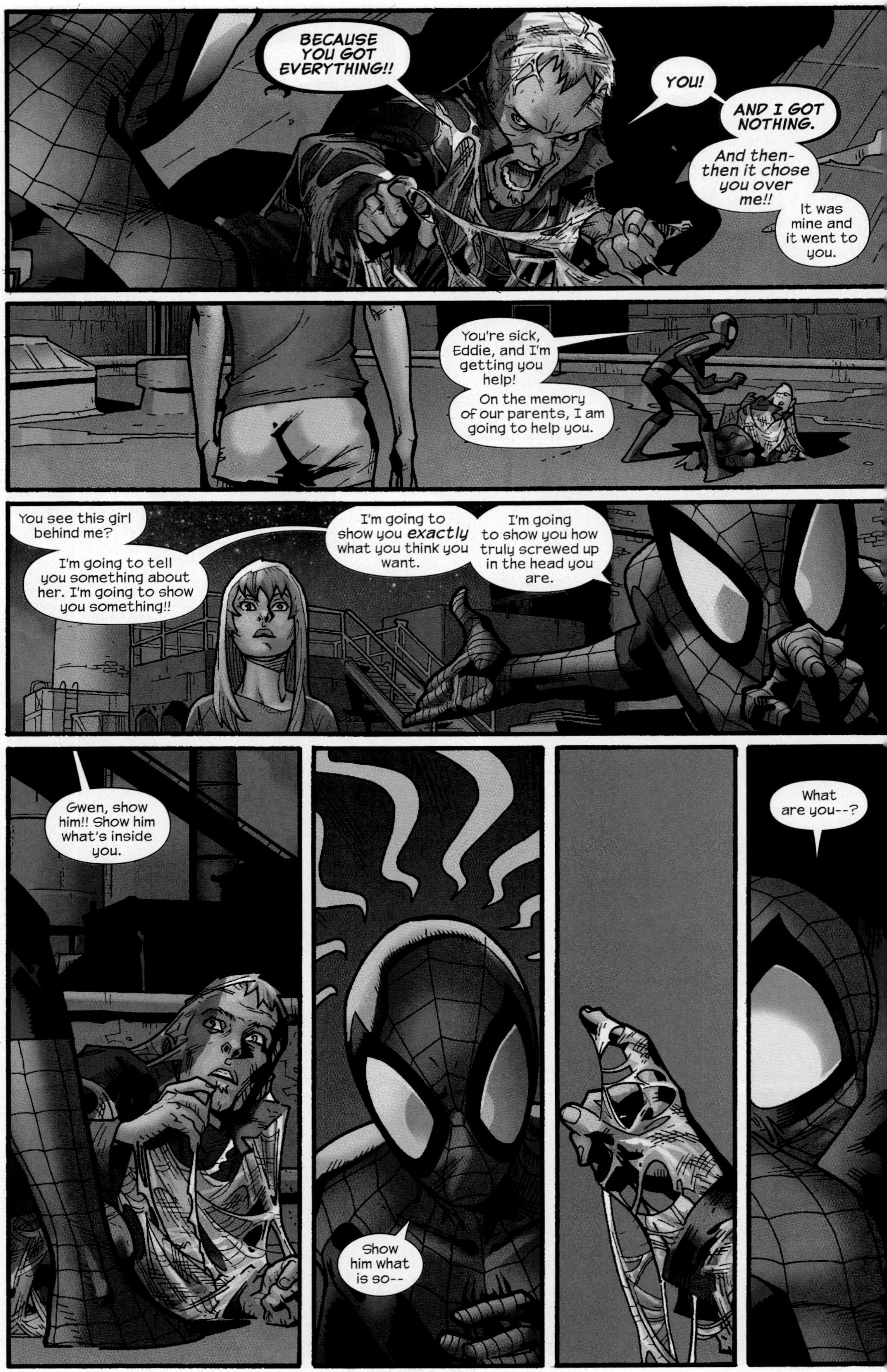
BECAUSE YOU GOT EVERYTHING!!
YOU!
AND I GOT NOTHING.
And then- then it chose you over me!!
It was mine and it went to you.
You're sick, Eddie, and I'm getting you help!
On the memory of our parents, I am going to help you.
You see this girl behind me?
I'm going to tell you something about her. I'm going to show you something!!
I'm going to show you *exactly* what you think you want.
I'm going to show you how truly screwed up in the head you are.
Gwen, show him!! Show him what's inside you.
Show him what is so--
What are you--?

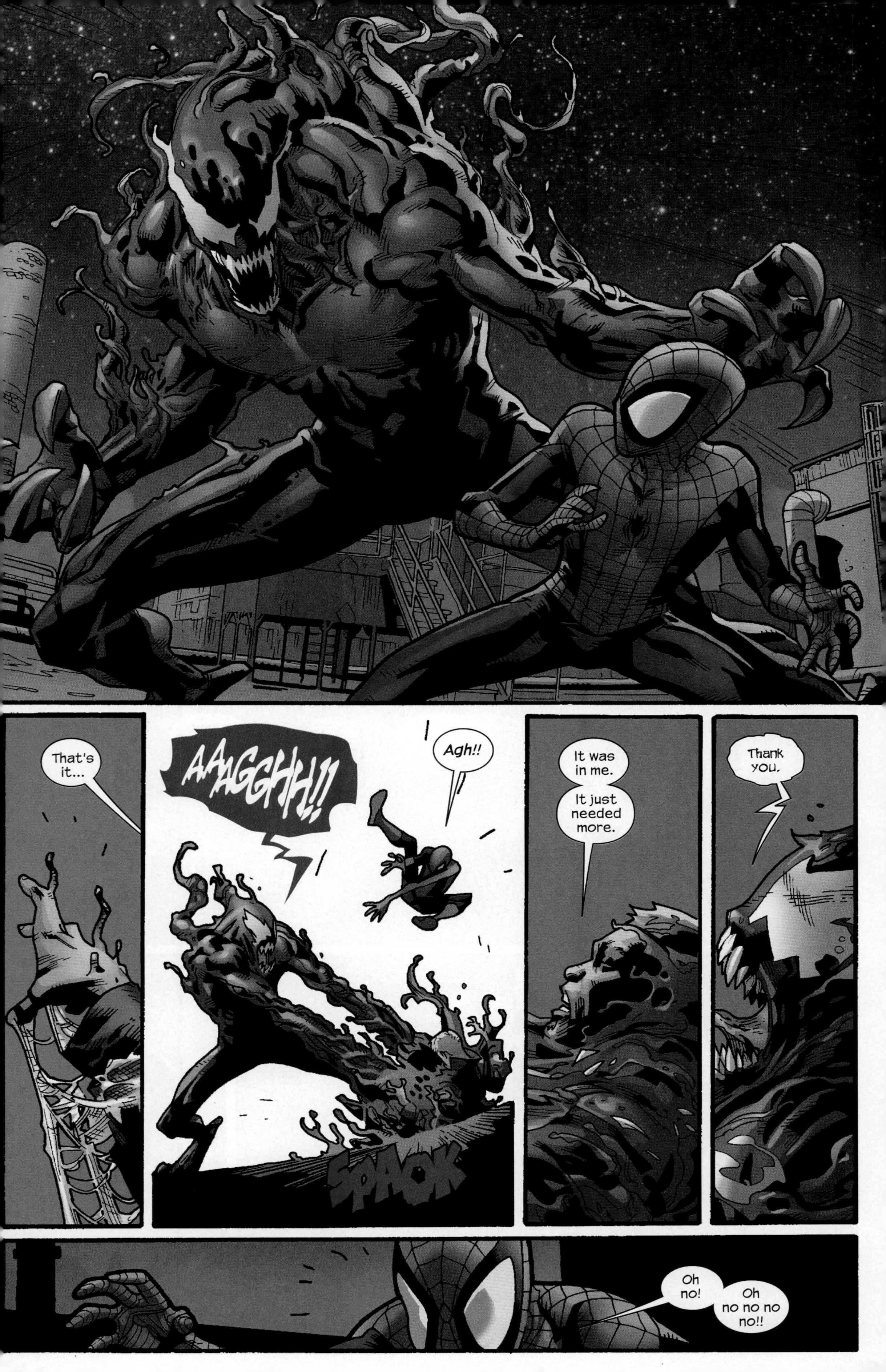
That's it...
AAAGGHH!!
Agh!!
SPLAK
It was in me.
It just needed more.
Thank you.
Oh no!
Oh no no no no!!

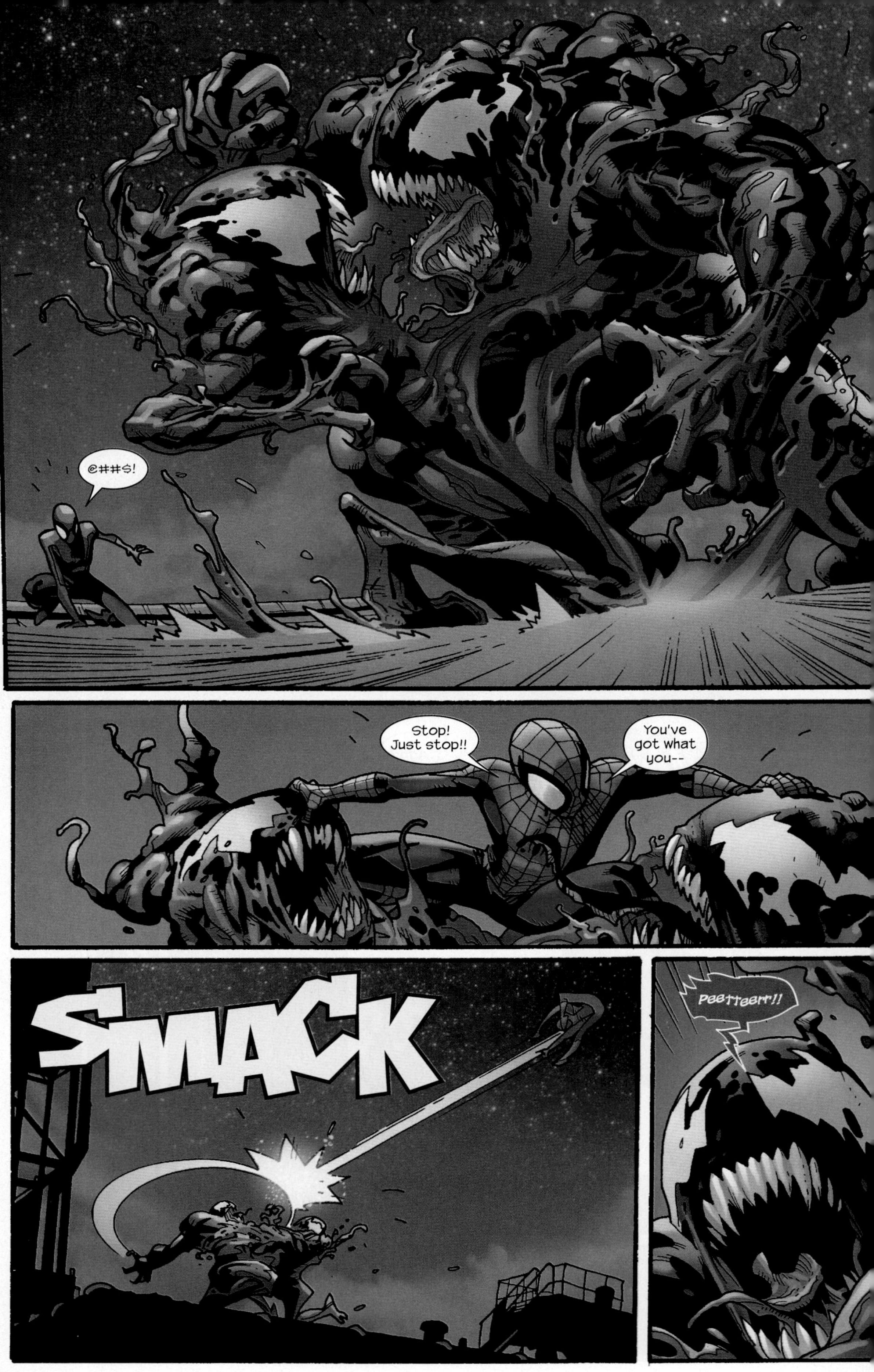
@##$!
Stop! Just stop!!
You've got what you--
SMACK
Peetteerr!!

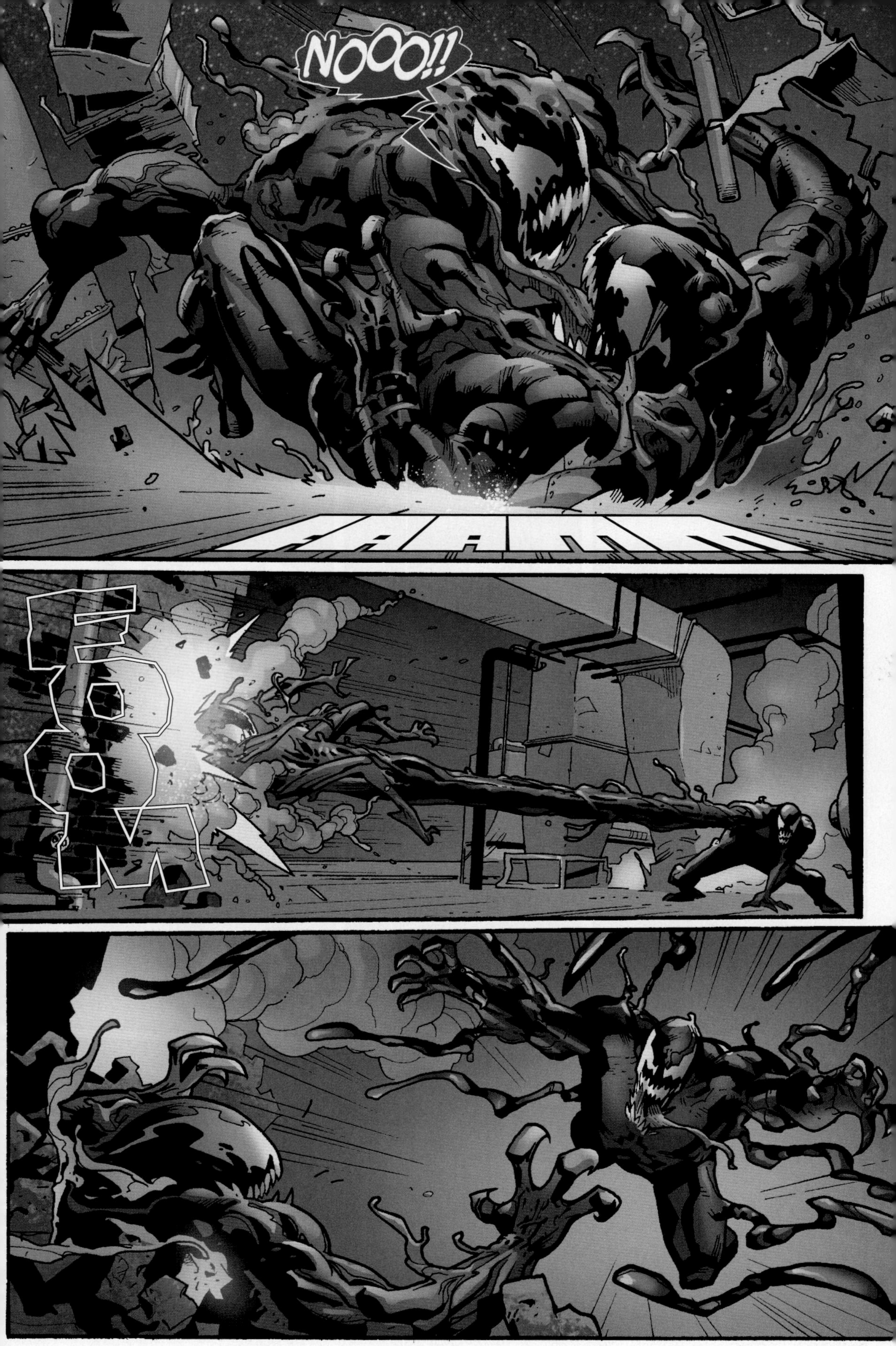
NOOO!!
FOOM

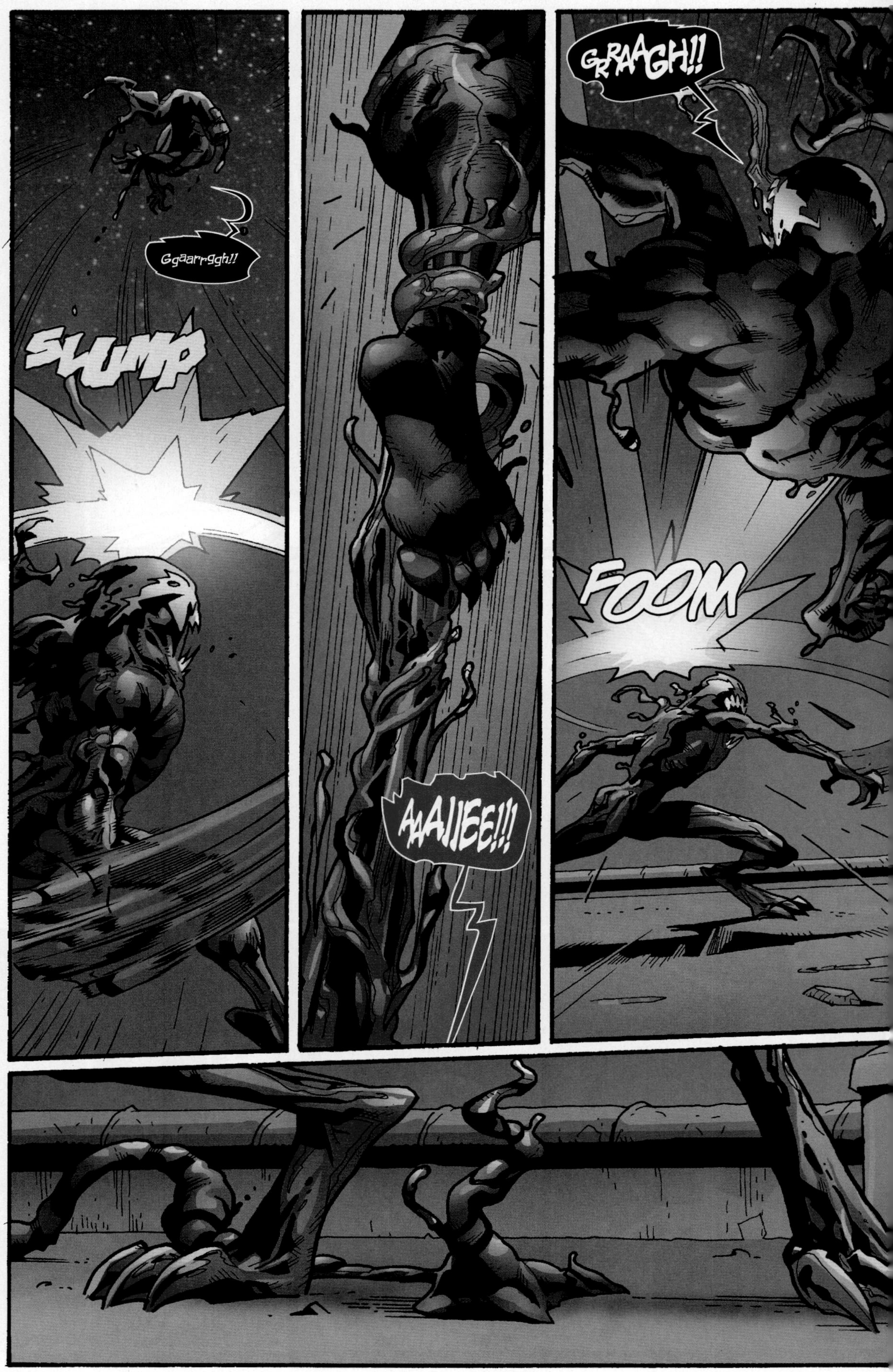
Ggaarrggh!!
SLUMP
AAAIIEE!!!
GRRAAGH!!
FOOM

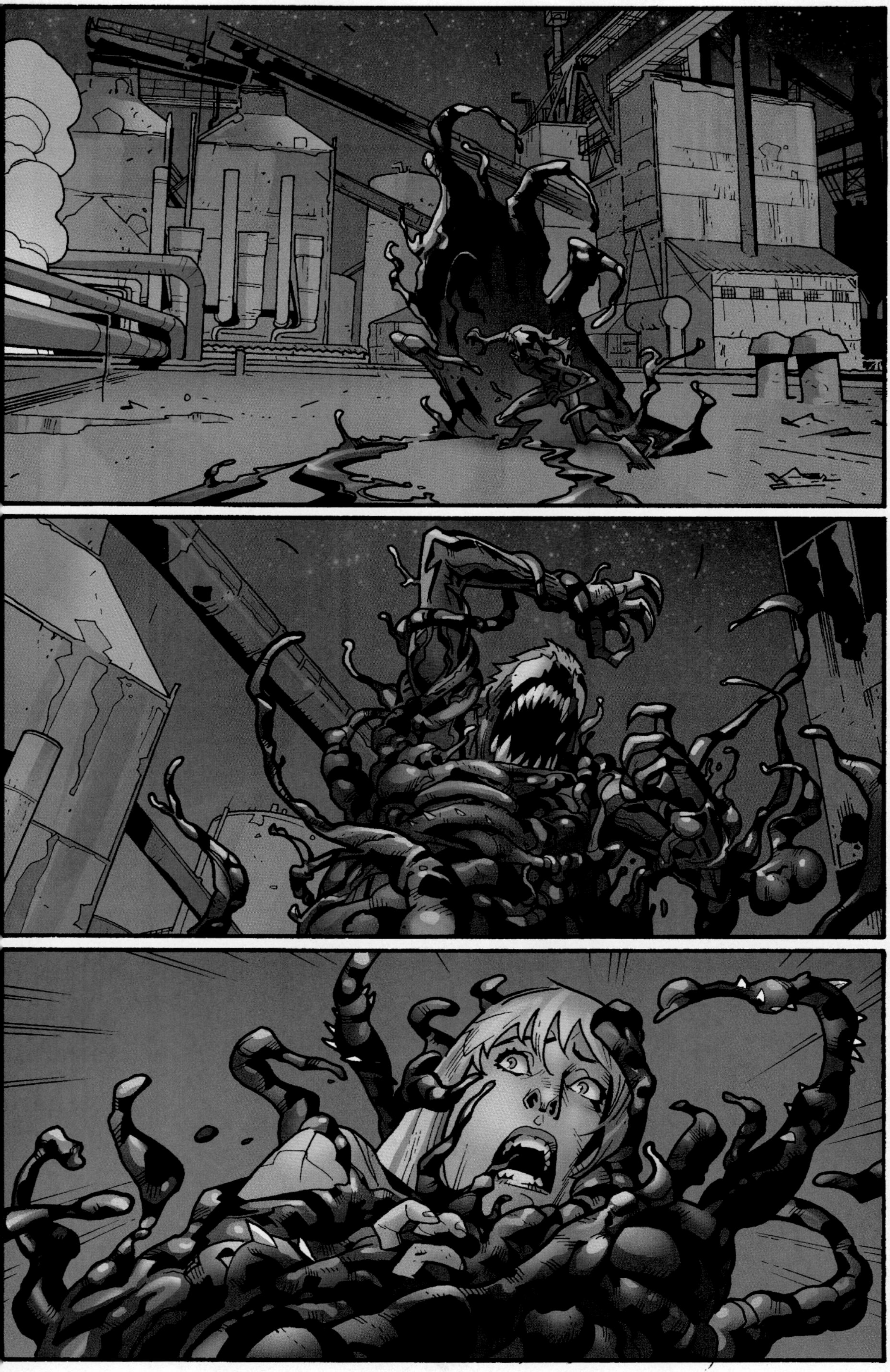

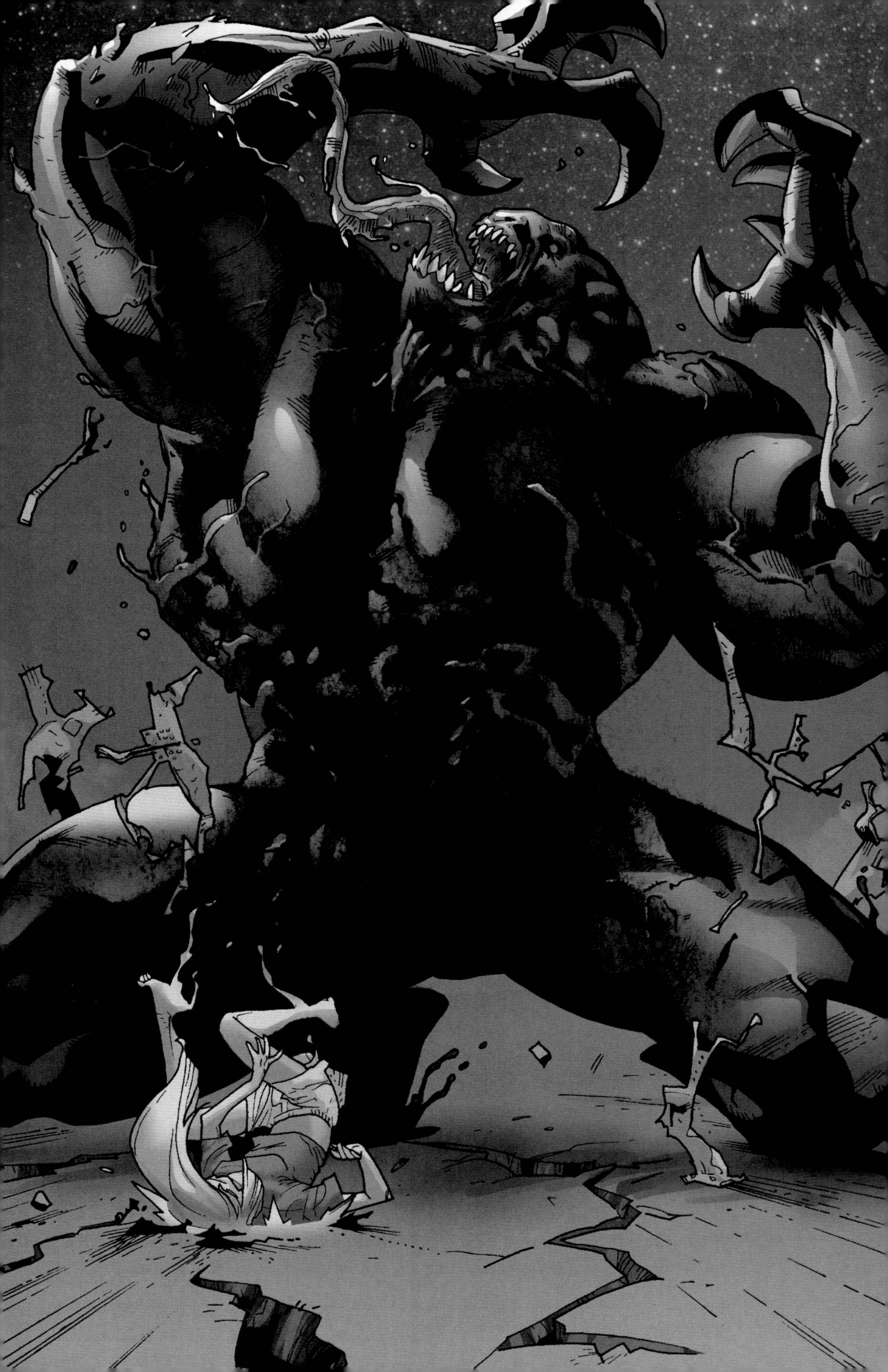

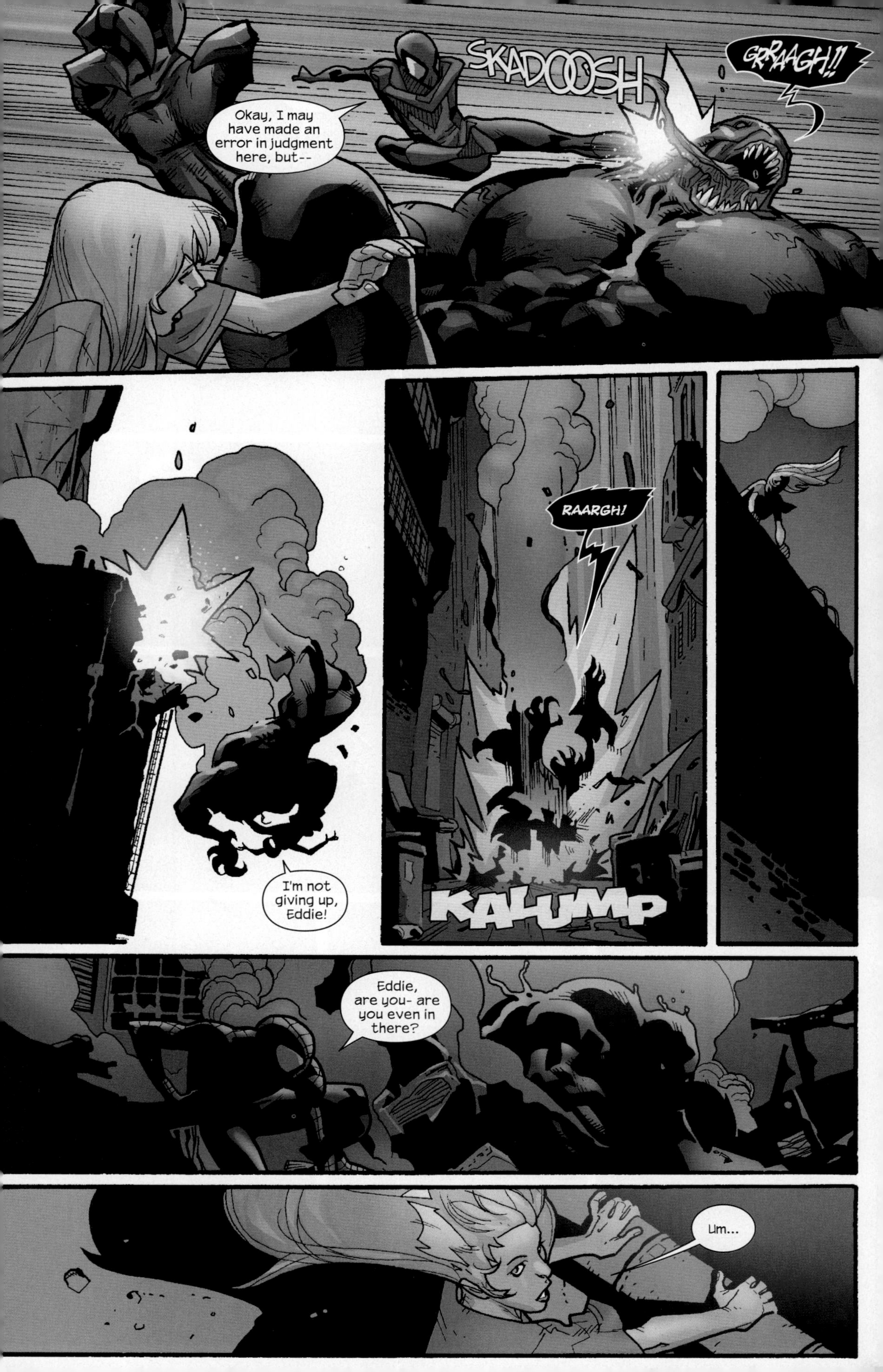
SKADOOSH
GRRAAGH!!
Okay, I may have made an error in judgment here, but--
I'm not giving up, Eddie!
RAARGH!
KALUMP
Eddie, are you- are you even in there?
Um...

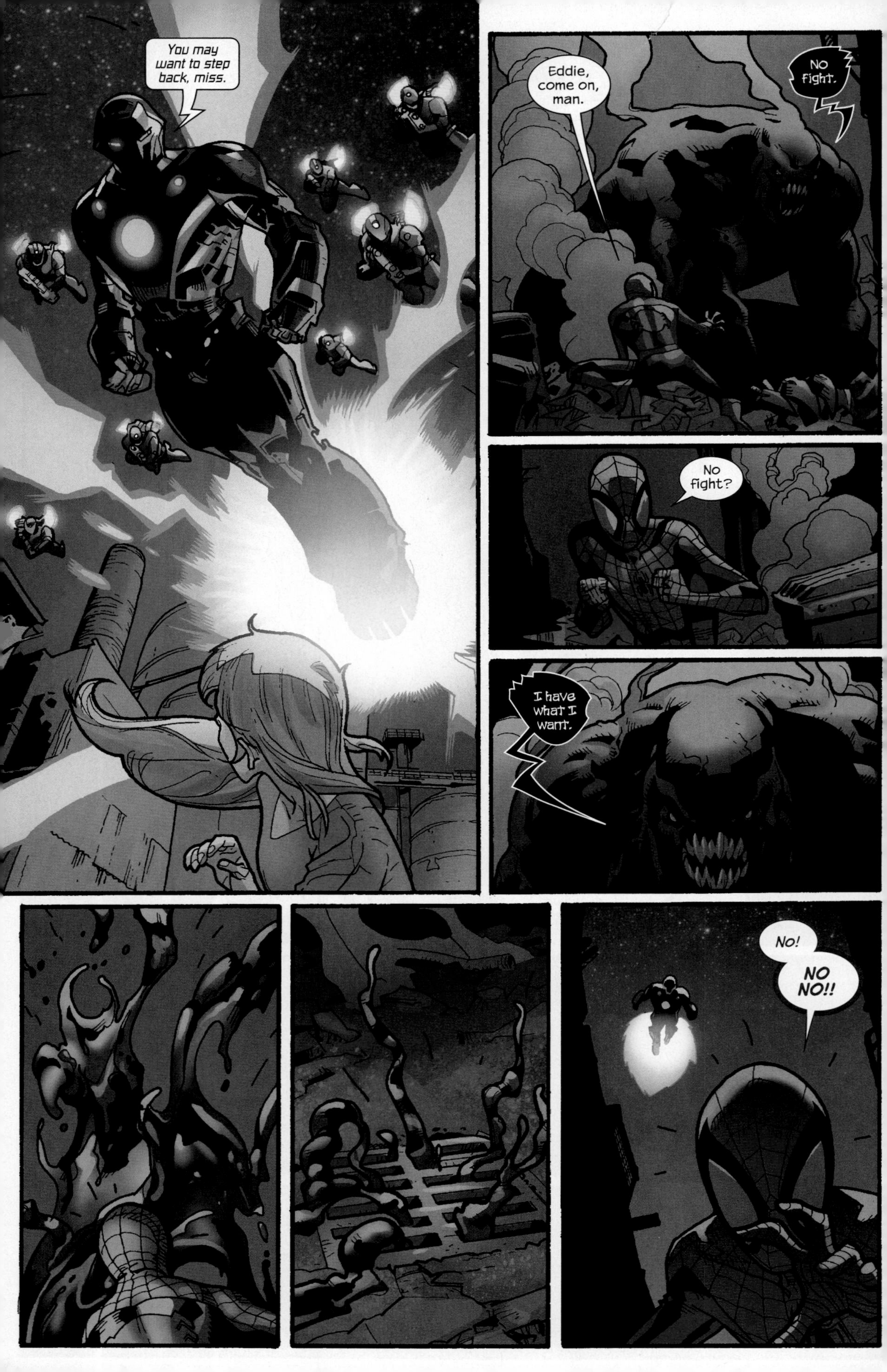
You may want to step back, miss.
Eddie, come on, man.
No fight.
No fight?
I have what I want.
No!
NO NO!!

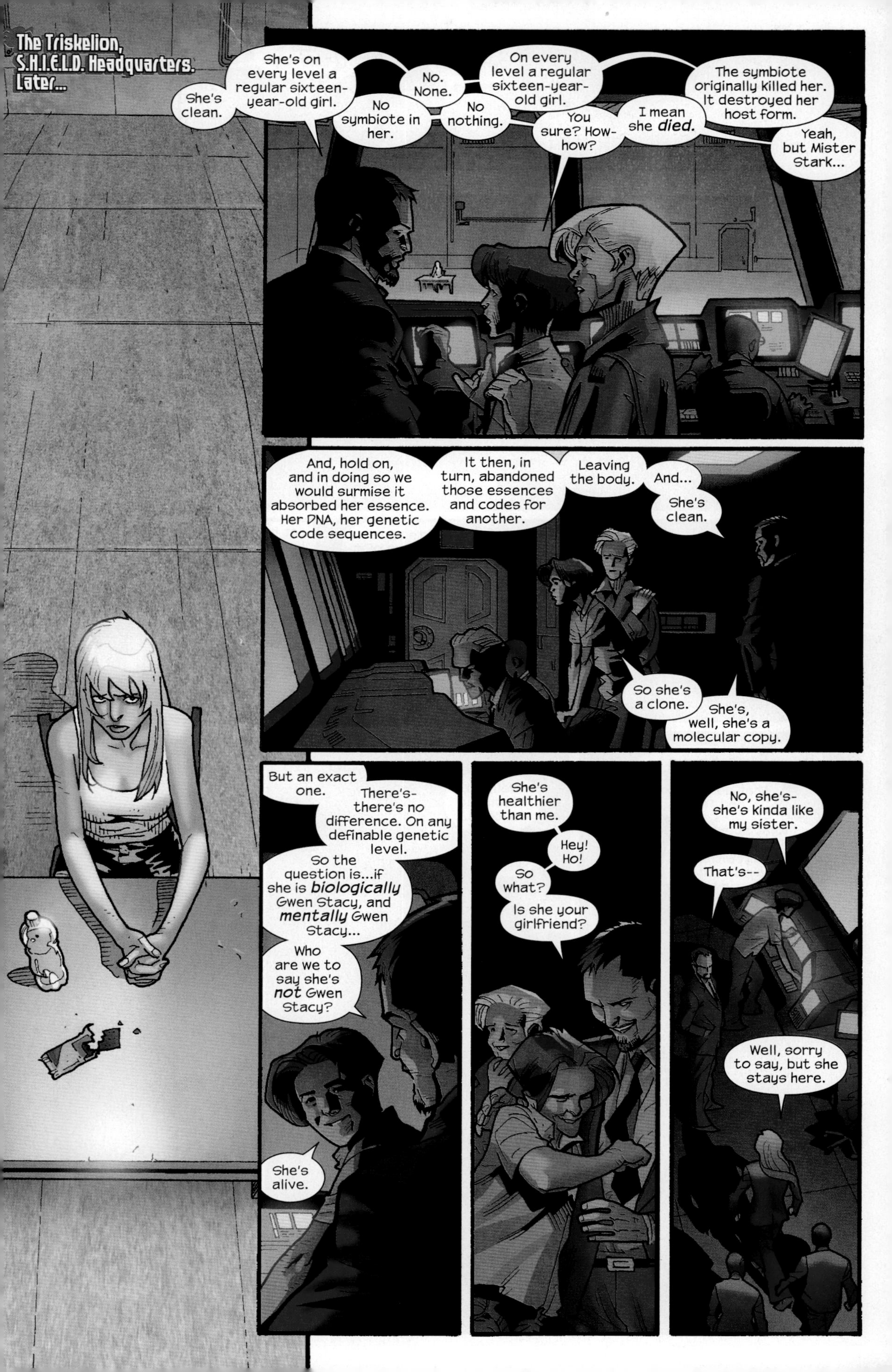
The Triskelion, S.H.I.E.L.D. Headquarters. Later...
She's clean.
She's on every level a regular sixteen-year-old girl.
No symbiote in her.
No. None.
No nothing.
On every level a regular sixteen-year-old girl.
You sure? How-how?
I mean she *died.*
The symbiote originally killed her. It destroyed her host form.
Yeah, but Mister Stark...
And, hold on, and in doing so we would surmise it absorbed her essence. Her DNA, her genetic code sequences.
It then, in turn, abandoned those essences and codes for another.
Leaving the body.
And...
She's clean.
So she's a clone.
She's, well, she's a molecular copy.
But an exact one.
There's- there's no difference. On any definable genetic level.
So the question is...if she is *biologically* Gwen Stacy, and *mentally* Gwen Stacy...
Who are we to say she's *not* Gwen Stacy?
She's alive.
She's healthier than me.
Hey! Ho!
So what?
Is she your girlfriend?
No, she's- she's kinda like my sister.
That's--
Well, sorry to say, but she stays here.

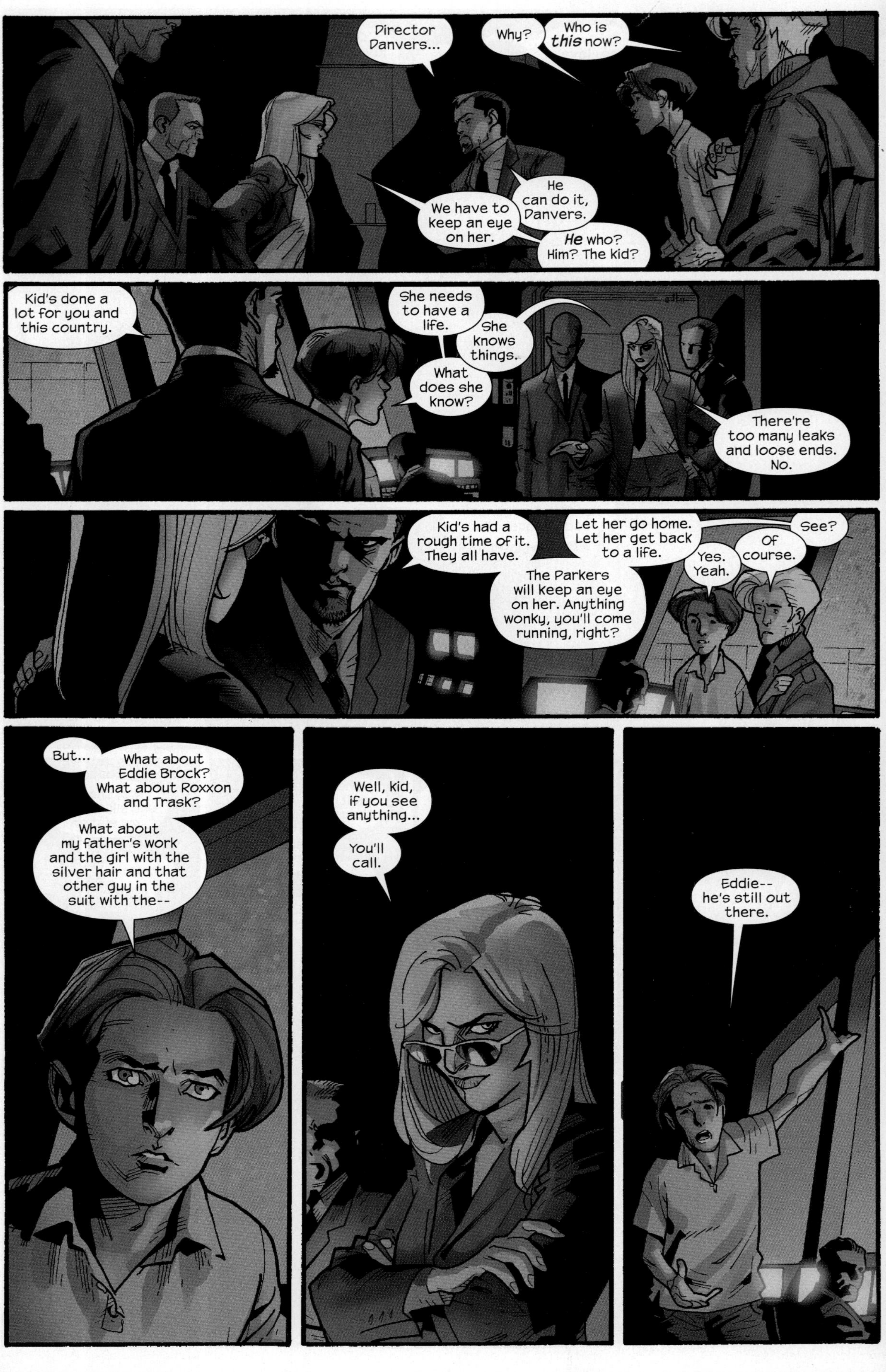
Director Danvers...
Why?
Who is *this* now?
We have to keep an eye on her.
He can do it, Danvers.
He who? Him? The kid?
Kid's done a lot for you and this country.
She needs to have a life.
She knows things.
What does she know?
There're too many leaks and loose ends. No.
Kid's had a rough time of it. They all have.
Let her go home. Let her get back to a life.
See?
Of course.
Yes. Yeah.
The Parkers will keep an eye on her. Anything wonky, you'll come running, right?
But...
What about Eddie Brock? What about Roxxon and Trask?
What about my father's work and the girl with the silver hair and that other guy in the suit with the--
Well, kid, if you see anything...
You'll call.
Eddie-- he's still out there.

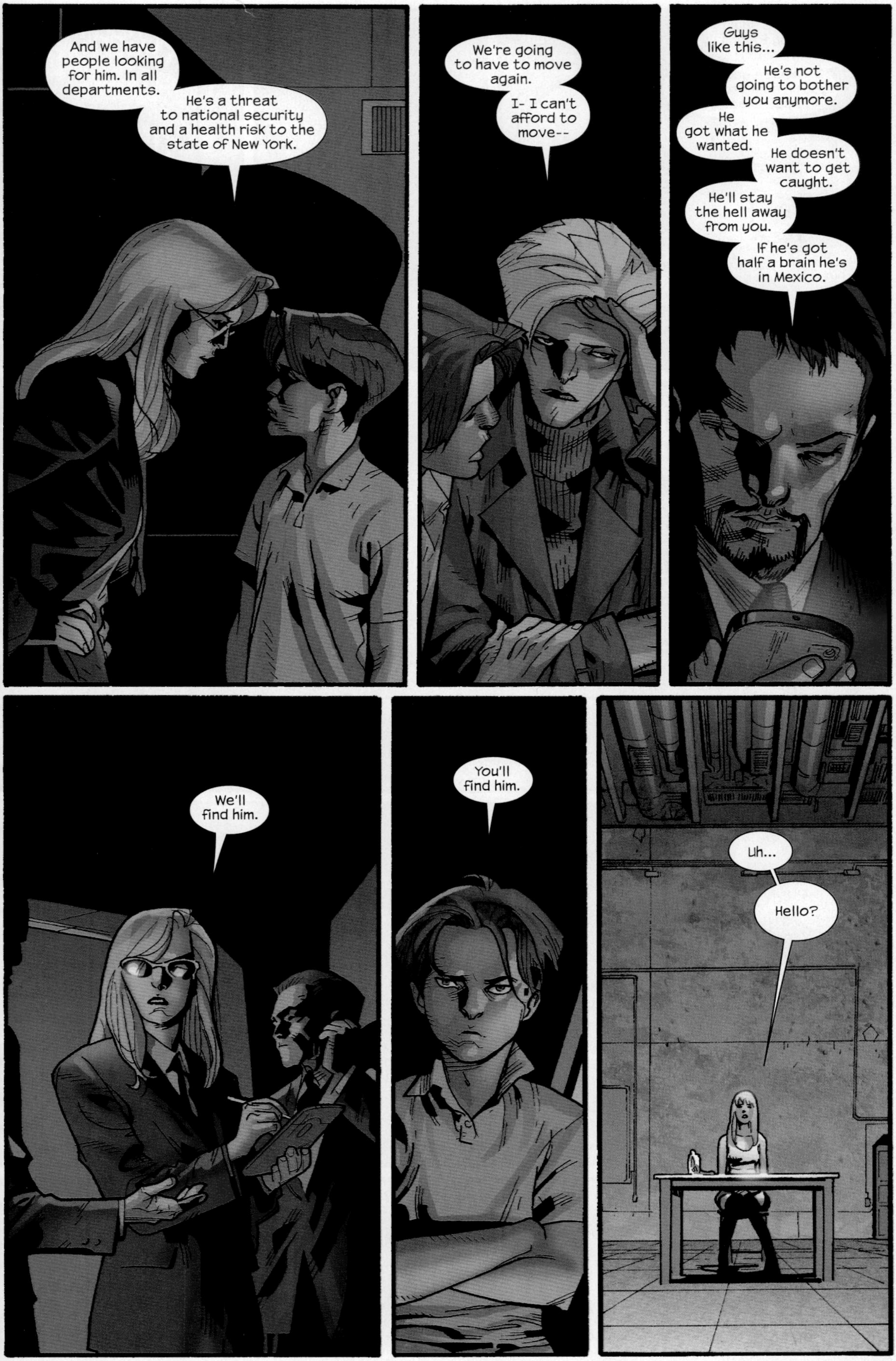
And we have people looking for him. In all departments.
He's a threat to national security and a health risk to the state of New York.
We're going to have to move again.
I- I can't afford to move--
Guys like this...
He's not going to bother you anymore.
He got what he wanted.
He doesn't want to get caught.
He'll stay the hell away from you.
If he's got half a brain he's in Mexico.
We'll find him.
You'll find him.
Uh...
Hello?

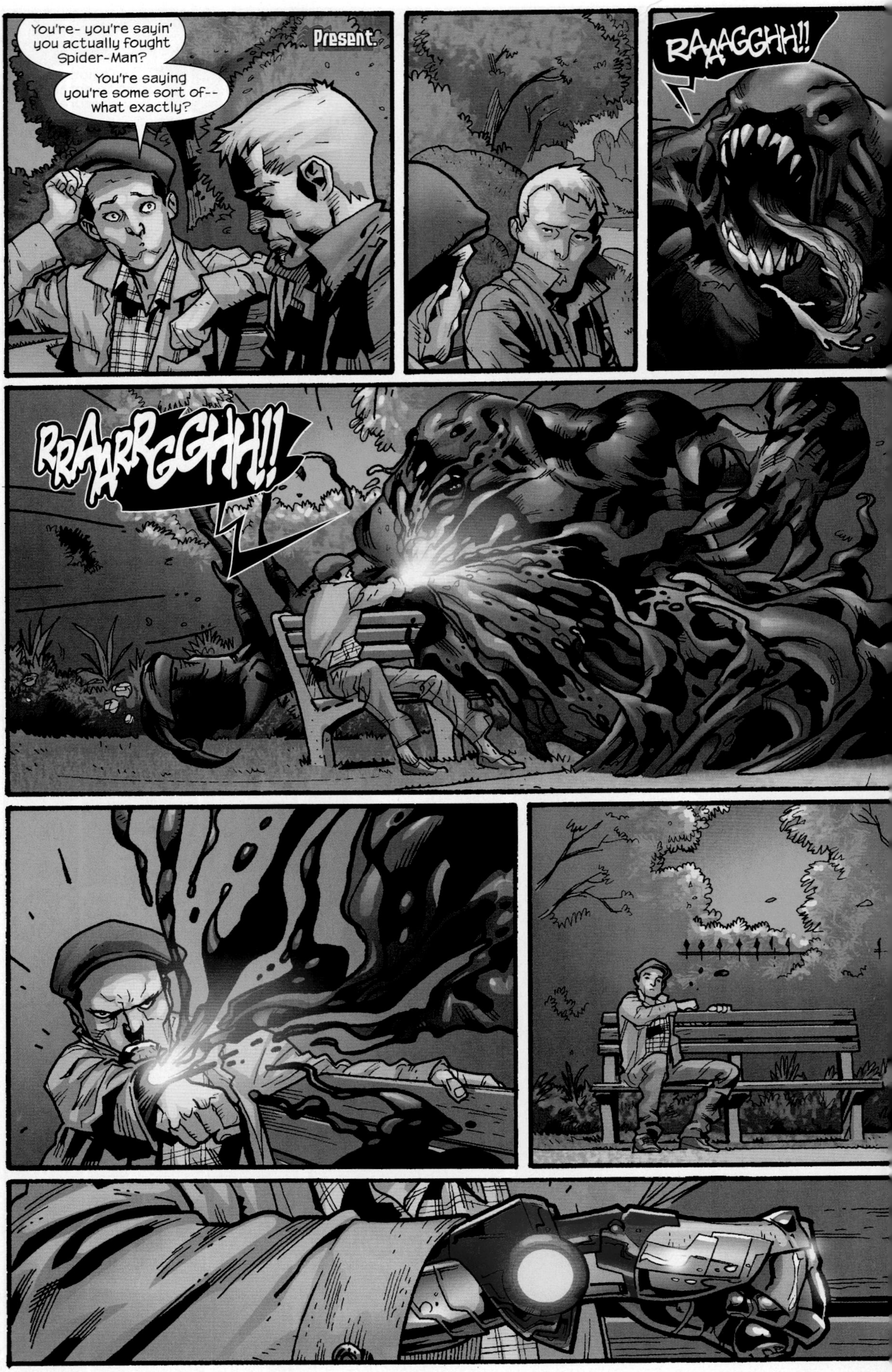
You're- you're sayin' you actually fought Spider-Man?
You're saying you're some sort of-- what exactly?
Present.
RAAAGGHH!!
RRAARRGGHH!!